THE FUTURE OF HUMAN RIGHTS

Upendra Baxi

OXFORD
UNIVERSITY PRESS

OXFORD
UNIVERSITY PRESS

YMCA Library Building, Jai Singh Road, New Delhi 110 001

Oxford University Press is a department of the University of Oxford. It furthers the
University's objective of excellence in research, scholarship, and education
by publishing worldwide in

Oxford   New York

Auckland   Bangkok   Buenos Aires   Cape Town   Chennai
Dar es Salaam   Delhi   Hong Kong   Istanbul   Karachi   Kolkata
Kuala Lumpur   Madrid   Melbourne   Mexico City   Mumbai   Nairobi
Sao Paulo   Shanghai   Singapore   Taipei   Tokyo   Toronto

and an associated company in Berlin

Oxford is a registered trade mark of Oxford University Press
in the UK and in certain other countries

Published in India
By Oxford University Press, New Delhi

© Upendra Baxi and Oxford University Press, 2002

First published 2002
Second impression 2002

ISBN   019   565 2894

Printed at Roopak Printers, Delhi-110 032
Published by Manzar Khan, Oxford University Press
YMCA Library Building, Jai Singh Road, New Delhi 110 001

Preface

I. Human Suffering and Human Rights

This book seeks to decipher the future of protean forms of social action assembled, by convention, under a portal named 'human rights'. It problematizes the very notion of 'human rights', the standard narratives of their origins, the ensemble of ideologies animating their modes of production, and the wayward circumstances of their enunciation. If the ways of state sovereignty often emerge as rocks upon which many a human rights wave flounders, at times it also comes to pass that many a human rights cause and movement gathers the strength of a storm that crumbles the citadels of state sovereignty as if they were sandcastles. The histories of contemporary human rights thus emerge as chronicles of contingency. So must narratives concerning the futures of human rights.

Of necessity, concern with the future of human rights extends to many disparate themes and traverses many a moment in human rights theory and practice. Though grounded on a full understanding of the *lawyer's law* of human rights, this work does not offer an exegesis on specific regimes of human rights. Lawyerly ways of grasping human rights continue to remain important for future development. I remain concerned here to grasp the portents of the future from the perspectives of social theory of human rights. It is my hope that the next two volumes (on the right to food and the right to development) will be more focused on the heterogeneous social and hermeneutic histories of specific clusters of human rights.

Important though the *lawyer's law* is for the promotion and protection of human rights, it can scarcely exhaust sources of meaning and movement in human rights. The politics of intergovernmental desire that results in constitutional, or international, law enunciations of human rights is not the sole, nor even primary, source of origin of human rights. A principal message of this work is that the originary authors of human rights are people in struggle and communities of resistance, which standard scholarship demotes to a lowly status. Once claims to 'authorship' stand thus pluralized, it follows simply that 'human rights' are not the *gifts of the West to the Rest*; the dominant discourse is diversionary when it locates the origins of human rights in Euroamerican tradition and experience (Chapter 2) and when it pursues endless debates over 'universality' and 'relativism' of human rights (Chapters 5 and 6).

What is more, the semiotic entity 'human rights' invites deconstruction (Chapter 1), even to the point of demonstration of its incoherence. 'Human rights' constitute not just a multitude of normative orderings but also distinct realms of human experience. One way of mapping that experience is to construct attitudinal dispositions that manifest in many forms of human rights weariness and wariness (Chapter 3) and concerns about there being too few, or too many, human rights (Chapter 4).

If this provides insufficient provocation for the dominant human rights discourse, I construct *just orders of anxiety* concerning the future of human rights through several conceptual distinctions. Throughout the work, I insist on the distinction between politics *of* human rights and politics *for* human rights. Much of the argumentative platform collapses if this distinction is rendered insensible. Similar results follow were you to find unsustainable my distinction (Chapter 8) between the paradigms of universal human rights and trade-related, market-friendly human rights, or the distinction between human rights *movements* and human rights *markets* (Chapter 7).

The troubled relationship between human *suffering* and human *rights* is my central concern here. I describe it as a 'troubled' relationship for many reasons.

First, the taught tradition in international law with its doctrinal distinction between the international law of war and peace, reserves languages of pain and suffering for the development of international humanitarian law. The Grotian doctrine of *temparementa belli*, in its origin and development, addresses the conduct of war, and war-like, operations. The obligation to minimize human suffering in such situations,[1] grounded in an order of non-negotiable moral obligations of 'civilized' behaviour even in situations of armed conflict, does not

---

[1] The four Geneva Conventions, for example, seek to protect non-combatants, civilians, prisoners of war, sick and wounded, and inmates of regimes of belligerent occupation.

attach to states of peace, even when 'peace' appears to millions of people as forms of belligerency by other means.[2] In other words, languages of suffering are not writ as large in times of peace as they are in times of war.

Second, while the very notion of human rights *violation* presupposes a sort of concern with *violence*, human rights languages do not always import the same order of heavy consequences for actors that produce human suffering in peacetime as in war-like situations. The emerging standards of international criminal law in war-like situations do not extend to systematic, sustained and planned peacetime denials of the right to satisfaction of basic human needs, such as food, clothing, housing, and health. Obligations to minimize human suffering emerge in contemporary human rights discourse as slow motion, rather than fast forward, kind of state and public policy orientations. This diffuseness of contemporary human rights discourse dissipates human and social suffering, and renders it almost socially illegible. The millions of *rightless* peoples have different stakes in the future of human rights than many epistemic human rights communities. While the latter find in every human rights enunciation a signature for a better human future, the rightless peoples, all too often, find these enunciatory moves rather callous.[3]

Third, it is thus clear that the very notions of sovereign self-determination, as the insignia of the right of each and every state to equality by international law, within a community of states, bears an ambivalent relation to human/social suffering. The notions of self-determination attribute to peoples a will to statehood; and the doctrine of equality among sovereign states assumes that 'states' can indeed *represent* peoples. In so far as these notions signify the illegitimacy of colonialism and imperialism, they remain human rights friendly. However we all know situations of state failure, where predatory sovereignty formations, thriving on ad hoc, 'instant' regimes of the dominant 'legalities' based on force and fraud, tyranny and terror, render peoples rightless. Human rights movement and discourse grapple

---

[2] Conditions of extreme impoverishment, forced labour, markets for systematically organized rape through sex trafficking, child labour, planned displacement of peoples in the name of 'development', for example, represent from the standpoint of the violated the same order of liquidation of human potential as war and war-like situations.

[3] Even on the eve of the Golden Jubilee celebrations of the Universal Declaration, the World Food Summit promised action to reduce by half, by the year 2015, the suffering of 800 million starving people!

with ways in which the practices of self-determination and state sovereignty may be converted into opportunities for rights realization. In the present opinion, this endeavour needs redirection in terms of more sustained engagement with human/social suffering, especially in understanding the ways in which the very languages of human rights may turn out to be a factor of production of human suffering.

Fourth, human rights reflexivity compels the recognition that the connection between human suffering and human rights is incredibly complex. Chapter 2 highlights ways in which the birth and growth of 'modern' human rights entailed legitimation of the suffering of the non-Euroamerican Other. In contrast, 'contemporary' human rights normativity renders altogether obsolete imperialism and racism as the cornerstones of 'civilized' international law and order. Violent social exclusion, in all its protean forms, constitutes human/social suffering that the languages and logics of 'contemporary' human rights contest everywhere, at every conceivable opportunity for global social action. At the same time, contemporary human rights theory and movement finds its own distinctive ways to normalize lived and embodied histories of social hurt and harm. Linking doctrinal disputations concerning the universality, interdependence, indivisibility and inalienability of human rights rhetoric to these histories will, I believe, constitute an immeasurable advance towards the future of human rights.

Fifth, the politics *of* human rights, performative acts of the worlds of desires of global power and of NGO diplomacy, weave many a compromistic web of textual politics; practices that shape the production of human rights norms and standards. These practices generate a paradoxical situation. The number of the *rightless* peoples also grows even as human rights norms and standards proliferate. The more people stand endowed with normative human rights by international and constitutional instruments, the greater and keener emerges the suffering of people existentially deprived of realization and enjoyment of human rights. The politics *of* human rights, interestingly, creates conditions for the politics *for* human rights. The normativity of human rights enunciations is deployed by the latter practices to describe, and often define, the illegitimacy of the power structures; these always seek to legitimize democratic, though not always peaceful, resistance to pave ways for a better human future. In their most creative moment, the labours of politics *for* human rights emerge as Herculean; in more stressed moments, these resemble the ordeals of a Sisyphus.

Put another way, human rights logics and paralogics presuppose theories that at once delegitimate state sponsored, civil society collaborative violation and justify *necessary* imposition of human suffering on the perpetrators. But theories about imposition of human suffering also exploit the rich indeterminacy of that rhetorical resource. Grammars of governance often marshal unto themselves the moral hierarchy of orders of pain and suffering enacted by the very languages of 'progressive realization' of social, economic and cultural human rights. So do the grammars of global governance that increasingly organize and sustain markets for human rights, which in turn lead to commodification of human suffering.

When human rights languages steadily supplant all other ethical languages, when almost each and every 'new' social movement tends to coalesce with the logics and paralogics of human rights, when all resistance to formations of power begins to present itself as morally *worthy* only when it shapes itself in human rights talk, the politics *of* human rights brings to us both human hope and hazards. The hope lies in the construction of visions of an 'ethical' state. The hazards lie in the acts of mystification of the modes of production of human misery and suffering. Perhaps, a way out of this lies in summoning the potential of the distinction I draw between forms of politics *of* and *for* human rights, the former serving the ends of *Realpolitik*, the latter seeking to combat modes of governance (national, regional or global) that command the power to cause unjustifiable human suffering, and impose orders of radical evil.

II. Reader Response

This work stands addressed to a whole variety of 'implied' readers and interpretive communities, including variegated conglomerations of international human rights lawyers, human rights activists, and human rights enunciators and peoples/communities in struggle. It, perforce, runs a thousand narrative risks!

A majority of international human rights lawyers, as already noted, may remain disappointed with this work as transgressive of customary, and therefore familiar, ways of reading the human rights 'law' and jurisprudence. Some may even go so far as to say that this book has little to do with human rights, let alone their futures. To the latter, I immediately need to say that no enterprise at reading the future of human rights is possible within the existing technocratic doctrinal thought formations. To those concerned with the 'lack' of human rights law in this book, that is the lack of specificity concerning both forms of the *is*, and the *oughts*, of 'positive' human rights 'law', I need to urge a momentary 'willing suspension of disbelief'.

I remain aware of the potential for alienation that this work carries for social action and human rights communities, to which I myself belong, even if in a minuscule measure. The language of analysis of 'human rights markets' (in Chapter 7) will, I know, generate a sense of hurt, even though this may be somewhat redeemed when they receive with some warmth my reflections on the paradigm shift rights (Chapter 8) and the critique of the emergence of the 'modern' human rights paradigm (Chapter 2). The uneven reception that I thus anticipate sustains my belief that we (those who struggle for the achievement of human rights and amelioration of human suffering *here* and *now*, on an, as it were, ASAP basis) need to be reflexive about our own practices in struggle and solidarity.

Statebashing *libidinal drive* (without which the contemporary human rights activist impulse is simply inconceivable) provides the movement and theory of human rights an animating platform for a critique of ways of domination and governance. So does the free-market bashing platform that many activist human rights lawyers and NGO communities occasionally share. At the very same moment, even as we critique state and market failures in terms of human, and human rights, violation, any advance serving the future of human rights also requires rigorous reflexivity by the movement people. Not to accept this premise is to retard that future by a human rights activist performativity centred excessively around the state or good corporate governance. To accept this premise is, at the same time, to also accept the notion of a *progressive state*, when not an oxymoron, empowering it to combat civil society formations that gnaw at the heart of human rights. Human rights movements entail both the 'progressive' empowerment and disempowerment of the 'State'. Human rights praxes thus remain deeply dilemmatic.

The managers and agents of contemporary economic globalization will find this work, in the main, irritating as well as diversionary. Irritating because of its polemical content and diversionary because it counters pet dogmas, which celebrate economic growth for some globalizing elites as *all-round* human development. But in proffering a human rights oriented critique of globalization, I do at least invite them to rethink the notions of 'good' corporate governance that remain seriously deficient from the standpoint of suffering peoples everywhere—from Bhopal to Ogoni-land, and beyond. Primitive capitalist accumulation that privileges profits over people is, I suggest to them, an insensible corporate governance strategy in the epoch of late capitalism. Equally dysfunctional are forms of whitewashing, greenwashing, and 'mainstreaming' human rights strategies. For, these pay no heed to the power of those movements of politics *for* human rights, which remain immune to cooptation.

III. Human Rights Futurology

Social prediction is necessarily a hazardous occupation. Predicting the future of human rights is even more so for many reasons. First, we have as yet no historiography, nor an adequate social theory of human rights. The lack of historiography enables continuous reproduction of fancy, and horror, stories concerning the exclusively Euroamerican origins of human rights. The lack of sustained enquiry into analogues or anticipations of human rights in non-Western cultures, either at the level of history of ideas or histories of practices of power, has several consequences.

The more human rights are hailed as the patrimony of the West, the greater is the inclination in most Euroamerican societies towards world hegemony. Also keener, as a result, is the intergovernmental desire in some non-Euroamerican societies to reject the underlying aspiration affirming equal worth of all human beings. Not merely repressive regimes but also progressive intellectuals in these societies remain ambivalent towards contemporary human rights enunciations. And (as Chapter 6 illustrates) progressive Eurocentrism inclines us all towards a postmodernist critique of notions of human rights. Authentic intercultural, or even inter-faith, dialogue remains a casualty of warped approaches to histories of human rights ideas and practices.

Second, the lack of what I name as a social theory of human rights is similarly disempowering. We lack an adequate sociological understanding of the genealogy of the 'modern' as contrasted with the 'contemporary' human rights discursive formations. We lack meaningful exploration of human rights movements as social movements, whether 'old' or 'new.' Analyses of the impact of mega-science and hi-tech on the theory and practice of human rights have yet to inaugurate themselves. And the costs of human, and human rights, violations have yet to be fully addressed in terms of law and economics and political economy. This work attempts to redress this lack in some preliminary ways. I hope that what gets said here will at least demonstrate that the epistemic base necessary for a meaningful forecast concerning the future of human rights is, in the present state of knowledge, simply inadequate. In the absence of significant reversals in the given asymmetrical international North/South divide in the mode of human rights knowledge production, the lack is unlikely to be redressed. That, by itself, should be sufficient for a concern with the future of human rights.

Third, contemporary international human rights norms and standards constitute, in the eye of human history, *a very recent moral human invention*. Contemporary human rights present at best the sites of heavily conflicted State and social movement consensus. In a sense, an enterprise that has so little and so brittle a past, some may say, simply does not bear the weight of interlocution in terms of the future. All there is to human rights theory and practice, some may say, is its *historical present*.

We live, it may be said on the other hand, in an era of extraordinary global transformation, which has already devoured many a powerful vision and language of alternate human futures. We live in an era of a heavily globalized human future that fully confiscates the sight and sound of *alternatives* to global capitalism. On this progress narrative of global capitalism, the future is already happening *now*, accelerating historic time and space that render obsolete many a fighting faith of the yesteryears. On this register, the question concerning the future of human rights stands already ahistorically posed, because it is a moral language (like those of 'social justice', 'equity' and 'redistribution') that is now simply *exhausted*. It fails outside a few contexts (notably, of regime-inspired or -supported torture and terror) to resonate with the globalizing middle classes around the world. Any work, like the present, on this sort of view, can only address *past futures,* the narratives of unrealized and even unattainable human rights.

IV. 'Too Little, Too Late'

It is thus either *too soon* or *too late* to raise issues concerning the future of human rights. The 'too soon' stance, affirming the potential of here-and-now struggles, marginalizes issues concerning a better future, or at least a future, for human rights. It reaffirms the historic potential of current structures of human rights engagement. These in the main address the conditions of globality, which provide grammars of human rights norm-creation and implementation, addressing human rights responsibilities even now and primarily to state structures. On this view, the tasks of human rights, in terms of making the state ethical, governance just, and power accountable, are tasks that ought to continue to define the agendum of activism. Any historically premature concern with the future of human rights is, then, a tragic moral mistake.

The 'too late' stance, in contrast, insists that the party, as it were, is over and the sooner we get rid of the deadweight of infatuating languages of human rights, the better it is for human futures. State structures can deliver the rhetoric but not the reality (materiality) of satisfying basic human (material and non-material) needs. Now that aberrations of 'welfarism', and 'socialism' are said to be 'safely' over, the State must reincarnate itself as the Night Watchman, facilitating the rights and interests of global capital, which alone through its manifold concentrations of technoscientific power, can create conditions of general progress towards satisfaction of basic human needs and rights. On this view, moral languages, especially those of human rights, become counterproductive when they oppose the progress, as well as the potential, of technoscience power.

These dauntingly complex tasks raise intractable questions concerning *agency* (who raises these questions) and method (how these are posed). The issue of *agency* is, indeed, crucial, entailing two related, but distinct, questions: *Who speaks through us when we speak about human rights? And on whose behalf may we speak?*

Inescapably, those who venture to raise questions concerning the future of human rights must confront their own historic subject-positions, and remain reflexive concerning human rights choices they make.[4] No matter how fluid and contingent we may make these subject-positions, theories about human rights do not quite manage to make audible that 'small voice of history', conveying the undertones 'of harassment and pain',[5] which countless human beings *somehow* endure as politically ordained *fate*. Howsoever problematic the category of the *subaltern* may be, or be made to appear by post-modernist analyses, stories plotting the future of human rights are sensible for the violated only when human rights discourses convey a *sense of suffering*. I endeavour, in this work, to articulate a distinctive subaltern perspective on human rights futures.

But rights discourse gets even more complex with the second question: *Whose* violation and suffering do we *highlight,* and whose do we *ignore,* in this endless discursivity on human rights? Since human, and human rights, violation is egregious, even the struggle to articulate

---

[4] Ranajit Guha, 'The Small Voice of History', in *Subaltern Studies IX*, I at 10–12 (1996).

[5] John Rawls in *The Law of Peoples* (1999) and Amartya Sen *Development as Freedom* (1999) exemplify for us the potency of such choices for the future of human rights. Both these works enhance our capacity for moral altruism in constructing *just* human futures.

the 'small voice of history' of those who suffer, remains often beyond hope. Putting human rights to work straddles both the structures of engagement and structures of postponement. Thus arises in human rights theory and movement the enactment of (what Veena Das names in a different context) the 'moral hierarchy of human suffering'. This work, at least partly, addresses the ways in which the grammar and idiom of contemporary human rights languages entail the 'sublimation' of human suffering.

Of course, much depends on how the narrative voice is appropriated to marshal the power to *enact* visions of human futures. The power it marshals becomes a *material force that enacts the anticipated futures*. Both the triumphal eras of bourgeois human rights formations and of revolutionary socialism of Marxian imagination marshaled this narrative hegemony for remarkably sustained practices of politics of cruelty. The former enforced imagined futures on the rest of the world (with its notions of the collective human right of the *superior races* to subjugate the *inferior ones*), while the latter legitimated many a *gulag*. Alternative ways of the *reinvention* of tradition (as in some situations of states claiming legitimacy from 'political' Islam, Judaism, Christianity or Hinduism), like both these 'visions', augment practices of politics of fierce cruelty.

It does not matter too much from the standpoint of the violated, whether enormous infliction of human suffering as well as the denial of the right to be and to remain human has been, and continues to be, justified in cosmological or secular discursivity. Of course, the narrative strategies of resistance differ materially with each version of imposition of suffering and human violation. What makes contemporary human rights movements precious is the fact that they contest *all* bleak and terrifying power of these narrative hegemonies.

They deny all cosmological, as well as terrestrial, justifications for the imposition of unjustified human suffering. And they insist on a dialogical construction of suffering that may be considered 'just'. In this, they also contest the notion of politics as *fate:* that is, the power of the *few* becoming the *destiny* of millions of human beings. Even this enterprise has to legitimate the *shifting* boundaries between '*necessary*' and '*surplus*' human suffering.

The power that they thus contest is 'political' power, the power of ideological and repressive apparatuses of the State and of global governance formations. Increasingly, however, digitalization and biotechnologies mark the emergence of *technoscientific* formations of power. These thrive on appropriation of languages and logics of human rights for capital-intensive corporate owned production of scientific knowledges that point to the emergence of (what I describe in Chapter 8 as) *trade-related, market-friendly* human rights paradigm, subverting the paradigm of universal human rights of all human beings. The subversion is profound: all over again the notion of being *human* stands periclated. That *human* now stands represented, in an era of digital capitalism, as networks of information, wholly capable of corporate ownership, whether in terms of electronic or genetic databases. The various Human Genome Projects, and the contemporary justifications of emergent technologies of human cloning as redemptive of human suffering, present a remarkable, if not an ultimate, challenge to half a century's attainment of an Age of Human Rights.

Technoscience, a regime of representation codifying new material practices of power, affects the very imagination of human rights praxis, not the least because the bearer of human rights stands recast either as a cyborg or a genetic storehouse. Old notions of what it means to be, and to remain, 'human' have been steadily, but spectacularly, rendered obsolete by technoscience. The notion of human rights, still sensible in relation to state violation, now becomes inchoate with regimes of technoscientific power that sustain the New World Order, Inc. The task now is not merely to *understand* these developments but to *transform* them in directions more compatible with competing notions of human rights futures.

The book in your hands obviously raises more questions than it answers. Even the questions it poses need a more sustained refinement and reformulation of activist theory. My task would have been amply done were you to consider these at all relevant, to human rights theory and practice.

Upendra Baxi

Acknowledgements

I dedicate this book to the lamented Neelan Tiruchelvam, a friend for over three decades, who will now forever be missed as an authentic voice for the future of human rights. This book owes more than can be acknowledged in words. Neelan-san (as I fondly called him) wished to preserve a distinct and authentic postcolonial future for the rights of the 'minorities', in an embattled world. He declined the prerogative of a safe globalizing expatriate life as a way of making the future of human rights more secure. He remained close to the scene of many a crime against human futures. In the senses that formal words of dedication of a book can describe, I 'dedicate' this book to his living presence amidst us.

This work owes a great deal to my students at various academic sites: The Law Schools at the Universities of Delhi, Warwick, Toronto and New York, Duke University, American University and the National Law School University of India, Bangalore. They made significant contributions to concerns I address here and it is a matter of considerable satisfaction that many of them have begun to address these in their preferred career paths.

As work in progress, various aspects of the themes of this book were presented to seminars and colloquia: the Indian Academy of Social Sciences, Pune Congress; the Australasian Law Teachers Golden Jubilee symposium at the University of La Trobe; the Universities of Copenhagen and Lund; the Center of Ethnic Studies, Colombo; the Center of Middle Eastern Studies at Princeton University; the University of New York Law School Faculty Workshop; the Harvard Human Rights Program; the Roundtable on the Future of Human Rights at the University of Warwick; the University of Delhi Law School and the National Law School University of India; the Australian National University, Canberra and the University of Iowa.

Professor S.P. Sathe alerted me to the perils of an infelicitous style of writing. Professor Lord Bhikhu Parekh not merely reassured me that this book was worth doing; he went so far as to graciously assist me in chasing up a couple of recalcitrant bibliographical references!

Professor David Kennedy in presenting aspects of this work at the NYU Faculty Workshop gently reminded me of the heterodoxy of my footnote citations, queried the viability of many binary distinctions I draw (especially in the genre of 'progress narratives'), and raised the important issue of how far my work may be said to belong to the conventional corpus of human rights scholarship. Professors Norman Dorsen and Ted Meron wondered whether the appropriation of human rights languages by multinational corporations might not be, after all, a 'good' happening for the future of human rights. Other distinguished participants at the faculty workshop (notably Professors Frank Upham, Christine Harrington, and Ruti Trietel), however, agreeing with the notion of trade-related, market-friendly human rights, interrogated the terms of description. So did Professors Nathan Glazer and Henry Steiner, at the Harvard Human Rights Program discussion.

Professor Burns Weston and Stephen Marks raised many friendly interrogations concerning my distinction between the 'modern' and 'contemporary' human rights paradigms. Weston agonizingly queried my notions of markets for human rights and commodification of human suffering. Professors Talal Asad and Veena Das raised questions concerning my approaches to the anthropology of human rights. Professor Dorothy Nelkin graciously offered detailed comments on an early draft of Chapter Eight. Professor Jane Kelsey (University of Auckland) drew my attention to the need for a more empirical narrative of fiscal and monetary aspects of contemporary economic globalization. I remain deeply appreciative of their friendly collaboration, although unsure that the book in your hands finally meets their expectation.

Among activist friends who have contributed to my understanding of human rights in action are: Clarence Dias, Vasudha Dhagamwar, Shulamith Koenig, Ward Morehouse, Rani Jethmalani, Professor Manubhai Shah, Fr. Joseph, Pandit Chintamani, Swami Agnivesh, Harivallabh Parekh, and the Bhopal activists (under the dedicated leadership of Shri Jabbar Khan).

The acknowledgement of activist friends is not complete without the mention of judicial activist friends. It is my privilege to record in full measure the 'churning' made possible by Justices V.R. Krishna Iyer, P.N. Bhagwati, D.A. Desai and O. Chinnappa Reddy. Till today I

...ain exposed to Justice Krishna Iyer's tempestuous summons, protesting the 'Little Done, the Vast Undone'. Many activist friends at the Bar, fortunately too numerous to be mentioned by name here, have contributed inestimably to my understanding of the bright side as well as the dark moments of the struggle for human rights in India.

While I have 'written' this book, its authorship remains composite. The heavily silent burdens of the labour of writing this book have been graciously borne by Prema. To Bhairav, Pratiksha, Shalini and Viplav, many thanks for the culinary mischief, stories and symphonies. I have no way of knowing how obsolete this work will appear to our granddaughter Paripoorna, now sixteen months 'old'. She will, I hope, at least read this work charitably by 2021 in a post-patriarchal and yet ironically post human rights world.

To the Oxford University Press editor, especially Rasna Dhillon and Aparajita Basu, I owe enormous debts for rendering the manuscript worthy of publication.

Without diminishing in any way any of these individual and collective debts, I need to say that the work in your hands owes much to the *real authors*, in ways that necessarily lie beyond traditional labours of authorial acknowledgement. If there is anything creative in this work, it is owed to my association for well over two decades with social action and human rights struggles. In particular, I owe a very great deal to the valiant struggle of over 200,000 women, children and men afflicted by 47 tonnes of MIC, in the largest global peacetime industrial disaster, orchestrated by Union Carbide Corporation. From them, and the geographies of injustice constituted by the 'organized irresponsibility' and 'organized impunity' of global corporations, I have learnt more about human violation and suffering than the work in your hands can ever possibly convey. I also dedicate this work to the *suffering of the just*, by no means an 'abstract' category.

Contents

1

An Age of Human Rights?

I. Towards a 'Common Language of Humanity'?

Much of the Christian twentieth century, and especially its later half, will undoubtedly be recalled as an Age of Human Rights. No preceding century in human[1] history has been privileged to witness such a profusion of human rights enunciations on a global scale. Never before have the languages of human rights sought to supplant other ethical languages. No previous century has witnessed the proliferation of endless normativity of human rights standards as a core aspect of the politics of *inter-governmental desire*. Never before has this discourse been so varied and diverse that it becomes necessary to regularly publish and update, through the unique discursive instrumentality of the United Nations system, in ever-exploding volumes of fine print, the various texts of instruments relating to human rights.[2] The Secretary General of the United Nations was, perhaps, right to observe (in his inaugural remarks at the 1993 Vienna Conference on Human Rights) that human rights constitute a 'common language of humanity'.[3] Indeed, it would be true to say that in some ways a human rights sociolect emerges, in this era of the end of ideology, as the only universal ideology in the making,

---

[1] I use the term 'human' as an act of communicational courtesy. Human is marked by the presence of man; so is person. My preferred non-sexist version is, therefore, a combination of the first letters of both words: huper. I await the day when the word 'huper' will replace the word 'human'.

[2] *The United Nations Human Rights: A Compilation of International Instruments* (1997).

[3] Boutros Boutros-Ghali, The Common Language of Humanity in *United Nations: World Conference on Human Rights, The Vienna Declaration and Program of Action* (1993).

enabling both the legitimation of power and the *praxis* of emancipatory politics.[4]

At the same time, even as sonorous declarations on human rights proliferate, the Christian twentieth century has been tormented by its own innovations in the practices of the politics of cruelty. Echoes of the Holocaust and Hiroshima–Nagasaki suffering vibrate in the Universal Declaration of Human Rights (hereafter UDHR) as well as in the millennial dream of turning swords into ploughshares. A distinctively European contribution to recent human history, the politics of organized intolerance and ethnic cleansing, has been universalized in the killing fields of post-colonial and post-socialist experience. The early, middle, and late phases of the Cold War[5] orchestrated prodigious human suffering[6] as well as exponential growth of human rights enunciations. Besides, if the Cold War practices were deeply violative of basic human rights, the 'post-cold war' practices of politics in terms of 'ethnic wars', to cite just one example, are no less so.[7]

Alhough not radically ameliorative of here-and-now human suffering, international human rights standards and norms do empower peoples' movements and conscientious policy-makers everywhere to interrogate practices of politics. That, to my mind, is an inestimable potential of human rights languages not readily available in the previous centuries. Human rights languages are perhaps *all that we have* to interrogate the

[4] For the notion of ideology as a set of languages characterized by reflexivity or as 'sociolect'—*see* Alvin Gouldner, *The Dialectic of Ideology and Technology: The Origins, Grammar and Future of Ideology* (1976), 61–5; J.B. Thompson, *Studies in the Theory of Ideology* (1984). A more recent variant of this is the use of the phrase 'dialects of human rights': *see* Mary Ann Glendon, *Rights Talk: The Impoverishment of Political Discourse* (1991).

See also, Upendra Baxi, 'Human Rights Education: The Promise of the Twenty-first Century?', in *Human Rights Education* (1997), 142–54. For a full version see http://www.pdhre.org; David Jacobson. *Rights without Borders: Immigration and the Decline of Citizenship* (1996), 2–3. The state, he rightly stresses, is becoming less constituted by sovereign agency and more by 'a larger international and constitutional order based on human rights'. Human rights provide 'a vehicle and object of this revolution'.

[5] Periodization of 'cold war' is crucial to any understanding of how the intergovernmental politics of desire pursued its own distinctive itineraries. The 'cold war' condenses many instances of practices of cruelty while simultaneously registering innovation in human rights enunciations.

[6] *See*, Clive Ponting, *The Twentieth Century: A World History* (1991).

[7] *See*, for an insightful analysis of 'ethnic wars' surrounding the former Soviet Union, M. Kazanov, *After the USSR: Ethnicity, Nationalism and Politics in the Commonwealth of Independent States* (1995).

barbarism of power, even when these remain inadequate to fully humanize the practices of politics of cruelty.

II. The Open and Diverse Futures

In this work, I ponder the *future of human rights*. This future is, as all futures are, open and diverse. However, not every human 'achievement' endures in time and space. Some become relics of a bygone time, of interest only to connoisseurs of human diversity. Some others furnish residues, out of which are fashioned the future practices of the reinvention of the past, or the politics of invention of nostalgia. Yet others live on as cult practices of a precocious minority in a vastly transformed world. In the eye of the future, that which we now term 'human rights' may live on only in the ruins of memory.

The notion that 'human rights' may have such radically contingent futures may seem outrageous to many of us (even when those many merely constitute an oasis) deeply committed to the alleviation of human misery and social suffering. Some of us who have devoted our entire lives to the struggle for implementation of 'human rights' may regard such an enquiry as morally offensive to the collective histories of embodied and lived hurts. It is precisely for that very reason, however, that it is crucial for us to recall that 'contemporary' human rights theory and practice is a very recent human invention, perhaps safely dated as no more than only half a century old; an archive of emancipatory secular human praxis. At the end of the second Christian millennium, the reminder of the contingency of human rights achievement is, perhaps, a richer resource for their future than the fond illusion that 'human rights' are here to stay, well-nigh irreversible. While we may not succumb to any 'future hype' in being so disposed, this approach has at least the merit of reminding us of the fact that the 'future' of human rights stands imperilled by a whole variety of developments in theory and practice which draw attention to:

- the *genealogies of human rights*, 'modern, and contemporary', their logics of exclusion and inclusion and the construction of ideas about 'human';
- the realities of overproduction of human rights norms and standards, and their significance for human rights futures;
- the politics of difference and identity, which views human rights as having not just an emancipative potential but also a repressive one;
- the postmodernist suspicion of the power to tell large global stories (the 'metanarratives') which carry the potential of

converting human rights languages into texts or tricks of governance or domination;

- the resurfacing of arguments from ethical and cultural relativism interrogating the politics of universality of human rights, making possible, in good conscience, toleration of vast stretches of human suffering;
- the danger of conversion of human rights movements into human rights markets;
- the emergence, with the forces and relations of production of 'globalization' (attested by the dominant ideologies of 'economic rationalism', 'good governance', 'structural adjustment') of a trade-related, market-friendly paradigm of human rights seeking to supplant the paradigm of the UDHR.

In addressing these tasks, I take it as axiomatic that the historic mission of 'contemporary' human rights is to give voice to human suffering, to make it visible, and to ameliorate it. The notion that human rights regimes may, or ought to, contribute to the 'pursuit of happiness' remains the privilege of a miniscule of humanity. For hundreds of millions of the 'wretched of the earth' human rights enunciations matter, if at all, as and when they provide shields against torture and tyranny, deprivation and destitution, pauperization and powerlessness, desexualization and degradation.

I do not pursue the task of bringing diverse voices of suffering to the reality of human rights. That is a subject for another kind of work. Not all voices necessarily speak to the world of global human rights. Not every human violation is necessarily a human rights violation, regardless of the overall normative poverty of international and constitutional human rights norms and standards. I strive, however, to do the next best: I endeavour to relate the theory and practice of human rights to the endless variety of preventable human suffering. Recovery of the sense and experience of human anguish provides the only hope there is for the future of human rights.

Before I address these themes, some approaches to keywords may be helpful, since I shun the self-proclaimed postmodernist virtue that, even at its best moment, celebrates incomprehensibility as a unique form of intelligibility.

True, the worlds of power and resistance to power are rife with complexity and contradiction. True, also, that the production of human rights *truths* contesting those of power stand marked by 'over-determination' or a surplus, a surfeit, of meaning. For those who suffer violation, an appeal to public virtues, no matter how creatively ambiguous, remains a necessity. In contrast, brutal clarity characterizes regimes of political cruelty.[8] All the same, clarity of conviction and communication is a most crucial resource for the promotion and protection of human rights. Success in this performance is never assured, but the struggle to attain it is by itself a human rights *task*.

III. The Haunting Ambiguities of 'Human Rights'

The very term 'human rights', which I invoke constantly, is indeed problematic. In rights-talk, the expression often masks the attempts to reduce the plenitude of its meanings to produce a false totality. One such endeavour locates the unity of all human rights to some designated totality of sentiment such as human 'dignity', 'well-being', and 'flourishing'. Another mode invites us to speak of human rights as 'basic', suggesting that some others may be negotiable, even dispensable. Those who are deprived, disadvantaged, and dispossessed may indeed find it hard to accept any justifications for the very notion of human rights that may end up in a denial of their right to be human. Yet another mode of totalization makes us succumb to an anthropomorphic illusion that the range of human rights is limited to human beings; the new rights to environment (or what is, somewhat inappropriately, even cruelly, called 'sustainable development')[9] take us far beyond such a narrow notion. As descriptive ventures, such attempts at totalization of human rights reduce to a 'coherent' category the forbiddingly diverse world of actually existing human rights. As prescriptive ventures, such modes simply privilege certain preferred values over others. In both cases, the normative complexity and existential outreach of human rights norms and standards are made to yield their historic futures to the demands of a uniform narrative. This, overall, obscures the contradictory nature of development of 'human rights'. There is not *one* world of 'human rights' but many conflicting worlds. Insofar as the ventures in totalization close doors of perception of the conflicted

---

[8] There is no indeterminacy in or about the perpetrator 'justification' for the Holocaust or its contemporary forms of ethnic cleansing. The 'devout' Nazi or contemporary neo-Nazis are rarely affected in their belief or practice by any ambiguity, which agonize human rights intellectuals in every single direction of the professed 'universality', 'indivisibility', and 'interdependence'.

[9] *See*, Andrew Rowell, *Green Backlash: Global Subversion of the Environmental Movement* (1996), 4–41; and for the extraordinary relation between Nazism and deep ecology, *see* Luc Ferry, *The New Ecological Order* (1992), 91–107.

normativity and social reality of 'human rights', one wonders whether the expression itself, despite its vast symbolic potential, invites its own constructive demise.

The practices of 'human rights' shelter an incredibly diverse range of *politics of desire-in-dominance* and *politics of desire-in-insurrection*. These histories of desire, in myriad forms of cruelly mortal conflict, resist encapsulation in any formulae; the best one may hope for is to let the contexts of domination and resistance articulate themselves as separate but equal perspectives of the meaning of 'human rights'. I hope to address these contexts in the rest of this work.

Rights, furthermore, may be considered in several different images:

> rights as boundary, and as access; rights as markers of power, and as masking lack; rights as claims, and protection; rights as organization of social space, and as a defence against incursion; rights as articulation, and mystification; rights as disciplinary and antidisciplinary; rights as a mark of one's humanity, and as reduction of one's humanity; rights as expression of desire, and as foreclosure of desire.[10]

These images can be put another way, as defying 'easy identification':

> Thus, rights are sometimes treated as concepts, as argumentative trumps, as factors of production, as preconditions of bargaining, as bearer-enabling entitlements, as totems, as sources of social solidarity, as legitimation devices …[11]

Too many images crowd consciousness of human rights. The preferred or 'perspectival'[12] image is not just the act of privileged epistemic choice (arising from reading of the 'right' books or following the 'right' canon) but also a function of (what Heidegger called) one's *thrownness* in the world. At the same time, the different images about rights heavily suggest the *dialectical* character of 'rights'. From that single subject position, human rights may be both 'emancipatory' and 'repressive' markers of 'articulation' of counter-power as well as of 'mystification' of power structures, signatures of a triumphant 'humanity' of the theoretical Everyone, and the register of lived depletion of that

---

[10] Wendy Brown, *States of Injury: Power and Freedom in Late Modernity* (1995), 96, f.n. 2.

[11] Pierre Schlag, 'Rights in the Postmodern Condition', in *Legal Rights: Historical and Philosophical Perspectives* (1997), 263 (footnote indicators omitted from the quote).

[12] To invoke, somewhat non-rigorously, 'the' Nietzschean notion of 'perspectivism' as the very 'geography of being'. *See*, Jean Granier, 'Perspectivism and Interpretation', in *The New Nietzsche* (1985), 190.

'humanity'. 'Human rights' constitute different constellations of diverse subject positions in, and through, agency-in-structure.

This having been said, I need to add several footnotes to this theme. The plurality and multiplicity of the fecund expression 'human rights' is worthy of celebration only if we are able to designate the distinctive modes of the sustaining networks of meaning and the logics of popular action that protest against all forms of human violation. If the notion of 'human rights' means many things to different people, these meanings need to be configured in some patterns without violating the richness of difference. I essay it tentatively under the following different rubrics.

(a) *Human Rights as Ethical Imperatives*

Some speak of 'human rights' in terms of ethical values that ought to inform collective and individual action. 'Human rights' are here not thought of in terms of the political practices of enunciation, as rationalization of interests. Rather, the ethic of human rights insists on what communities and individuals *ought* to desire. The core ethical values (such as human dignity, integrity, and well being) furnish a standpoint from which the dominant human rights paradigms (knowledge/power formations) may be constantly subjected to interrogation. The ethics of human rights emerges as a tradition of *critical morality* by which the *positive morality* of human rights practices themselves may be judged.

The source and scope of these values remain contested sites. The project of human rights, however, is seen as distinctly ethical. The visions of moral development vary profoundly as contemporary discourses on feminist ethics and eco-ethics abundantly testify. At least one core value seems to command consensus. Respect toward the Other as a co-equal human is the groundwork of an ethic of human rights, furnishing universally valid norms for human conduct and the basic structure of a just society. That respect, as Emmanuel Levinas memorably reminds us, does not consist of the 'imperialism of the Same'.[13] Rather, it consists of the full recognition of human rights as a 'sole source of solidarity among strangers', conceding 'one another the right to *remain* strangers'.[14]

In this perspective 'human rights' emerge as a moral–ethical discourse furnishing standards of critical morality for the evaluation of any

---

[13] Emmanuel Levinas, *Totality and Infinity: An Essay on Exteriority* (1969), 87.
[14] Jurgen Habermas, *Between Facts and Norms: Contributions Towards a Discourse Theory of Ethics* (1996), 308.

existing state of affairs. Unlike most ethical discourses that primarily address issues of distribution in the basic structure of a given society and tradition, the ethical 'human rights' discourse also addresses the society of states in historically evolving circumstances of globality.[15] 'Human rights' becomes an expression that carries the burden of a transformative vision of the world, in which the state (and the community of state and state-like global institutions) incrementally becomes ethical, governance just, and power (in all its hiding places) accountable.

(b) *Human Rights as Grammar of Governance*

Practices of governance ambivalently sustain the network of meanings called 'human rights'. Human rights address the problem of legitimacy of power to rule. Human rights provide a corpus of constraints on public decision-making power and the languages of transparency in public choice. However, even as these provide obstacles to free play of power, rights standards also provide opportunities for it. Rights-oriented governance structures and processes—the rule of law formations—also shape, and at times determine, the form and content of human rights. The rule of law conceived as the lawyers' law (that is, the public processes of protection and promotion of 'human rights') remains consistent with structural violation by virtue of its capacity to reproduce legitimate law. The sovereign power constantly negotiates the imperatives of the rule of law in ways that, for example, somehow render as legitimate the affluence of a few with the extreme impoverishment of many, locally and globally. This form of reproduction of rights and legality often, at least from the standpoint of those violated, combines, and recombines, the rule of law with the reign of terror.

The normative quest for governance structures that produce legitimate laws with a more serious regard for human rights, emphasizes the *democratic rights of the peoples* to redress this non-structural vision of human rights. It emphasizes escalating orders of participatory rights of the people—such as their rights to constitute governance through periodic free and fair elections; self-determination through at least genuine modes of devolution of power; identity rights, and the right to cultural and physical survival as communities or groups. This realm

[15] John Rawls, 'The Law of the Peoples', in *On Human Rights: The Oxford Amnesty Lectures* (1993), 41. Professor Rawls has since elaborated the thematic in his germinal monograph (1999).

does not so much pertain to the daily activity of a state but to the rights-integrity of its structures that furnishes an approach to the solution to the problem of the very legitimacy of the law itself.[16]

In both the realms of rights, practices of governance become contested sites, sustaining loyalty as well as mobilizing democratic deficit or even legitimation crises. Human rights in either sense relate to governance practices by way of complicity or struggle. In either situation, the diverse theory and practice of human rights carry the potential for a pervasive impact on the practices of state-formation.

(c) *Human Rights as Languages of Global Governance*

An incredible range of activities or phenomena nestles within this expression. Although axiomatic, it is now the talk of the town (and also the gown!) that practices of global governance may legitimate themselves best by recourse to human rights languages. How this may happen is, of course, deeply problematic as, for example (and these are unwieldy illustrative domains) in the United Nations discourse on 'sustainable development' and 'global governance'. It is unsurprising that human rights standards and norms, which are products of diplomatic and international civil service desire within the ever-expanding United Nations system, lend themselves to a whole variety of foreign policy and global corporate uses and abuses under the cover of 'international' consensus. The amazing aspect, however, is the resilient autonomy of human rights normativity that periodically interrogates such acts of expropriation of human rights in the pursuit of severely self-regarding national or regional interests.

(d) *Human Rights as Syndrome of Shared Sovereignty*

The dissipation, as well as reconfiguration, of sovereignty occurs (in the production and maintenance of meaning/signification systems called 'human rights') through four principal mechanisms. Each of these puts to its distinctive use the languages of 'human rights'.

First, postmodernist confederations of power, of which the European Community provides a most singular, even spectacular, example that intertwines governance with rights languages: whether these

---

[16] Habermas, *supra* note 14 at 104–32. The Habermasian enunciation does not include many governance practices that mock the logic of participatory rights: for example, the collective right of peoples and communities to immunity from corrupt practices of governance.

arrangements reinforce the power to govern or the democratic rights of peoples subject to governance remains an open question.[17]

Second, the distinctive regimes of related global (the World Trade Organization) and regional trade arrangements (for example, NAFTA, APEC, ASEAN) emerge as organisms generating powerful antibodies to the 'epidemic' of human rights, conceived both as civil liberties and democratic rights. These regimes regard all human rights as irritating impositions, insofar as these retard global capital's mission to create conditions and circumstances of 'development', only within which human rights may envision their practical and foreseeable future.

Third, the ever-increasing complex linkages between 'development aid' and donor country conditionalities present sites of intersection between 'human rights' and the tasks of global governance. Were the Northern donors not to insist on gender equality or 'democratic' elections, internationally supervised, the groundwork (as it were) for political reformation in the aided nations, it is felt, would remain forever innocent of 'human rights' aspirations. Many South-based international NGOs work admirably, and tirelessly, to promote such 'human rights' conditionalities. In seeking to constrain the governance practices of the 'nation-state', these formations also become subjected to the emerging paradigms of 'global governance' no matter how benignly presented as human rights friendly.

Fourth, the extraordinary incursions into national autonomy of 'political' decision-making by international financial institutions in the pursuit of promotion, if not protection, of 'human rights' in their cumulative effect may well be regarded as mechanisms for dissipation and reunification of 'human rights' unfriendly hegemonic sovereignties.

(e) *Human Rights as Insurrectionary Praxis*

Through myriad struggles and movements throughout the world, 'human rights' become an arena of transformative political practice that disorients, destabilizes, and at times even helps destroy deeply unjust concentrations of political, social, economic, and technological power. Movements for decolonization and self-determination, elimination of apartheid, 'women's rights as human rights', ecological integrity and the right sexual orientation provide archetypal illustrations of the potential for transformative practice.

---

[17] *See*, the insightful analysis by Peter Leuprecht, 'Innovations in the European System of Human Rights Protection: Is Enlargement Compatible with Reinforcement?', 8, *Transnational Law and Contemporary Problems* (1998), 318.

The perplexities here lie in deciphering the 'upward' and 'downward' linkages between 'mass' movements and aspirations for transformation and their representation by an incredible variety of NGOs (now renamed, and perhaps not innocently, as CSOs—civil society organizations)[18] in close interaction between national, regional, and international power formations. The NGOs who so pre-eminently lead these movements vary in their levels of 'massification' in terms of their potential for articulating the voices of the violated and authenticating their visions of a just world. As such, they do not as yet, fortunately, exhaust their emancipatory potential. At the same time, these movements pluralize meanings of human rights far beyond doctrinal disputations concerning 'relativism' and 'universality' that, at the end of the day, subserve the global interests in the making.

(f) *Human Rights as Juridical Production*

Not many of even the most pre-eminent international lawyers carry in and through their lifework, this incredible range of human rights meanings or significatory practices. Those, however, who do devote their singular talents to systematizing human rights law and practice or to sculpt alternate structures (like the International Criminal Court) create systems of meanings for 'human rights,' almost equally available for the ends of governance and insurrection.

The dogmatic tradition of scholarly human rights discourse is *prudential* in the best, even Thomistic, sense of the term, stressing the evolutionary character of the emerging law of human rights entailing convergence, though agonizingly haphazard, of state practice around specific norms and standards. In contrast, the critical, even radical, scholarly human rights practices tend to view human rights emergences in terms of breaks, discontinuities, and fissures in the canonical narratives of state sovereignty and legitimacy. They perceive international relations and organizations as having a dialectical relation between power and resistance at the level of agency and structure. Put in another way, this scholarly genre focuses upon the critical practices of non-'sovereign' but still self-determinative peoples in the development of international law generally and international human rights law in particular. Both types of theoretical practices have a bearing on theorizing repression, but only critical practice takes this as an explicit objective.

---

[18] *See*, Upendra Baxi, '"Global Neighborhood" and "Universal Otherhood"': Notes on Report of the Commission on Global Governance', 21, *Alternatives* (1996), 525–49.

Theorizing repression, however, requires also, besides the articulation of an authentic cry of deep human anguish, enormous labours of erudite understanding of ways of power and governance, which remain the focus of the dogmatic approach with all its technologizing constructions of human rights. To be sure, a state-sensitive dogmatic approach remains liable to servicing the ends of power and governance. This, however, also brings to view the pathologies of Realpolitik in rich detail. This is useful, even important, because the devil often lies in the detail!

(g) *Human Rights as 'Culture'*

In this discourse, riven with contestation on 'universality' and 'particularism', human rights are conceived as cultural systems. It is the case that every societal culture encapsulates beliefs, sentiments, symbols that impart sense to the notion of being human, no matter in how many different registers of inclusivity. Similarly, every societal culture has traditions of understanding concerning what rights human beings ought to have. No culture then is devoid of notions about human rights, even when that which constitutes these rights varies within the same culture in time and place, and these vary across comparable cultures. Within societal cultures, distinctive legal cultures give rise to the practice of rights. In this sense, perhaps, human rights may be described as 'cultural software'; 'a set of mechanisms of hermeneutic power'[19] that make, in a constantly dynamic way, new understandings of what it means, and ought to mean, to be *human*.

These societal human rights cultures relate to global cultures of human rights. It is trivial to say that they are shaped by the global cultures and in turn shape them. What matters are the perception and the reality of this mutuality of determination. If the global cultures of human rights are dominant, societal human rights cultures would be confronted by a relation of submission and struggle. However, even at this level sensitivity to the tyranny of the singular is critical. If societal human rights cultures are diverse, so are global human rights cultures. The relations of submission and struggle at all levels are intensely complex and contradictory.

---

[19] J.M. Balkin, *Cultural Software: A Theory of Ideology* (1998), 273–85. Balkin of course, does not address human rights as cultural software. However, human rights as cultural software enable us not only to 'understand but in doing so helps us produce the "we" that understand' (p. 274). It 'produces the hermeneutic power that binds members of a culture together' and makes 'cultural conventions possible' (p. 278).

The cultural software of global human rights is not, of course, exhausted, though typified, by human rights norms and standards. There is more to global human rights culture than can be exhausted by often, indeed all too often, lifeless human rights instruments. The kiss of life is given by interactions of solidarity within the emerging archipelagos of human rights activism in the United Nations system even when increasingly dominated by sovereign states and, in recent times, by meta-sovereign global corporations. The global cultures of human rights, ceaselessly driven by a Nietschzean Will to Power of myriad NGO initiatives, are equally so driven by the hegemons in a post-Cold War era of *pax Americana*. A fallout of this synergy is the constant rewriting of the societal cultural software of human rights. If one were inclined to this view, it would be odd to regard global human rights culture as (to borrow an evocative phrase of Sharon Traweek in the context of practices of technoscience) the 'culture of no culture'.[20] Of course, those who contest, at the level of knowledge/power practices the universality of the human rights thematic need to narrativize a global human rights culture precisely in these terms. All available evidence, however, points to the reality that the global human rights culture, far from being a culture of no cultures, is intensely multicultural, a culture of many cultures.

IV. Discursivity

By 'discursivity' I refer to both the orders of erudite and ordinary practices of the 'rights-talk'. Rights-talk (or discursive practices) occurs within traditions (discursive formation).[21] Traditions, themselves codes for power and hierarchy, allocate competences (who may speak), construct forms (how may one speak; what forms of discourse are proper), determine boundaries (what may not be named or conversed about), and structure exclusion (denial of voice). What I call 'modern' human rights offers powerful examples of the power of the rights-talk tradition.

[20] Sharon Traweek, *Beamtimes and Lifetimes* (1988).

[21] For example, rights-talk (discursive practice) gives rise to distinct, even if related, regimes (discursive formations): the civil and political rights regime in international law is distinct from the social, cultural and economic rights regime. The ways in which discursive formation occur determine what shall count as a violation of human rights. The prohibition against torture, cruel, inhuman degrading punishment, or treatment in the civil and political rights formation also inhibits rights-talk, which equates starvation or domestic violence as a violation of human rights. The latter gets constituted as violation only when discursive boundaries are transgressed.

What I call 'contemporary' human rights discursivity illustrates (though not always and everywhere) the power of the subaltern discourse. When that discourse acquires (in moments of rare solidarity) the intensity of a discursive insurrection, its management becomes a prime task of human rights diplomacy. Dominant or hegemonic rights-talk seeks, but never fully achieves, the suppression of subaltern rights-talk.

Human rights discursivity is marked by complexity and contradiction between (to invoke a Filipino template) the statist discourse of the educated (*illustrado*) and the subversive discourse of the *indio* (the indigenous).[22] It is this vital distinction which we need to address in Jurgen Habermas' germinal endeavour to assign to the 'public sphere' the future of human rights; that is, the belief in 'the procedural core' of deliberative public politics.[23] To put the point simply (but hopefully accurately) such practices of politics must entail equality of discourse between the *illustrado* and the *indio*. This, in turn, presupposes that the dominant power structures are *already* constrained (or that they could be so significantly constrained) to strive towards equal dignity in discourse among the literate and the illiterate, the haves and the have-nots, the tormentors and the tormented, those who suffer from a lack of the basic necessities of life and those that suffer but only the surfeit of pleasure. The Habermasian 'post-metaphysical' discourse ethics at its very best addresses the future of human rights in terms of 'post-industrial societies'. This, while crucial for the future of human rights in *illustrado* discursive realms, points to an equal *but* not separate need to re-imagine the future of human rights for the *indio*.

Further, discourse theorists often maintain that discursive practice constitutes social reality; there are no violators, violated, and violations outside discourse. However, such discourse theory ignores or obscures *non*-discursive or material practices of power and resistance. This way of talk *disembodies human suffering here and now*, for future ameliorative/ redemptive purposes, whose status (at least from the standpoint of those that suffer) is *very obscure, indeed to a point of cruelty of theory*. The non-discursive order of reality, the materiality of human violation, is just as important, if not more so, from the standpoint of the violated.[24]

---

[22] Anthony Woodiwiss, *Globalization, Human Rights and Labor Law in the Pacific Asia* (1998), 104.

[23] Habermas, *supra* note 14 at 304–8.

[24] A point cruelly established, for example, by the 'productive' technologies entailed in the manufacture and distribution of landmines or weapons and instruments of mass destruction. It would be excessive to say that these are constituted by

V. Logics and Paralogics of Human Rights

By the use of the notion of 'paralogics' I conflate the notions of logic and rhetoric. Paradigmatic logic follows a 'causal' chain of signification to a 'conclusion' directed by the major and the minor premise. Rhetorical logic does not regard argument as 'links in the chain' but rather as the legs of a chair.[25] What matters in rhetorical logic is the choice of *topoi*: literary conventions that define sites from which the processes of suasion begin. These are rarely governed by any pre-given *topoi*, but rather dwell in that which *one thinks one ought to argue about*.[26] 'Human rights' logic or paralogics are all about how one may or ought to construct '*techniques of persuasion (as) a means of creating awareness*'.[27]

The human rights *we-ness* that enacts and enhances these techniques of suasion is multifarious, contingent, and continually fragmented. That *we-ness* is both an artifact of power as well as of resistance. Human rights discourse is *intensely partisan*; it cannot exist or endure outside of the webs of impassioned commitment and networks of contingent solidarities, whether on behalf and the behest of dominant or subaltern ideological practice. *Both* claim the ownership of a *transformative vision of politics, of anticipation of possible human futures*. The historic significance

---

discursive practices and do not exist outside those practices. The materiality of non-discursive practices, arenas, and formations is relatively autonomous of discourse theories.

It is another matter that human rights discursive practices are able, at times, to highlight victimage caused by deployment of these technologies as human rights violative. Insofar as it is possible for the last word to be said, David Harvey has come closest to saying it: 'Discourse and language may be a vital locus of struggle. But they are not only or even necessarily the most important places of struggle.' David Harvey, *Justice, Nature and the Geography of Difference* (1996), 113.

[25] Julius Stone, *Legal Systems and Lawyers' Reasonings* at 327 (1964).

[26] Expressed brilliantly by Umberto Eco thus:

For example, I can argue as follows: 'What others possess having been taken away from me is not their property; it is wrong to take from others what is their property; but it is not wrong to restore the original order of Property, putting back into my hands what was originally in my hands.' But I can also argue: 'Rights of property are sanctioned by the actual possession of the thing; if I take from someone what is actually in their possession, I commit an act against rights to property and therefore theft.' Of course, a third argument is possible, namely: 'All property is per se theft; taking property from property-owners means restoring equilibrium violated by original theft, and therefore taking from the propertied the fruits of their theft is not just a right but a duty. Umberto Eco, *Apocalypses Postponed* (1995), 104 (emphasis added).

[27] Ibid. at 105. I borrow Eco's phrase explaining the task of rhetoric in general.

of 'human rights' (no matter what we perform with this potter's clay) lies in the denial of administered regimes of disarticulation, even when this amounts only to the perforation of the escutcheon of dispersed sovereignty of state power.

VI. Future(s) of Human Rights

A sense of unease haunts my heavy invocation of the notion of the future of human rights. In a sense, this future is already the *past* of human rights time, manner, and circumstance. In a sense, what may constitute the future history of human rights depends on how imaginatively one defines, both in theory and movement, the challenges posed by the processes of globalization: already we are urged to appreciate the 'need to relocate' human rights in the 'current processes of change'.[28] On this view, what stands mandated is the very mode of *structural adjustment of human rights reflexivity itself.* Prospects of recycling moral languages of human rights appear rather bleak in our 'globalizing' human condition in ways that these did *not* to the forerunners and founders of human rights: from a Grotius to a Gandhi.

A contrasting vision stresses 'rooted Utopianism'. It constructs human rights futures as entailing non-technocratic ways of imaging futures. The technocratic imaging takes for granted 'the persistence of political forms and structures, at least short of collapse through catastrophe'. In contrast, the non-technocratic ways derive sustenance from exemplary lives of citizen–pilgrims 'at work amidst us' who embody a 'refusal to be bound by either deference or acquiescence to statism' and 'relate fulfilment to joy in community, not materialist acquisition'.[29]

This work straddles uncertainly the many worlds of human rights between the globalization (doomsday) possibility of human future and the vision of Utopian transformation animated by the exemplary lives of countless citizen–pilgrims.[30] It must, however, be acknowledged

---

[28] UN Commission on Human Rights, *The Realization of Economic, Social and Cultural Rights: The Relationship Between Enjoyment of Human Rights... and Income Distribution* (Final Report of the Special Rapporteur Jose Bengoa), UN Doc. E/CN.4/Sub.2/1997, 30 June 1997.

[29] Richard Falk, *Explorations at the Edge of Time: The Prospects for World Order* 1950, 101–3.

[30] Professor Falk mentions (Note 29 *supra*) Mother Teresa, Bishop Desmond Tutu, Paulo Friere, Lech Walesa, Kim Dae Jung, and Petra Kelly. However, alongside these

that human rights as languages of power and of insurrection have not one but many futures.

VII. Suffering

Save when expedient, the statist human rights discourse in its enunciations of human rights does not relate to languages of human pain and social suffering. In contrast, people's struggles against regimes practising the politics of cruelty stand rooted in the direct experience of pain and suffering.

Even so, human rights languages problematize notions of suffering. Suffering is ubiquitous to the point of being *natural*. Pain and suffering are egregious; some forms of suffering are considered 'necessary' and some 'unnecessary'. Different cultural traditions weigh social suffering as 'justified' and 'unjustified', making the construction of suffering difficult. Successful social and human rights movements create new forms of justifiable suffering. Gender equality makes patriarchs suffer everywhere. The overthrow of apartheid in the United States has made many a white supremacist suffer. Prison guards and officials suffer when their custodial sovereignty is assailed by prison reform favouring the rights of the inmates. People in high places suffer when movements against corruption achieve a modicum of success and we all get e-mail from Chilean groups that urge us to think of the suffering imposed on Pinochet by the extradition proceedings. The militant practices of the right to self determination by insurgent groups claiming autonomous state and communitarian identity often entail incredible human and social suffering. At the threshold of relating human rights to suffering, the analytic standpoint urges us to accord these forms of suffering an equal dignity of discourse that we extend to practices of the politics of cruelty and catastrophic practices of power.

Human rights oriented and caused, human suffering is both creative and destructive of human potential. It is, in the best sense of that word, the imposition of *secular* social suffering. In this sense, unlike suffering legitimated by religious traditions through a cosmology,[31] secular

---

charismatic figures there are 'countless other women and men we will never know'. Behind every legendary human rights life lie the lives of hundreds of human beings, no less exemplary. The task of historiography of human rights is to roll back the orders of anonymization. This task gets complicated in some troublesome ways by innumerable media-porous, UN accredited, and self-certified NGOs who obscure from view the unsurpassed moral heroism embodied in everyday exemplary lives.

[31] *See*, e.g., Thomas Aquinas, *The Literal Exposition on Job: A Sciptural Commentary Concerning Providence* (1989).

human rights traditions bear only the hope of here and now human redemption. That venture at redemption, however, stands marked by many a boundary between necessary/unnecessary suffering,[32] sensitive to the problematique of cultural/professional appropriation of human suffering.[33]

Crucial for our present purposes is the fact that *even* human rights instruments, regimes, and discursivity enact a hierarchy of pain and suffering. Statist human rights regimes seek to legitimate capital punishment (despite the normativity of progressive elimination); provide for suspension of human rights in situations of 'emergency' (howsoever nuanced); promote obstinate division between the exercise of civil and political rights, on the one hand, and that of social, economic, and cultural rights on the other. Similarly, some global human rights' policing via the emergent post-Cold War regimes of 'sanctions' and direct armed intervention *justify*, in the name of making human rights secure, massive, flagrant, and ongoing violations. Even non-statist human rights' discursivity (and at first sight 'progressive') justifies imposition of human suffering in the name of self-determination, autonomy, and identity movements. Further, the processes of globalization, in seeking to render human rights languages irrelevant to the theology of free trade and investment, enact a new dramaturgy of *justifiable* human suffering.

The visions of future of human rights depend on our power not just to name an order of evil but in our ability to articulate a normative theory concerning the ethical *unjustifiablity* of certain forms and formations of human suffering that the regime of radical evil incarnates.

VIII. An Age of Radical Evil as Well as an Age of Human Rights

From this standpoint it is worth recalling, over and over again, that the Age of Human Rights is also, at the same time, the Age of Radical Evil. That Kantian notion bears reiteration in Hannah Arendt's enunciation of radical evil as a 'structural element in the realm of human affairs' in which human beings 'are unable to forgive what they cannot punish and . . . unable to punish what has turned out

---

[32] Maurice Glasman, *Unnecessary Suffering: Managing Market Utopia* (1996).
[33] *See*, e.g., Arthur Kleinman and Joan Kleinman, 'The Appeal of Experience; The Dismay of Images: Cultural Appropriations of Suffering in Our Times', in *Social Suffering* (1997), 25.

to be unforgivable'.[34] 'All we know', she maintains, 'is that we can neither punish nor forgive such offences and that they therefore transcend the realm of human affairs and the potentialities of human power.'[35]

Arendt wrote in the aftermath of the Holocaust about the not consistently heroic moral ways of its redressal that led to the *invention* of the Nuremberg (and Tokyo) principles, and paved the way for the addressal in some normative modes of the *catastrophic* practices of politics, national and global, since then. Since then too, practices of *radical evil* have been universalized and innovated through sundry gulags. The radical evil that we may neither punish nor forgive has grown apace. Curiously, however, (contrary to a Humean standpoint) the *moral ought* stands derived from an *inhuman is*. Put in another way, radical evil is the womb that nurtures the embryo of the 'contemporary' human rights.

The notion of radical evil provides simultaneously the dynamism for the birth and growth of 'contemporary' human rights as well as intimations of their mortality. In coping with violations that exceed the possibility of punishment and forgiveness, situations of radical evil (as we see shortly) also take us beyond the human rights norms and standards they help us establish. Even as situations of radical evil accelerate normative consensus against such evil, actual ways of handling the aftermath of radical evil lead us to action that repeatedly flouts that new born normativity. On this terrain, the anomie (in the same of violent normlessness) of the perpetrator unites with the anomie (in the sense of the powerlessness) of the violated.

If we were to think of radical evil in these terms, the future of human rights must indeed appear very bleak. Radical evil is the imposition of suffering beyond redress, remorse and rights, and even recall. That is why it perhaps appears unwise to think about colonization (and its Siamese twin, imperialism) as an order of radical evil in the same way that one thinks of it in the context of modern genocidal politics. Also, perhaps the same prudential mood characterizes our unwillingness and inability to name the Cold War as an order of radical evil. There has been no endeavour to establish the pervasive Cold War violation of human rights as crimes against humanity, no acknowledgement of responsibility, no conversation about forms of reparation and

[34] Hannah Arendt, *The Human Condition* (1958), 24. *See*, however, Carlos Santiago Nino, *The Ethics of Deliberative Democracy* (1996). *See also* the diverse postmodern meditations on this notion in Joan Copjec (ed.), *Radical Evil* (1996).
[35] Ibid.

restitution. This organized moral amnesia undermines the very foundations of contemporary human rights; human rights cultures may not be robust for the future when based on such comprehensively organized politics of oblivion of the horrific past and recent human violation.

The very conceptualization of 'radical evil' may lead us to think of its Other as the routine, everyday evil with which, and somehow, human rights norms and standards may wrestle more effectively. There are many reasons why we may not leave this issue unexamined, at least from the standpoint of the suffering of those violated.

The notion of radical evil addresses, at least in the context of the emergent international law, the problem of how to deal retroactively with massive violations of human rights by the 'exceptional' state or regime. In this sense, it identifies radical evil with genocidal practices of power. It focuses juristic and popular energies on the problem of how best to temper justice with mercy, truth with reconciliation, past and future.

Radical evil, however, flourishes outside histories of colonialism, imperialism, and the Cold War, though in some situations it is still determined by these. Necrophilic forms of power indwell many structural sites, a fact mercifully (from the point of view of the violated) somewhat cognized in the contemporary international human rights law and jurisprudence that address

- civil society sanctioned, culturally grounded human violations such as the oppression of women;
- the *dharma*–sanctioned caste system, which still justifies in embodied suffering the violations of those born into untouchability;
- the plight of the forgotten peoples (indigenous communities under threat of extinction, recalled only as sites of human genetic diversity that must be rescued for technoscience before they are extinct);
- millions of women and girl-children condemned to sexual slavery through forced trafficking in women;
- children and young persons conscripted into state or insurgent militia;
- people living under conditions and contexts of mass impoverishment.

The danger, of course, is that this kind of diaspora of the notion of radical evil surrenders its majesty and power. However, that diaspora of the notion is necessary in 'contemporary' human rights engagement, at least from the point of view of the violated. The future of 'contemporary' human rights depends, from this standpoint, a great deal on a more comprehensive understanding of radical evil, both as the practices of concentrated catastrophic politics and as everyday structural violation.

In this sense, the quest to relate human rights to human suffering is fateful for the future of human rights. This is, however, by no means an easy task. Human rights languages, being products of inter-governmental and NGO politics of desire, of necessity privilege some forms of suffering over others. In particular, moral negotiation of suffering seeks to redress the 'past' of outrageous human violation through constructions of a future liberated from a systemic propensity for such violation. Such constructions entail contradictory happenings. Even when the violated acquire narrative voice, the narrative authority resides elsewhere. The truths that emerge are not insurgent truths but truths that are nationalized. The past is allowed to speak only so as to serve the future, and yet there is no assurance that that future will be tethered to making human rights secure. Nor are the violated put in a position of any authority to sculpt that future, even as they yield to projects of national reconstruction their biographies and histories of pervasive human suffering, which have irrevocably extinguished their life projects in a litany of torture, tyranny and terror.

I refer here to devices, barely a quarter century old, of truth and reconciliation commissions.[36] These mark a moral, and human rights, movement forward. *No such devices emerged in the wake of* decolonization. To this day, no imperial/colonial power has even thought it possible to *apologise* to the ex-colonial peoples! Nor are any reparations even *imaginable*. Viewed from this perspective, the device,

---

[36] *See*, Marc Osiel, *Mass Atrocity, Collective Memory and the Law* (1997); Harvard Human Rights Program, *Truth Commissions: A Comparative Assessment* (1997); Priscilla B. Hayner, 'Fifteen Truth Commissions 1974 to 1994: A Comparative Study 16' *Human Rights Quarterly* 597; John Duggard, 'Reconciliation and Justice: The South African Experience' 8, in *The Future of International Human Rights* (1999); *Transitional Justice: How Emerging Democracies Reckon With Former Regimes* (3 vols. 1995; Neil J Kritz ed.); *Impunity and Human Rights in International Law and Practice* (1995), Naomi Roht-Arriaza (ed.); Judith N. Shklar, *Legalism: Law, Morals and Political Trials* (1986); Carlos Santiago Nino, *Radical Evil on Trial* (1996); Martha Minow, *Between Vengeance and Forgiveness: Facing History After Genocide and Mass Violence* (1998); Geoffrey Robertson, *Crimes Against Humanity: The Struggle for Global Justice* (1999).

as noted, does mark a noteworthy singular moral advance, led by the nations of the Third World.

At the same time, all this occurs within a peculiar formation of what must be called the *political economy of 'contemporary' human rights*. That formation precludes any determination of complicity and culpability of hegemonic world powers which install, arm, and promote (or otherwise aid and abet) regimes that thrive all along on catastrophic politics of cruelty. Also, as truth commissions tend to become the order of the day, the moral negotiation of suffering thus entailed remains deeply flawed, incapable of addressing the *efficient causes of human violation*.

The processes also remain deeply flawed from the perspectives of the violated. They emerge only as narratees before compromistic structures of accountability, in the shaping of which they are accorded *no primary voice*. Their testimony becomes the raw material for 'national reconstruction'; their primary suffering and violation becomes 'nationalized' all over again.[37] Also without any assurance of augmentation in the human rights sensitivity of apparatuses and agents of national and global governance, such moral negotiation of suffering thrives on the *ethic of the violated*; even to the Buddhist doctrine of *karuna* (compassion) in the case of Pol Pot just before his death.[38]

Contemporary human rights cultures hover between 'retribution' to the violators and the displays of forgiveness of those violated, manifesting somehow the ethical superiority of those irreversibly violated. Perhaps

---

[37] 'Since memory is a very important factor in struggle (really, in fact, struggles develop a kind of conscious moving forward of history), if one controls peoples' memory, one controls their dynamism. And one also controls their experience, their knowledge of the previous struggles....' Michel Foucault, 'Film and Popular Memory' in *Foucault Live* (*Interviews*, 1966–84) (1989), 89 at 92.

Control over administration of public memory and of forms of organizing oblivion are clearly preferred forms of goverance and regime styles for managing political transition. The violated, however, have their own history, which should ideally make this project of power contingent upon moments of collision between the 'narrative truths of power and insurgent truth of victims', putting to stress 'the power of power to erase victimage' and tormenting forms of state power itself, when 'anxious about the basis of its legitimation. It is the agony of power, ... that the possibility of justice indwells.' Upendra Baxi, 'Reflections on Narrative Rights and Victimage', in U. Baxi, *Inhuman Wrongs and Human Rights: Unconventional Essays* (1994), 28 at 32.

[38] Similarly, in asking Pinochet to express public remorse (just before the British extradition proceedings began) at massive and flagrant violations of human rights, even Ariel Dorfman in an initial articulation invoked the higher ethic of the violated. The South African Truth and Reconciliation Commission continually appealed to the ethic of forgiveness.

the future of human rights depends on how this moral negotiation of suffering is in the decades to come made more inclusive, participatory, and just from the standpoint of those violated rather than that of the perpetrators, perhaps *not*.

In raising these anxious questions, I do not wish to belittle the small, and even significant, steps thus far taken. The praxis of making catastrophic practices of the politics of cruelty accountable is akin to the work of ages involved in building the great formations of coral reef. Yet, the current wonder of the human rights world remains fragile in the absence of constant reflexivity on how the modes of negotiating human suffering may be moved by invention of anguished forms of new human solidarity.[39]

Perhaps this solidarity may thought to be disturbed, and even destroyed, by any endeavour to extend a human rights sensibility seeking to indict the very sources of global power that cause egregious human, and human rights, violation by the neo-colonial, practices of global governance by a coterie of Euro-American hegemonic powers. In the present view, unless these causative, even *originary powers of radical evil,* stand confronted by human rights languages, the future of human rights must forever remain deeply insecure. What is at stake for that future is not merely the punishment of sundry perpetrators of horrendous human violation in the Third World but also the accountability of the world of *illustrado* that so remorselessly, and cruelly, engages in the global mode of production of human, and human rights, violation of the *indio*.

---

[39] Veena Das has shown that the 'inner world' of the violated 'too has history', that is the history of resistance to confiscation of memory. She asks:

> What kind of human solidarity can one establish with people in the face of the recognition that there is an impulse to transform this suffering into a moral commentary? Is there is a way in which Durkhiem's contention, that pain shared collectively can be transformed to bear witness to the moral life of the community, may be resurrected? To what notions of creations of moral community may we summon that state and society in the face of such terror?

Veena Das, *Critical Events: An Anthropological Perspective on Contemporary India* (1995), 190–1.

2

Two Notions of Human Rights: 'Modern' and 'Contemporary'

I. Authorship and Ownership

The very notion of human rights (or the 'rights of *man*') is generally presented as the gift of the West to the rest. The non-Western traditions are usually considered bereft of notions of human rights. Neither did they experience the rise of capitalism with which the origins of 'modern' human rights is thought to be inextricably interlinked; nor did they attain the 'flourishing of theoretical knowledge (*savior*) through which European humanity passed on its way towards its modernity'.[1] Such consciousnes of human rights that occurred in non-Western societies is said to be purely due to the patterns of imposition and diffusion of the Enlightenment ideas and ideals among them. It was the mimetic adaptation of these ideas that enabled, even empowered, the non-West communities with the knowledge and power to interrogate their traditions devoid of notions of human rights and to transform these in heroic confrontation with colonization and imperialism. Even today Third World theory and action is thought to be mimetic, picking up cognitive bits and pieces from the smorgasbord of the critique of Enlightenment from Marx, Nietzsche, Freud, Heidegger, Habermas, Rawls, Foucault or Derrida. Overall, human rights discursivity was and still remains, according to the narrative of origins, the patrimony of the West.

To be sure, such things that were the commonplaces of thought in the preceding three centuries are never articulated any longer with such overt epistemic racism. Such attitudes do however persist, and this

[1] Emmanuel Levinas, *Outside the Subject* (1987), 119 (italics omitted).

bodes ill for the future of human rights. The presentation of human rights notions as enclosed in originary Western metanarratives entails many consequences, intended or otherwise.

First, it disables any intercultural, multi-civilizational discourse on the genealogy of human rights. The originary claims concerning the invention of 'human rights' in the West lead to a continuing insistence on the oft-reiterated *absence* of human rights traditions in the 'non-West'. From this it is but a short practical step for the 'West' to impart, by coercive and 'persuasive' means, to others the gift of human rights. This leads to a rank denial, even in a post-colonial and post-socialist age, of equal discursive dignity to other cultures and civilizations. It also imparts a loss of reflexity, in terms of intercultural learning, for the Euro-American traditions of human rights.

Second, this originary metanarrative leads to imagining *human* futures within which futures of human rights have their being. The 'Enlightenment' epoch that gave birth to the liberal, 'modern' notions of human rights (especially to human rights to property, making the power of a few the destiny of millions of people) in effect globalized Social Darwinism. Planned destruction of 'traditions', cultures, and *peoples* was considered necessary and desirable, during the violence of the long dark night of colonialism, for the ideas and practices of bourgeois legality and rights to flourish worldwide. The project of world socialism, though inspired by very different visions and values, followed the same itinerary for the construction of new human futures. Equally so does the project of contemporary economic globalization, where free trade, investment, and commerce (so free as to cause the state to become a clone of global capital) are presented, in the long run, as the harbingers of a secure future for human rights. Communities in struggle and people in resistance have contested, often at the price of unspeakable human violation, these hegemonic versions of human futures and human rights.

Third, the originary stories about human rights equip dictatorial regimes in the Third World (no doubt supported and shaped by the often obscene Realpolitik of the Cold War) to deny wholesale, and in retail, even the most minimal protection from human rights violations and serves such regimes with an atrocious impunity of power.[2]

---

[2] *See*, Malaysia-Human Rights: Reopen East West Debate on Rights, Inter-press Service, 1 August 1997, available on Lexis, cited in Stephen Marks 'From the "Single Confused Page" to the "Decalogue for Six Billion Persons"': The Roots of the Universal Declaration of Human Rights in the French Revolution', 20 *Human Rights Quarterly* (1998), **459** at 461–2. *See also* Amartya Sen, 'Human Rights and Economic Achievements', in *The East Asian Challenge for Human Rights* (1999), 88–102.

The future of human rights is serviced only when theory and practice develops the narrative potential to pluralize the originary metanarratives of the past of human rights beyond the time and space of the European imagination, even in its critical postmodern incarnations.

This work does not even begin this task. It needs reiteration however that such an endeavour must rest on the premise that all nations come as *equal strangers* to the task of protection and promotion of human rights. To say this is not to deny that the Euro-American discourse made a headstart from the seventeenth century onwards in elaborating the 'modern' conceptions of human rights. It does, however, imply that these conceptions (as we see later) were 'tradition-constituted' and 'tradition-constitutive'[3] and were consistent with the catastrophic practices of cruelty towards the non-Euro-American Other. Since all concepts are history laden, one also needs to make similar inquiries requiring the invention of non-Western traditions of thought in ways that anticipate and reinforce the contemporary human rights discursivity. The progress of interlocution of non-Western traditions lies, perhaps, on the following paths:

- In what ways did the classical traditions of thought (African, Buddhist, Confucian, Hindu, Islamic and indigenous civilization) configure the notion of what it meant to be *human*?
- How did these entail ideas and ideals of equality, dignity, and justice in social and political relations?[4]
- To the extent that these traditions had no linguistic or semiotic equivalents to the 'modern' notions of rights, what *other* tropes carried the burden?[5]

---

[3] *See*, for an elaboration of this insightful distinction, Alasdair MacIntyre, *Whose Justice? Which Rationality?* (1988), 1–11, 326–88.

[4] *See*, for example, the corpus of Han Yongun, especially his *Treatise for the Reform of Korean Buddhism* (1913); An Pyong–Jik 'Han Yougun's Liberalism: An Analysis of the Reformation of Korean Buddhism', 19, *Korea Journal* (1979), 13–18. Yongun traced the complex relationship between the Buddhist notions of equality and salvation in ways that achieved a spiritual foundation for the political practice of the principle of self-determination. Freedom from Japanese rule for Korea was but an aspect of struggle against global militarism and imperialism; a struggle fully warranted by a radical reinterpretation of the Buddhist tradition.

[5] For example, the nearest classical Hindu jural equivalent of rights were: *hak* (akin to legally enforceable claims), *adhikar* (authority that a right commands), and *lokadhikar* (close to the notion of 'democratic rights' of the peoples).

- Were there no notions about just governance or the ethic of power?[6] If there were, in what precise ways may these be said to anticipate non-Western lineages of human rights?
- What interplay exists between the 'modern' and 'contemporary' human rights languages and those to be discovered in traditional thought practices? How best may we trace complexity and contradiction among these?

Aside from all this, it is indubitable that these traditions, in confrontation with colonialism and imperialism, which Enlightenment thought sustained for so long, innovated much of Western human rights discursivity. The latter was brutally incoherent of an Indian Lokmanya Tilak who dared (in the first decades of the Christian twentieth century) to enunciate the maxim '*Swaraj* [self-determination] is my birth-right and I shall have it', or a Mohandas Gandhi who challenged the early, but still vicious, forms of apartheid in South Africa. Both these praxes de-traditionalized the Eurocentric traditions of the rights of men. So did, at the turn of the nineteenth century, a freed American slave, Fredrick Douglas. Their heroic resistance may be traced to a multicultural tradition of human rights that resulted decades later in the maturation of *jus cogens* of international law,[7] which delegitimated the Enlightenment legacy more powerfully than critical theory and assorted forms of contemporary postmodernisms may ever accomplish.

When, if ever (given the present mode of production of knowledges about human rights) the originary history of human rights is written from non-Euro-enclosed perspectives, the future of human rights will be more secure than it is now.

II. 'Modern' and 'Contemporary' Human Rights

I wish to suggest ways of constructing the contrasting paradigms of 'modern' and 'contemporary' human rights. The basic contrasts seem to me to be as follows. First, in the 'modern' paradigm of rights the logics of *exclusion* are pre-eminent whereas in the 'contemporary' paradigm the logics of *inclusion* are paramount. Second, the relationship

---

[6] For an insightful elaboration of the paradigmatic notions in the Buddhist and Hindu traditions of *rajdharma*, *see* Stanley J. Tambiah, *World Emperor and Renouncer: A Study of Buddhism and Polity in Thailand Against a Historical Background* (1976).

[7] Now reflected in the UN instruments enshrining the rights to self-determination, elimination of all forms of racial discrimination, xenophobia and intolerance, and proscription of slavery and practices akin to slavery and forced labour.

between human rights languages and governance differ markedly in the two paradigms. Third, the 'modern' enunciation of human rights was almost ascetic; in contrast, contemporary enunciations present a carnival. Fourth, the contemporary paradigm inverts the inherent modernist relationship between *human rights* and *human suffering*.

The terms I use, *faute de mieux*, may mislead. My description of the paradigms is distinctly oriented to the European imagination about human rights. An adequate historiography will, of course, as indicated, locate the originating languages of human rights far beyond the European space and time. I focus on the 'modern' precisely because of its destructive impact, both in terms of social consciousness and organization, on that which may be termed clumsily and with deep human violation, as 'pre-' or 'non-' modern.

Countless variations exist even within European space and time. 'Modernity' was constructed there as oppositional to the 'Ancients' constituted by traditions of Hellenic thought, as any reader of Leo Strauss' germinal essay, *The Three Waves of Modernity*[8] surely knows. What I call 'modern' also embraces a Hugo Grotius with his memorable emphasis on *temperamenta belli* (insistence on minimization of suffering in war) and a Francisco Vittoria who valiantly proselytized against the Church (to the point of heresy) and the Emperor (to the point of treason) the human rights of the New World. However, the pre-eminent notions of European modernity did not, at the end of the day, contest that Idea of Progress under which the politics of cruelty entailed in colonialism stood somehow, and overall, ethically justified.

What I call the 'contemporary' human rights paradigm stands, in some of its major moments, marked by a vision of human rights that confronts the politics of cruelty so far justified, and held justifiable. The 'contemporary' is, however, also heterogeneous. It is characterized by practices of Realpolitik, above all conscripting human rights languages to the brutal ends of superpower rivalry in the phases of the Cold War and of the emergent post-Cold War politics. In many senses, the distinction between 'modern' and 'contemporary' human rights masks continuity in the *raison d' état* regimes, but critical differences remain.

III. The Logics of Exclusion and Inclusion

The notion of human rights—historically the rights of *man*—has been confronted with two perplexities. The first concerns the nature of *human* nature (the *Is* question). The second concerns the question:

---

[8] Leo Strauss, *Political Philosophy: Six Essays by Leo Strauss* (1975).

Who ought to count as human or fully human (the *Ought* question). While the first continues to be debated both in theistic and secular terms,[9] the second question, 'Who should count as human? occupies the centre stage of the modern enunciation of human rights. The criteria of individuation[10] in the European liberal tradition of thought furnished some of the most powerful ideas in constructing a model of human rights. Only those beings were to be regarded as 'human' who were possessed of the capacity for *reason* and autonomous moral *will*. What counted as reason and will varied in the course of the long development of the European liberal tradition. However, in its major phases of development 'slaves', 'heathens', 'barbarians', colonized peoples, indigenous populations, women, children, the impoverished, and the 'insane' have been, at various times and in various ways, thought unworthy of being bearers of human rights.

These discursive devices of Enlightenment rationality were devices of *exclusion*. The 'Rights of Man' were human rights of all men capable of autonomous reason and will; and a large number of human beings were excluded by this peculiar ontological construction,[11] although by no means the exclusive prerogative of 'modernity'.[12]

Exclusionary criteria have provided the signature tune of the 'modern' conceptions of human rights. The foremost historical role performed by these was to accomplish the *justification of the unjustifiable*: namely, *colonialism* and *imperialism*. That justification was inherently racist:

[9] The theistic responses trace the origins of human nature in the Divine Will; the secular in contingencies of evolution of life on earth. The theistic approaches, even when recognizing the holiness of all creation, insist on Man being created in God's image, and therefore capable of perfection in ways no other being in the world is; secular/scientific approaches human beings as complex psychosomatic systems co-determined both by genetic endowment and environment, and open to experimentation, like all other objects in 'nature'.

These differences could be [and have been] described in more sophisticated and wider ways: a task attempted by various naturalist thinkers, *see*, e.g., Julius Stone, *Human Law and Human Justice* (1965).

[10] *See*, Bhikhu Parekh, 'The Modern Conception of Rights and its Marxist Critique' in *The Right to be Human* (1988), 1–22; *see also* Raymond Williams, *Keywords*, (1983), 161–5.

[11] *See*, Peter Fitzpatrick, 'The Mythology of Modern Law', 92–145 (1992); Mahmood Mamdani, *Citizen and Subject: Contemporary Africa and the Legacy of Late Colonialism* (1996), 62–137.

[12] Religious traditions specialized, and still do, in ontological constructions that excluded, for example, Untouchables, rendering them beyond the pale of the *varna* system: see Upendra Baxi, 'Justice as Emancipation: The Legacy of Babasaheb Ambedkar', in *Crisis and Change in Contemporary India* (1995), 122–49.

colonial powers claimed a collective human right of 'superior' races to dominate the 'inferior' ones. The Other in many cases ceased to exist before the imperial law formations as the doctrine of *terra nullius*, following Blackstone's scandalous distinction between the inhabited and uninhabited colonies, illustrates with vivid cruelty.[13] Since the Other of the European imperialism was by definition not human or fully human, it was not worthy of human rights; at the very most, Christian compassion and charity may fashion some devices of legal or jural paternalism. That Other, not being human or fully human, was also liable to being merchandised in the slave market or to constitut the 'raw material' of exploited labour within and across the colonies. Not being entitled to a right to be and to remain a human being, the Other was made a stranger and an exile to the language and logic of human rights being fashioned, slowly but surely, in (and for) the West. The classical liberal theory and practice of human rights, in its formative era, was thus innocent of the universality of rights though no stranger to its rhetoric.

The natural collective human right of the 'superior' races to rule the 'inferior' ones is the only *juristic* justification, if any is possible, for colonialism/imperialism (and its contemporary neo-imperialist incarnations), and it comes in many shapes and forms. One has but to read the 'classic' texts of Locke or Mill to appreciate the range of talents devoted to the justification of colonialism:[14] and the related but different logics combined to the production of a belief in the collective human right of the well-ordered societies to govern the 'wild' and 'savage' races. All the well known devices of the formative era of classical liberal thought were deployed: the logics of rights to property and progress; the highly manipulable dichotomy between the state of nature and civil society; Social Darwinism combining the infantalization and maturity of 'races' and stages of civilization. The collective human right to colonize the less well-ordered peoples and societies for the common 'good' of both as well as of humankind was also by definition indefeasible, not in the least weakened by the contradictions of evolving liberalism.

IV. Human Rights Languages and Power of Governance

The languages of human rights are often integral to tasks and practices of governance, as exemplified by the constitutive elements of the

[13] Fitzpatrick, Note 11 *supra* at 72–91.

[14] Bhikhu Parekh, 'Liberalism and Colonialism: A Critique of Locke and Mill, in *The Decolonization of Imagination* (1997), 81–98.

'modern' paradigm of human rights, namely, the collective human right of the colonizer to subjugate 'inferior' peoples and the absolutist right to property. The manifold, though complex, regime of justifications offered for these 'human rights' ensured that the 'modern' European nation-state (*imagined communities* on one register) and 007 James Bond type *communities* (on another register) was able to marshal the *right to property*, as a right to *imperium* and *dominium*.

The construction of a collective human right to colonial/imperial governance is made sensible by the co-optation of languages of human rights into those of *racist* governance abroad and *class* and *patriarchal* domination at home. The hegemonic function of rights languages, in the service of *governance* at home and abroad, consisted in making whole groups of people socially and politically *invisible*. Their *suffering* was denied any authentic voice, since it was not constitutive of human suffering. 'Modern' human rights, in their originary narrative, entombed masses of human beings in shrouds of necrophilic administration of regimes of silence.

In contrast, the 'contemporary' human rights paradigm (as we see shortly) is based on the premise of radical self-determination. Self-determination insists that every human person has a right to a *voice*, a right to bear witness to violation, a right to immunity against disarticulation by concentrations of economic, social, and political formations. Rights languages, no longer so *exclusively* at the service of the ends of governance, thus open up sites of resistance.

V. Ascetic Versus Carnivalistic Rights Production

The 'contemporary' production of human rights is exuberant.[15] This is a virtue, when compared to the lean and mean articulations of human rights in the 'modern' period. In the 'modern' era the authorship of human rights was both *state-centric* and *Eurocentric;* in contrast, the processes of formulation of contemporary human rights are increasingly inclusive and often marked by intense negotiation between the NGOs and governments. The authorship of contemporary human rights is multitudinous. The United Nations and regional networks of collaboration provide an incredible register of diversity of conceptions of human rights. As a result, human rights enunciations proliferate, becoming as specific as the networks from which they arise and also in turn sustain. The 'modern' notion of human rights forbade such

[15] *See*, for an insightful overview, Burns H. Weston, 'Human Rights', 20, *Encyclopaedia Britannica* (15th edn 1997), 56.

dispersal; the only major movement made being in incremental affirmation of the rights of labour and minority rights. The way collectivities now stand installed in human rights enunciations is radically different: not merely do they reach out to 'discrete' and 'insular' minorities,[16] but also extend to wholly new, hitherto unthought of, justice constituencies.[17]

VI. Human Suffering And Human Rights

Even at the end of the Christian twentieth century, we lack a social theory about human rights. Such a theory must address a whole range of issues,[18] but for our present purpose it is necessary only to highlight the linkage between human suffering and human rights. The 'modern' human rights cultures, tracing their pedigree to the Idea of Progress, Social Darwinism, racism and patriarchy (central to the 'Enlightenment' ideology), justified global imposition of cruelty as 'natural', 'ethical', and 'just'. This 'justification' boomeranged in the form of the politics of

[16] This historic phrase comes from the famous footnote 4 in *United States v. Carolene Products Co.* 304 US, 152 n.4 (1938).

[17] Contemporary enunciations thus embrace, to mention very different orders of example, the rights of the girl child, migrant labour, indigenous peoples, gays and lesbians (the emerging human right to sexual orientation), prisoners and those in custodial institutional regimes, refugees, and asylum-seekers' children.

[18] By a social theory of human rights, I wish to designate bodies of knowledge that address, (a) genealogies of human rights in 'pre-modern', 'modern', and 'contemporary' human rights discursive formations; (b) contemporary dominant and subaltern images of human rights; (c) tasks confronting projects of engendering human rights; (d) exploration of human rights movements as social movements; (e) impact of high science and hi-tech on the theory and practice of human rights; (f) the problematic of marketization of human rights; (g) the economics of human rights.

The listing is illustrative of bodies of reflexive knowledges. In select areas these knowledges are becoming incrementally available but still remain in search of a new genre in social theory. Even as the era of 'grand theory' in the imagination of social thought seems to begin to disappear, a return to it appears imperative if one is make sense of a whole variety of human rights thought and practice. Daunting difficulties entailed in acts of totalization of human rights stand aggravated by this aspiration, but I continue to feel that the endeavour is worthy.

Valuable beginnings in some of these directions have been made by Richard Falk, *Explorations at the Edge of Time* (1995); Boaventura de Sousa Santos, *Towards a New Commonsense: Law, Science and Politics in the Paradigmatic Transition* (1995); Wendy Brown, *States of Injury: Power and Freedom in Late Modernity* (1995); Roberto Mangaberia Unger, *What Should Legal Analysis Become?* (1996); Shadrack B.O. Gutto, *Human Rights and People's Rights for the Oppressed: Critical Essays on Theory and Practice from Sociology of Law Perspectives* (1993); Issa G. Shivji, *The Concept of Human Rights in Africa* (1989).

genocide in the Third Reich, often resulting in cruel complicity, unredeemed by even the *Schindler's List*, by 'ordinary' citizens in the worst foundational moments of the present day forms of ethnic cleansing.[19]

The 'modern' liberal ideology that gave birth to the very notion of human rights, howsoever Euro-enclosed and no matter how riven with contradiction between 'liberalism' and 'empire',[20] regarded the imposition of dire and extravagant suffering upon individual human beings as wholly justified. Practices of politics, barbaric even by the standards of the theological and secular thought formations of the Enlightenment, were somehow considered justifiable overall by state managers and ideologues, and the political unconscious that they generated (despite, most notably, the divergent struggles of the working classes).

Making human suffering *invisible* was the hallmark of 'modern' human rights formations. Suffering was made invisible because large masses of colonized peoples were not regarded as human or because a considerable number of human beings were regarded as not fully human, in need of tutelage. Although sentient objects of conquest and subjects of European property rights regimes, the colonial subject was closer to the order of things or beasts whose suffering was not sufficiently important to trump the career of the Enlightenment project. Indeed, their suffering had no voice, no language, and knew no rights. As their Lordships of the Privy Council succinctly put it in 1919, some natives may be 'so low in the scale of social organization as to render it idle to impute to such people a *shadow of rights known to our law*'.[21]

In contrast, the post-Holocaust and post-Hiroshima/Nagasaki *angst* registers a normative horror at human violation. The 'contemporary' human rights discursivity is rooted in the illegitimacy of all forms of politics of cruelty. No doubt, what counts as cruelty varies enormously even from one human rights context/instrument to another.[22] Even so, there are now in place firm *jus cogens* norms of

---

[19] Is this point of view any more contestable? *See* Daniel Jonah Goldhagen, *Hitler's Willing Executioners: Ordinary Germans and the Holocaust* (1996); Richard Weisberg, *Poethics: and Other Strategies of Law and Literature* (1992).

[20] Uday Mehta, *Liberalism and Empire* (1998).

[21] In re:Southern Rhodesia(1919) AC at 233–4 (emphasis added).

In contrast, the *insufficiently human* were capable of suffering but their suffering was to be ameliorated by an expansion of the rights (as power) of those who were sufficiently human (thus the *patriae potesta* power of the husband or the father over women).

[22] For example: Is capital punishment in any form and with whatever justification a practice of cruelty? When does discrimination, whether based on gender, class or

international human rights and humanitarian law, which de-legitimate as well as forbid barbaric practices of power in state as well as civil society. From the standpoint of those violated, this is no small a gain; the community of perpetrators remains incrementally vulnerable to human rights cultures, howsoever variably, and this matters enormously for the violated. In a non-ideal world, human rights discursivity seems to offer if not an 'ideal', the 'second best' option.

No matter how many contested fields stand provided by the rhetoric of universality, indivisibility, interdependence, and inalienability of human rights, contemporary human rights cultures have constructed new criteria of legitimation of power. These increasingly discredit any attempt to base power and rule on the inherent violence institutionalized in imperialism, colonialism, racism, and patriarchy. Contemporary human rights make possible, in most remarkable ways, discourse on human suffering. No longer may practices of power, abetted by grand social theory, justify beliefs that sustain wilful infliction of harm as an attribute of sovereignty or of a good society. Central to contemporary human rights discourse are visions and ways of construction of an ethic of power that prevent the imposition of surplus repression and human suffering beyond the needs of regime-survival, no matter how extravagantly determined. The illegitimacy of the languages of immiseration becomes the very grammar of international politics.

The distinction between 'modern' and 'contemporary' forms of human rights is focused on *taking suffering seriously*. In the 'modern' human rights paradigm it was thought possible to take human rights seriously without taking human suffering seriously.[23] Outside the

---

caste, assume the form of torture proscribed by international human rights and norms? When may forms of sexual harassment at the workplace be described as an aspect of cruel, inhumane, and degrading treatment forbidden under the current regime of international human rights standards and norms? Do non-consensual sex practices within marriage relationships amount to rape? Do all forms of child labour amount to cruel practice, on the ground that the confiscation of childhood is an unredressable human violation? Are mega irrigation projects creating eco-exiles and environmental destruction/degradation acts of developmental cruelty? Are programmes or measures of structural adjustment an aspect of the politics of imposed suffering? This range of questions is vast and undoubtedly more may be added.

For an anthropological mode of interrogation, *see* Talal Asad, 'On Torture, or Cruel, Inhuman and Degrading Treatment', in *Social Suffering* (1997), 285–308.

[23] See the interesting analysis concerning 'minimization of suffering' in the formative period of modern human rights, Charles Taylor, 'Conditions of Unforced

domain of the laws of war between and among the 'civilized' nations, 'modern' human rights regarded large-scale imposition of human suffering as *just* and *right* in pursuit of a Eurocentric notion of *human 'progress'*. That discourse silenced human suffering. In contrast, the 'contemporary' human rights paradigm is animated by a politics of activist desire to render problematic the very *notion of politics of cruelty*.

VII. The 'Historic' Processes of Reversal

The processes by which this reversal happens in the 'contemporary' era of human rights are complex and contradictory, and require recourse to human rights modes of reading the histories of the Cold War. While no capsule narrative is ever reliable, I present here, in bare outline, five ways that shaped the theory and practice of 'contemporary' human rights.

(1) *Fragmented Universality of 'Contemporary' Human Rights*

It would not be too much to say that the defining feature of the contemporary world has been the rise and fall of the principle of self-determination. Beginning, in particular, its career with the historic assertion of the right to self-determination in India, the principle globalizes itself in the early phases of the Cold War, through a radical insistence on the illegitimacy of colonialism. Although severely denied to people living under actually existing socialism, the Soviet Union promoted self-determination abroad, through the grammar of wars of national liberation. Socialist ideology powerfully discredited justifications for imperialism and colonization, while manipulating a startling level of support among the 'new', 'non-aligned' nations for brutal repression in Hungary and Czechoslovakia.

The division of the rest of the world into two giant spheres of influence (itself a euphemism sheltering unconscionable human violation) had a profound impact on the formation of 'contemporary' human rights. The practices of the right to self-determination became incarcerated in the 'superpower' hegemony and domination.[24] The

---

Consensus on Human Rights', in *The East Asian Challenges for Human Rights* (1999) at 124, 140–3. Professor Taylor's observation that in contemporary times we 'have new reasons to minimize suffering but we also lack a reason to override the minimizing of suffering' is, perhaps, best understood in relation to the notion of radical evil discussed in Chapter 1.

[24] The US 'Monroe Doctrine' soon found its counterpart in the 'Brezhnev Doctrine', unredeemed by the principles of *panchshila* in the vision of the non-aligned world.

'self' proclaimed to be entitled to 'determination' thus stood constituted by the play of hegemonic powers. This necessarily implied that the birth of the 'New' Nations was a process also marked by the superpower imposition of enormous suffering and cruelty, justified by either the progress of world 'socialism' or global 'democracy'. In this sense, neo-colonialism is born just when the practices of the right to self-determination seem to succeed.[25]

Neo-colonialism not merely shaped the context for the birth of the 'new' states; it also worked its way to contain the newly found sovereignty of the Third World. The need to maintain 'spheres of influence' provided 'justification' for manufacturing, installing, and servicing regimes and cliques of power in the Third World that engaged over long stretches of time, with impunity, in all kinds of human rights violations.

The task of consolidation of the territorial boundaries of the former colonial states posed another limit situation for the universality of the right to self-determination. The 'new' nations of Asia and Africa somewhat understandably insisted that the right to self-determination extended only to situations of 'classic' colonialism, available to their 'peoples' only once in history: to determine their collective status as sovereign states within the meaning of international law. That right once exercised was extinguished for all times; this presumed that the 'logic' of colonialism, which made all sorts of different peoples, cultures, and territories vessels of imperial unity, should continue in the post-colony. The post-colonial state was somehow to create out of many nations a single 'nation-state'.[26]

---

[25] Factors and forces other than ideology also influenced politics of superpower rivalry. The spheres of influence also marked the imperial scramble for world resources: for example, fossil fuels, notably oils, minerals, forest wealth, and international waterways. The United Nations Charter was thus obscenely manipulated, for example, in Suez Canal, Algeria, the Congo and the West Asian 'crises-management' in superpower diplomacy. Imperialism incarnated itself all over again in the play of the theory and practice of self-determination. The decolonizing world was in the process, yet again, of recolonization.

[26] Also, within, the ideological recomposition of the world, the initiation by Nehru, Nasser, and Tito, of a 'non-aligned' community of states played a highly creationist role for 'contemporary' human rights. It deployed the symbolic capital of the voting majority in the UN General Assembly to richly improvise the creation of 'soft' international standards of human rights. These envisioned a just international order, but amidst the superpower rivalry created debris of human rights violations. To be sure, the regimes in the 'Third World' too, also and at the same time, deployed the Cold War 'justifications' for violation of human rights. In this period of the Cold War we see the emergence of a contradiction between human rights, norm-creation at the global level (politics *for* human rights) with a claim, in the title of 'nation-building' to violate these with impunity at home (politics *of* human rights). The

This enterprise proved hazardous in the extreme both for the new national governance élites and those who professed a radical right to self-determination that now perceived the claims of 'national unity' as a species of neo-colonialism. The Cold War provided both a creative stimulus and a bloody limit to this kind of assertion.

The 'creationist' logic of the right to self-determination gave language to the aspiration to the politics of identity and difference within the 'new' nations. The processes by which the right to self-determination was eventually de-radicalized did not comprise only interpretive or semiotic performances. They were also exercises in near-complete militarization of the ways of governance, as also of resistance. The two Superpowers, and their satellites, be it recalled, contributed heavily to militarization of the Third World states in ways that institutionalized the potential for horrific violations of human rights being perfected in that great normative workshop called the United Nations.

Far from being dead on arrival, the logics and paralogics of the human right to self-determination brought to the 'contemporary' worlds of power new forms of legitimation crises and democratic deficit. At the same time, from the standpoint of those who were denied self-determination, the postulate of 'universality' of human rights emerged as a deeply fragmented notion. The vaunted 'universality' of the right to self-determination thus stands fragmented in the very moment of its enunciation.

(2) *The Cold War 'Naturalization' of Human Rights Violations*

The politics of human rights in the formative era of the Cold War invented its own ways of naturalizing (or de-problematizing) human suffering. The Cold War, consistent with the traditions of political cruelty in the Euro-Atlantic states, restructured the modernistic criteria of exclusion. Those suspected of being 'communists' in the claimed spheres of 'Free' World and 'bourgeois sympathizers', 'capitalist roaders', or 'enemies of people' in the claimed spheres of the 'socialist' world were subjected to permanent states of emergency, the reign of terror and genocidal practices of politics. Enemies of 'democracy' in one sphere or of 'socialism' in the other were *excluded* from the realm of the newly proclaimed human rights norms and standards, marking a cruel continuity with the 'modern' in the emergent paradigm of 'contemporary' human rights. Human rights acquired a fragmented universality within this emergence.

'universality' of human rights gets fractured all over again along the axis of norm-creation and everyday violation.

As generations pass, these words lose the sense of lived histories of gulags in the 'liberal' as well as 'socialist' societies. These presented the globalization of US McCarthyism as 'natural' in the systematic massacre of hundreds of thousands of 'communists' (in Indonesia in the sixties, to mention just one example) or reigns of terror in the Soviet Union and associated states.

Not surprisingly, heroic individual and mass resistance ensued, despite the savage face of repression. The 'contemporary' human rights-in-the-making owe much to the practices of resistance and martyrdom, against forces of superpower politics seeking to *mute* the voices of the violated. Politics *for* human rights began to emerge as a force questioning the might of the politics *of* human rights. Not to understand the ways in which this happened is to forfeit the very future of human rights in the third Christian millenium. Those who would write the histories of 'contemporary' human rights only in terms of intergovernmental or the NGO politics of desire do a great disservice to the future of human rights.

(3) *Outlawry of Racism*

'Contemporary' human rights' normativity shows a remarkable insistence on the illegitimacy of institutionalized state racism.[27] Its enduring contribution resides in the delegitimation of an overtly racist national constitutionalism, which subsequently, and differentially, spreads into international human rights instruments outlawing intolerance and xenophobia in all their myriad forms. The new regime of human rights is thus aggressively protective of 'minority' rights. The right to self-determination acquired claims to visions of human futures radically different from those proclaimed through mainstream European Enlightenment.[28]

(4) *The Marxist Critique*

Through the foregoing processes, the Marxian critique of bourgeois human rights formation also universalized itself.[29] It exposed many 'genetic' fault-lines in bourgeois models of human rights. The varieties

---

[27] The single decade beginning with the UN Declaration on the Elimination of All Forms of Racial Discrimination, 1963, and ending with the International Convention on the Suppression and Punishment of the Crime of Apartheid, 1973, presents a memorable human rights convergence in a world rife with superpower rivalry and discord.

[28] *See*, Article 27, UDHR; GA Resolution on the Permanent Sovereignty Over Natural Resources (14 December 1962).

[29] Upendra Baxi, *Marx, Law and Justice* (1993); Wendy Brown, Note 18, *supra*.

of Marxisms (whether Marxist–Leninist or Euro–Marxist) helped to powerfully fashion articulation of lived critiques of the bourgeois human rights paradigm that propagated the sanctity of rights to private property over a minimal satisfaction of the basic needs of the masses. Socialist and radical feminism stressed causal linkages between universal structures of patriarchy and global capitalism,[30] though unable itself to negotiate the contradiction, above all, between class and gender, on the one hand, and the dictatorship of the Party and human rights of women, on the other.

Confronted by its own nemesis the 'Western'/'modern' tradition of human rights came to terms at least in part with its own reactionary rights-violative potential. It did so partly by arriving through a long and tortuous process of construction of a welfare state paradigm within the bourgeois formation in all its contradiction and complexity.[31] The Marxian critique of rights provided a powerful impetus for negotiation of many 'contemporary' international human rights enunciations.[32] Although the 'political' and 'civil' rights were severely compromised by Euro–Atlantic states that vigorously promoted them in the process of the 'export' of a counter-doctrine and practice of 'making the world safe for democracy', these nevertheless acquired saliency in the struggle against the export of socialist revolution that denatured Marxian insights on emancipation into all kinds of gulags. The politics *of* human rights flourished in this epoch, as a mode of production of models of governance, regardless of how enormous the toll of human suffering it entailed on all sides. If in the 'Free World' it was considered legitimate to promote 'purges' of all those suspected of communist leanings, at home and abroad, the socialist world also engaged in extirpating the 'capitalist roaders', and 'bourgeois' elements at home and within its spheres of influence with equally obscene cruelty. All this led to acute forms of militarization of the leading Western 'democratic' states, rendering, all over again, into killing fields the life of new nations in Asia and Africa, and the revitalized Monroe-doctrine-afflicted nations of Latin America.

---

[30] Allison M. Jagger, *Feminist Politics and Human Nature* (1983).

[31] Jurgen Habermas, *Between Facts and Norms: Contributions to a Discourse Theory of Law and Democracy* (1996).

[32] A mere listing, without adequate historical analysis, may mislead, but for the present purposes the relevant references are: the International Bill of Rights, the 1969 Declaration on Social Progress and Development, the Declaration on the New International Economic Order, the Declaration and Convention on the Elimination of All forms of Racial Discrimination, and the Declaration on the Right to Development.

(5) *New Forms of Global Solidarity*

The brutal ideological competition for global supremacy created, dialectically, the political space for solidarity on both sides for voices of civil society to emerge in a politics *for* human rights. The pattern of solidarity that emerges is overlaid with ideological contradictions, and not only through the contortions of Euro-Marxism. It raises questions about the ways of understanding the birth of a whole new form of global thought and action in which concern with human rights transcends national boundaries and pre-occupation with political thought and theory as a socially and ethically 'neutral' social practice.[33] All this awaits the discovery of a Foucaldian episteme for human rights.

As offering interlocution or a 'critique' for governance of paradigms and state power everywhere, 'human rights' become floating signifiers, not embedded in sovereign territoriality. The 'global institutionalization of human rights'[34] signifies the interpenetration of the world of politics *for* human rights with the worlds of power harnessing the politics *of* human rights. However, the worlds of 'contemporary' human rights, I submit, not merely have their origins in the Cold War formations but will remain conditioned, though no longer as determined, by these.

This capsule narrative is heavily suggestive of the matrices of *violence* within which the 'contemporary' human rights paradigm has emerged. It seems always the case that the emergent discourse on human rights remains heavily parasitic on human suffering.

(6) *The Emergence of Politics Of and For Human Rights*

This capsule narrative also renders legible my insistence that history of 'contemporary' human rights activism has its origins in practices of resistance to the Cold War global formations of the politics of cruelty. The circumstance of globality that gave rise to the manifold expression of 'contemporary' human rights activism, forms the historic script, no matter (though this is enormously important) how the dramatis personae may improvise it. It is always well worth recalling that if resistance is the Other of power, it is power that, after all, ordains the fate of activism, even of self-propelled, transcendent human rights activism.

Global, regional, national, and local human rights struggles and movements in the Cold War era witnessed new practices of the politics

---

[33] I have in mind here the transaction from Descartes, dictum: 'I think, therefore I am' to Albert Camus' motto: '*I rebel, therefore, we are*'.
[34] Ronald Robertson, *Globalization* (1992), 138.

of cruelty to a point that at times the whole world became a 'community' of gulags. Summoning images like 'democracy' and 'human rights' conveyed the reality of aggressive state terrorism. In the practices of resistance is born the distinction between the *politics of human rights* and the *politics for human rights*.

The politics *of* human rights deploys the symbolic or cultural capital of human rights to the ends of management of distribution of power in national and global arenas. 'Human rights' become the pursuit of politics, and even aggression and war by other means. The politics *of* human rights at times becomes associated with terroristic repression of realms of human autonomy and expression, where dissent becomes subversion and the sycophancy of the ruling ideology the commanding height of free expression; and international diplomacy deftly uses in this form of politics visions of global futures for the prodiction of ideological compliance.[35]

No phrase except a romantic one—*the revolution in human sensibility*—marks the passage from the politics *of* human rights to the politics *for* human rights. That new form of sensibility, arising from responsiveness to the tortured and tormented voices of the violated, speak to us of an *alternate politics* seeking, against heavy odds of a traumatically changeful human history; that order of progress which makes the *state more ethical, governance progressively just, and power increasingly accountable.* The struggles which these voices name draw heavily on cultural and civilizational resources richer than those provided by the time and space of the Euro-enclosed imagination of human rights, which they also seek to innovate.

The historic achievement of the 'contemporary' human rights movements consists in positing peoples' polity against state polity; or in the fashioning and articulation of visions of human future, through the practices of politics *for* human rights, that the shrivelled soul of Realpolitik must forever resist.[36]

At the same time, this struggle is overlaid by the historicity of 'contemporary' human rights. I turn in the next chapter to the ways of this happening, which constitute the mood, method, and message of the 'contemporary' human rights movements in deeply heterogeneous ways.

---

[35] Indeed, to a point that even in this so-called era former officials of the United States and communist party voices full and throatily seek to 'justify' horrors of a Stalin or a McCarthy regime and the various techniques of destabilization of democratic aspirations and regimes as politically 'sensible' programmes!

[36] This distinction gets further articulated in concrete detail. *See*, e.g., pp. 60–5.

3

The Practices of 'Contemporary' Human Rights Activism

I. The World of NGOs

Contemporary human rights production is heavily influenced by complex and contradictory practices of human rights movements. By common discursive practice, these movements are generally referred to as NGOs. Their overwhelming proliferation is, indeed, a fact of enormous significance in the second half of the twentieth century, and the ways in which they approach issues of human rights in the next few decades will, indeed, be decisive for our uncommon future. The history of the early precursors of the present day NGO communities and of the enormous diversity that characterize these today, has yet to be written.

The first task would itself entail a separate treatise. Here it should suffice to note, first, that international NGOs, in the early part of the twentieth century, though few in number, were vast in impact especially in the creation of regimes of humanitarian international law[1] and, second, that civil society NGOs were in fact indistinguishable from great social movements, such as the anti-slavery, labour and suffragette movements. The notions of human rights were prefigured in different modes in each of these movements but these were not human rights movements *as such*. I recognize the complexity of distinguishing between social and human rights movements later (Chapter Eight),

---

[1] As, for example, the Red Cross and the efforts by an international consortium of NGOs that led to the establishment of the High Commissioner for Russian refugees in 1921. *See*, e.g., David P. Forsythe, *International Humanitarian Assistance: The Case of the Red Cross*, 3, *Buffalo Journal of International Law*, 235 (1996); Steve Charnovitz, *Two Centuries of Participation*, 18, *Michigan Journal of International Law* (1997), 183.

but I believe that such a distinction remains important in any study of the formative histories of the NGOs.

It is the second task, namely the diversity of contemporaneous NGOs, that I address here briefly. This diversity is indeed staggering, in terms of the processes of naming or description, modes of organization and connectivity, range of resourcing, agenda, auspices and ideology. The histories of their formation and development also vary considerably.

(a) *Politics of Naming*

A threshold issue is that of the politics of naming. Increasingly, the term NGOs has been dispersed into several categories and histories, as revealed, for example, by terms such as: INGOs, CSOs, ISOs, NGDOs, ENGOs.[2] The shift in nomenclature is decisively reflective of internationalization of the bulk and generality of the NGO movement. Also as can be seen from the variety of naming practices, the internal differentiation among international NGOs also reflects a growing, and diverse, understanding of human rights and ways of their realization. Even so, it has become difficult to exclude 'non'-or 'anti'-human rights formations from the world of the NGOs.

The difficulty arises from at least two sources. First, any denial of NGO status to civil society-, market-, and regime- sponsored NGOs paradoxically entails the charge of denial of human rights to free speech and association. Sponsored by both specific industries and international coalitions of industry, the BNGOs (Business NGOs) claimed and enjoyed the same status as ENGOs, and even outnumbered these, at the recent Kyoto climate change conference.[3] It is also now common practice for regime-sponsored NGOs to offer more eloquent justification of violations of human rights, at available international fora, than state officials are in a position to do.

Second, the labelling of some NGOs as non-, or anti-, human rights groups becomes contentious, given the fact that the *right to interpret rights* is itself a basic human right. To take just two examples, neither the aggressive espousal of the right to life of unborn children nor religiously grounded objections to the progress towards cloning human beings is manifestly anti-human rights. These may be said to be so by

---

[2] International, civil society, development, environment NGOs. ISOs stand for International Solidarity Organizations, a term often used in Francophonic Africa.
[3] *See*, Chiara Giorgetti, 'From Rio to Kyoto: A Study of Non-governmental Organizations in the Negotiation on Climate Change', 7, *New York University Environmental Law Journal* (1999), 201.

those who, in the first instance, support (as I do) the autonomy of women in terms of reproductive rights or in the second by those who advocate radical regulation of the right to pursue scientific research and experimentation, given the corporatization of 'big' scientific research, as an aspect of the right to freedom of speech and expression. Conflicts of rights beget conflicted NGOs, pursuing their versions of socially and globally acceptable redefinitions of the content and scope of human rights.

There appears, however, a degree of unanimity concerning an *in limine* exclusion from the world of the NGOs of those formations that engage in practices of violent and militant practices of transformation of civil society and state. To be sure, recourse to 'symbolic' violence in NGO protest mobilization efforts seems already legitimated by contemporary NGO morality.[4] However, militant self-determination or autonomy movements that justify violent *present* denial of human rights (whether of incumbent power holders or of innocent bystanders) in the title of the *future* realization and enjoyment of human rights for all are considered manifestly human rights violative. It has been recently argued that the human rights NGOs may even have a specific 'mandate', without of course endorsing state terrorism, in relation to insurgent acts and formations.[5] In contrast, the use of violent means for construction of visions of a de-colonized world presented fewer, even different, problems. Impassioned commitment to future visions of a just and righteous world still regards insurgent violence as unconscionable and its links to future achievement for human rights tenuous. Both state terrorism and insurgent violence, even for a just social order, stand equally condemned. Only the humanitarian NGOs, pursuing the logics and paralogics of a Grotian *temperamenta belli*, seem to be securely ethically anchored. The future of human rights will be more secure when the world of contemporary NGOs is able to reflexively address issues of collective political violence as (in Robert Cover's memorable term) *jurisgenrative*.[6]

---

[4] The most vivid examples of such recourse are: the burning of a hazardous chemical plant in Phuket, the Karnataka *appiko* movement (uprooting state maintained nurseries of eucalyptus plants), and the recent Greenpeace destruction of GMO in England.

[5] *See*, Ravi Nair, 'Human Rights and Non-state Paramilitary Organizations', 1, *Yale Human Rights Development Law Journal* (1998), 2.

[6] Robert Cover, 'Foreword: Nomos and Narrative' 97, *Harvard Law Review*, 62 (1987) *Cf.* Upendra Baxi, 'From Human Rights to the Right to be Human', in Upendra Baxi, *Inhuman Wrongs and Human Rights*, 1, (1994), 13–16.

(b) *Modes of Organization*

The struggle for the achievement of associational existence and autonomy is now truly past. Not, however, wholly so: it continues to re-emerge in its earlier forms in some contemporary societies whose regimes are able to withstand or weaken (in relation to them) the otherwise powerful assertion of respect for minimal human rights to free speech and assembly. The growing networking of solidarity among human rights NGOs empowers these struggles in ways that much of the history of *modern* human rights did not.

Much of the history, and future of human rights lies congealed in this enunciatory struggle for the creation of human rights in which human rights *movements* faced undeniable repression, on their way to becoming legitimate and legal *organizations*. (Besides, to repeat, this struggle continues in many parts of the world.) This translation from illegitimacy to legality of social movements is an ineluctable aspect of juridical and social flourishing of civil society associations. Human rights *movements* undoubtdly need to articulate themselves into some sort of juridical form, conferring an order of comparative social and political advantage. Indeed, the histories of trade union movements richly illustrate everywhere the struggles of *movements* to become *organizations*, in ways that testify to the power of social movements to constrain and compel the state to acknowledge the legitimacy and legality of certain forms of associational activity. The conflicted history of the right of association is thus the proto-history of all human rights movements.

Outside the bloody and bruised history of trade union movements, and in stark contradictions to the paradigm of 'modern' human rights, lies the site of 'antisystemic' movements, the early intimations of the birth of NGOs.[7] The contradiction resides in the repressive denial of human rights movements in colonial possessions and their juridical flourishing in the metropolis. In a related, but a different mode it re-emerges during the career of the Cold War constitutionalism, a theme that I will not pursue here.

---

[7] Like the Pennsylvania Society for Promoting the Abolition of Slavery in 1775, the British and Foreign Anti-Slavery Society in 1839, the Henry Dunant (1863) Geneva Public Welfare Society (the precursor of the International Red Cross), and the international consortium, inclusive of the International Federation of Trade Unions, that led to the prototype High Commissioner of Refugees in 1921. *See*, Karsten Nowrot, 'Legal Consequences of Globalisation: The Status of Non-governmental Organizations Under International Law', 6, *Indiana Global Law Studies Journal* (1996), (henceforth referred to by author), 578 at 582.

For the present purposes, all we need to note is the transition from *organized* association activity to ever-expanding networks of NGO enterprise. The contemporary world of NGOs is marked by an extraordinary degree of social reproduction of cooperation in the creation, protection, promotion, exercise, and enjoyment of human rights and fundamental freedoms. The animating spirit is that of *somehow* putting human rights to work through collective coalitional international efforts rather than by localized heroic historic incursions. Not that these are discounted or discredited but increasingly the communities of global NGOs appear to feel more secure in their attempts at creating *global* spaces, that will nurture social action within the *local*. The most recent examples of the resilience of global social power of such network solidarity was provided by the notable successes of the anti-MAI coalition engaging 650 NGOs/CSOs from 70 countries[8] and the Seattle WTO Summit, furnishing powerful narratives of the redemptive profiles of (what Castells calls) the 'network society'.[9]

In addition to these coalitional efforts, and times underlying these, are forms of transnational NGOs that (like Amnesty International, OXFAM, Greenpeace) that command greater membership than the citizen-populace of some states[10] and resources at times far larger than those available to some of the so-called least developed countries.[11] Though neither as powerful as states or transnationals, some leading international NGOs command resources simply not available to their inaugural historic precursors in the late nineteenth and early twentieth Christian centuries. (This phenomenon is not altogether unrelated to the emergence and growth of human rights markets, which I tentatively explore in Chapter Eight.)

(c) *Agenda and Ideologies*

Admitting of no simple formulation, the agenda, overall, of most contemporary international human rights NGOs espouses four

---

[8] *See*, Miloon Kothari, 'Globalisation, Social Action and Human Rights', in *Development and Social Action*, 9 at 15–8.

[9] *See*, Manuel Castells, *The Power of Identity* 68–242 (1997).

[10] Amnesty International, for example, has more members than the citizens of 'mini-states' such as Nauru, Fiji, San Marino.

[11] The funds allocated to NGDOs, for example, reached US$ 956 million in 1993 and the Northern NGDOs quadrupled their income from private funding by 1993 to US$ 5.7 billion. *See*, Ignacio de Senillosa, 'A New Age of Social Movements: A Fifth Generation of Non-governmental Development Organizations in the Making?' in *Development and Social Action* (1999) 87, 91–2.

principles: the primacy of human rights, non-retrogression, the right to effective remedies and rights to participation.[12] However, what constitutes the totality called 'human rights' bears diverse meanings in the contemporary human rights NGO worlds; each of these principles presents a contested site. The principle of the 'primacy' of human rights gets embroiled in the issue of prioritization of human rights, mocking notions about the indivisibility and interdependence of universal human rights. 'Non-retrogression', (duties of states to respect, protect, and promote human rights obligations under treaty-regimes) flounders on its distinctive circularity, raising (outside the rare *jus cogens* situations such as slavery or genocide) questions of what duties states have actually assumed amidst a riot of reservations, understandings and declarations accompanying the treaty ratification. How far the right to remedies and participation may extend to global and economic regional trade and commerce arrangement is also a vexed issue, as the debate concerning the WTO social clauses abundantly shows.[13] I remain all along, in my activist persona, on the side of the angels! I must however say, at the very least, that the reason of human rights is as sufficiently troubled and contradictory as the unreason of the state.

The question of ideology is also very vexed. Despite the commonality of coalitional concern, there is always an active residue of the North–South divide. Changing conceptions of aid and development policies in the North state practices undoubtedly seem to affect the activist milieu: a recent study has identified at least five generations and areas of work of the Northern DNGOs.[14] It has even been said that these 'have ended up playing a subordinate, if ever more important, role in putting structural adjustment into practice', often with 'negative impact on autonomous social movements'.[15] Even claims of 'solidarity' have been put to question as reciprocity-deficient, lacking in 'personal commitment, despite the generosity with short term 'material aid' and by the lack of 'willingness to receive, not only to give'.[16] The active residue is manifest in other areas of hostile hermeneutics of the North–South divide on such crucial issues as women's rights as human rights

---

[12] *See*, Miloon Kothari, 'Globalisation, Social Action, and Human Rights', in *Development and Social Action* (1999), 9, at 14.

[13] Jagdish Bhagwati, *A Stream of Windows: Unsettling Reflections on Trade, Immigration and Democracy* (1998), 247.

[14] *See*, note 10 *supra* at 92–7.

[15] Ibid. at 101, quoting J. Petras and S. Vieux, *Hagan Jeugo!* (1995).

[16] Ibid. at 102, quoting an assassinated priest in San Salvador (Jon Sobrino SJ) (emphasis in original removed).

and 'sustainable development'. On the other hand is the nightmarish question of authenticity of voice affecting co-equally the North as well as the South NGOs: How after all does the quest for structuring innovative global spaces, *even places*, for human rights, empower the *local*?

One also needs to reflect upon ways in which the contemporary national, regional and global NGOs are emerging as salient actors. At least over the past quarter of a century their participation has been incrementally promoted by the United Nations system. In a sense, this process has resulted in the creation of a milieu of participatory culture of global governance, which then tends to universalize itself as a virtue of all forms of political governance. If the process has incrementally augmented the legitimacy of the ever growing corpus of the United agencies and auspices, including some exposed to very severe legitimation deficit,[17] it has no doubt also created a genuine transgovernmental space for global initiative for justice and rights.[18]

The only common ground then for the contemporary worlds of human rights NGOs stands furnished by the denial that associations of agribusinesses, pharmaceutical industries, mining conglomerations, petroleum industries, and the run of the mill federations of chambers of commerce and industries have as their prime, or even ancillary, purpose the task of protection and promotion of human rights. As we see in some detail in Chapter Eight, these formations assiduously promote their present role in a globalizing world in terms of a progress narrative. The power of such narratives is illustrated by the fact that some contemporary human rights NGOs seek partnership with them towards the construction of a viable future for human rights through the invention of forms of dialogical corporate human rights cultures. Even so, and despite momentary triumphs, some even memorable, it remains highly improbable that such feats may overcome the ceaseless quest for power and profit that constitute global corporate cultures. At any rate, the distinction between human rights NGOs and CSOs remains precious in any serious consideration of the future of human rights.

---

[17] *See*, World Bank, *NGOs and the Bank: Incorporating FY95 Progress Report on Cooperation Between the World Bank and the NGOs* (1966). The FY95 refers to the fiscal year in which approximately 41 per cent of the Bank projects contained provisions on NGO collaboration.

[18] For example, human rights NGOs have been salient in the articulation of the idea of an International Criminal Court: *see*, Steve Charnovitz, note 1 *supra*. I mention this example because it illustrates more than any other the historic longevity of proactive NGO pursuit the accomplishment of a very difficult structural transformation in the world order.

Without any desire to reduce the complexity of the contemporary worlds of NGOs, it seems justified to inventory these in the following terms of intended or achieved tasks/missions:

• *Future Inventing*: By this notion, in contrast to the rather effete term 'consciousness raising', I refer to a variety of practices that seek to innovate social consciousness and organization towards new visions of human future, de-legitimating the reigning conceptions. The simple but powerful practices interrogating racism, colonialism, violence, and discrimination against women, social exclusion, and environmental degradation, for example, create conceptions of alternate *just* as well as *caring* human futures.

• *Agenda-setting*: Many NGO practices seek to create an agendum of political and social action arising out of their conceptions of alternate human futures: the most conspicuous examples being provided by the environmental and women's rights movements.

• *Norm-creative*: NGOs arrive on the United Nations (and national) platforms either as first draftspersons or co-authors of human rights enunciations. Equally, they combat with great vigour developments that threaten the fragile normativity of human rights. The recent mobilization of informed public opinion against the MAI arresting its progression on behalf and the behest of multinational capital furnishes one striking example.

• *Implementational*: In the still dismal situation of continuing direct or regime-sponsored violations of human rights, NGOs perform a wide variety of tasks related or leading to implementation of human rights. These include ombudspersons, exposés, investigative, and lobbying roles. These roles entail close collaboration with the print and electronic media and all related learned professions.

• *Solidarity*: NGO practices seek to sustain, even empower, national and local level rights activism against practices of the politics of cruelty. Powerful global condemnation against the repression of human rights activists has created a global culture of empathy for those who struggle to implement human rights against all odds. It is this emerging network of solidarity between and among NGOs that endows them with a fiduciary power, which makes possible the pursuit of human rights (to deploy the sanitized United Nations prose) in 'difficult situations'.

At the same time, it is abundantly clear that there exist not *one* but *many worlds* of NGOs. Indeed, one might perhaps say with only slight exaggeration that there are, towards the end of the second Christian millennium, as many NGOs as there are human rights. One major task for a comparative social theory of human rights is to construct maps that chart the plural, multiple, and conflicted territories of NGOs. Since these possess incredible powers of self-definition, any endeavour to pattern the worlds of NGOs may seem foredoomed to failure. When we add to this the thinkers and ideologues, the epistemic communities who work with or influence the NGOs, the task becomes all the more formidable. Also, any such mapping will be fraught with a problematic mix of descriptive and prescriptive elements. This becomes immediately evident when one seeks agreement on conceptual categories such as the following:

- *reach:* how does one characterize NGOs in terms of the geography of difference (at the levels of existential location: local, regional, national, interregional, global)?
- *history*: what genealogical understanding may inform preferred narratives of persistence over time and in space?
- *agenda*: how best may one classify NGOs in terms of specific configurations of human rights they seek to promote and protect?
- *fluidity*: what accounts for capabilities for transformation of initially espoused agenda?
- *reflexivity*: what registers emerge for cumulative experential learning, enhancing scope for future transformative praxis?
- *autonomy*: how is autonomy, in relative terms, constructed in relation to forces of co-optation?
- *toleration*: how are patterns of respect and understanding for divergence and plurality within the inner dynamic of the day to day working of kindred NGOs developed?
- *accountability*: how is this elusive attribute crystallized in relation to the constituencies of violated peoples, rather than indirect forms that relate to accountability to donors and funders for human rights action?
- *excellence*: how does one construct and measure, by way of reflexive monitoring, human rights attainments, even achievement?
- *solidarity*: how are patterns of capacity developed to co-suffer with the violated, as distinct from the orders of human rights altruism manifest in 'networking' at a distance?

In the real world, NGOs are constantly exposed to evaluation by diverse instrumentalities: governments, security forces, the United Nations system, the donor and funding agencies, human rights advocates, and occasionally by consumers/beneficiaries of activism. I describe some of these ways in Chapter Seven through the metaphor 'human rights markets'. The questions raised above offer alternate ways of social audit or introspection.

In what follows, I seek to construct, by way of ideal types, varieties of scepticism and faith that affect most international NGOs that define themselves as 'progressive'.

II. Attitudes

Some international NGOs complain of *exhaustion* (which I term human rights *weariness*). Some suspect, given the history of politics *of* human rights, sinister imperialistic manoeuvres animating all human rights enunciation (which I term human rights *wariness*). Some activists celebrate virtues of dialogue among the communities of perpetrators and those violated (which I term human rights *dialogism*). Some celebrate human rights as *a new global faith or a new civic religion* (which I term human rights *evangelism*). Their fervour is often matched by those who think that the vocation of human rights lies in UN-sponsored human rights diplomacy, whether through historic redemption (by moving/removing the language in brackets in UN 'summit' declarations, programmes of action), a feat that I describe as human rights *romanticism*. Some human rights activists believe in 'aborting', as it were, global instruments favouring the rights of global capital opposed to the universal human rights of human beings (which I term 'free choice' politics *for* human rights). Some activist NGOs believe that human rights of human rights *normativity* can be best produced by manipulating the itineraries of global diplomatic, intergovernmental, regional and national careers of those who earn a living through the symbolic capital of human rights (this I term the *bureaucratization* of human rights). Some insist (like me) that the real birthplaces or sites of human rights are far removed from the ornate rooms of international conferences, being located in the struggles in the farm and the factory, home and hearth (this I term human rights *realism*).

These genres of 'contemporary' human rights attitudes and approaches carry implications for the construction of the future(s) of human rights. I include in the narrative voices not just from human rights NGOs but also human rights oriented thinkers who exercise a measure of influence on the contemporary worlds of activism.

III. Human Rights Weariness

Human rights weariness takes many forms. The first emerges as a normative weariness. It represents a kind of moral fatigue with rights languages and logics, marked by an ethical disposition that contests the very notion of human rights as a moral language and rhetoric. In a variation on Bentham's robust attack describing natural rights as 'nonsense on stilts',[19] the idea that the notion of human rights is itself incoherent leads to the conclusion that that there 'are no such rights and belief in them is one with belief in witches and unicorns'.[20] In much the same vein, it is said that, because human rights mean different things to different people,[21] rights have no 'robust ontological identity' and rights-talk only mystifies the question of such identity.[22]

The second weariness formation, related to the first, signifies nostalgia for old traditions for engagement with ethical and moral theory, which the rights-talk forever so wearisomely complicates. Instead of talking about 'virtue' and 'goodness', 'duty' and 'responsibility', rights languages seek to bring in conflicted and adversarial forms of social cooperation, displacing old notions about human perfectibility and communitarian harmony. To the extent that such displacement occurs, it is said, the gulf between the individual and community widens in ways that promote and enhance atomism over connectedness, abstraction over contextuality, rights over responsibility, independence over 'relational' rationality— a hallmark, overall, of a heavily feminist notion of human rights.[23]

This second type of manifestation of rights weariness represents moral anxieties that are worthy of attention, as against the first which suggests that the very idea of human rights is a *moral mistake*. It is unnecessary, for my present purpose, to deal with this form of contention,[24] but it is necessary to draw attention to this ethical enervation with the languages, logics, and paralogics of human rights.

[19] *See*, for example, the acute interrogation by Maurice Cranston, *Are There Any Human Rights?*, 112, *Daedalus* (1983), 1–17.

[20] Alasdair MacIyntyre, *After Virtue* (1981), 69.

[21] 'Rights are cast as substantialities, as relations, as frames. Rights are also cast as grounds of political redress or legal actions, as the mechanisms through which conflicts are resolved or mediated, as the endpoints in political and legal struggles. They are cast as acts scenes, agencies, and purposes. In short, rights can register on all sorts of matrices and networks ...' Pierre Schlag, 'Rights in the Postmodern Condition', in *Legal Rights: Historical and Philosophical Perspectives* (1997), Austin R. Sarat, and Thomas R. Kearns (eds), 263 at 264.

[22] Schlag, note 21 *supra* at 265.

[23] *See*, for an excellent analysis, Suzanna Sherry, 'Civic Virtue and the Feminine Voice in Constitutional Adjudication', 72, *Virginia Law Review* (1986), 543 at 590.

[24] The defence of the idea of human rights and the task of demonstrating that rights are not antithetical to community has been provided, germinally, by the life-work of Alan Gewirth. *See*, especially, his recent work *The Community of Rights* (1996).

IV. Human Rights Wariness

(1) *Types of Representational Powers*

Rights-wariness characterizes the communities of perpetrators of human rights violation as well as the communities of the violated, on whose behalf (though not always at whose behest) human rights activists speak to the world. Articulation of rights wariness involves the problematic of representational power.

Given the logic of sovereign representation of 'peoples' by 'states', and of states in turn by political regimes and cliques, it often becomes possible for the heads of states and governments (no matter how they reach the pinnacle of power) to speak on behalf of their peoples, and articulate typical forms of rights wariness. One is the representation of the contemporary human rights tradition as a threat to civilizational and cultural values, of which of course the leaders and the regimes present themselves as the most exemplary guardians and custodians. Another, and related, form consists in the representation that condemns contemporary human rights as being itself a form of radical evil; one that needs to be condemned in the name of God and the Holy. Yet another form of rights wariness takes an equally strident secular voice: contemporary human rights, 'Western' in their origin, are languages of neo-colonization, concealing new designs of a progressive Eurocentrism.[25]

However, this representational character is ambiguous and multiplex, impacting upon the practices of what I call the politics *of* and politics *for* human rights. Vigilant rights-wariness among critical communities, an attitude of confrontation with the politics *of* human rights, often collapses when otherwise indefensible regimes need to be supported against 'imperialism' of a solitary superpower. In these moments, a nationalist defence of state sovereignty and sovereign equality of all states becomes curiously unproblematic even for the practitioners of the politics *for* human rights. Indeed, an all too trigger-happy global policy of Pax Americana carries with it high costs of escalating human rights wariness in communities where enthusiasm for the protection and promotion of human rights has developed as a resource, howsoever fragile, for the transformative practices of politics. This bodes ill for the future of human rights.

At other moments, when characteristically repressive and brutal political regimes and élites are able to speak of the 'Asian', 'Islamic', 'Latin American', or 'African' approaches to human rights, rights-

[25] *Cf.* Slavoj Žižek, *The Ticklish Subject: The Absent Centre of Political Ontology* (1999), 219.

wariness is the only response available for those who are engaged in
the difficult politics *for* human rights. Such invocation by wicked or evil
regimes or 'leaders' of rich and diverse civilizational traditions amounts
to no more, from the perspective of the violated, than somehow seeking
an endorsement of the power to create and sustain their own gulags.
To the extent that this 'representational' feat is accomplished, human
rights wariness constitutes discursive power-formations that threaten
the future of human rights. However, to the extent that practices of
the politics *for* human rights succeed in relocating the authorship of
human rights to people in struggle and communities in resistance,
rights-wariness is a resource for a better future for human rights.

Increasingly however, human rights communities also seek to exercise
representational power on behalf of the violated, the very time and
space of what I term the politics *for* human rights. Just as state
managers often denounce human rights universalism, so do some
thoughtful activists. Some activist thinkers insist that a human rights
agenda is after all a global one that threatens the 'pluriverse' of thought,
action, and reflection.[26] They insist, and often with good reason, on
the 'need to break free from the oppressiveness of the Universal
Declaration of Human Rights'[27] (and its progeny) and struggle to
avoid locating inside oneself the 'recolonizing' 'contemporary Trojan
Horse' called Universal Human Rights.[28] This kind of manifestation
of human rights wariness manifests plurality and multiplicity of activist
perception that enriches and enervates at the same time the future
praxis of human rights. Explorations in the comparative sociology of
human rights are urgently required to assess the diverse potential of
rights-wariness for the future of human rights.

(2) *Coalescence*

There are other, less dramatic, occasions when communities of power
and of social activist thought differentially share a platform of rights
wariness. This happens through ideological practices that

- Demonstrate the dualism of standards in evaluation of human
  rights performances.[29]

---

[26] Gustavo Esteva and Madhuri Suri Prakash, *Grassroots Post-modernism: Re-Making the Soil of Cultures* (1998), 25.

[27] Ibid., at 126.

[28] Ibid., at 133–4.

[29] The North is unwilling, despite its proud boast to make the world safe for democracy, to create conditions within its own jurisdiction to eliminate circumstances and prac-tices that encourage massive, ongoing, and flagrant violations of human rights abroad.

- The North consistently refuses to assume human rights obligations to the South, whether in terms of *reparations* for past injuries and mayhems on ex-colonial societies and indigenous peoples of the world or in terms of the dedication of even a meagre percentage of its resources to alleviate conditions of extreme global impoverishment caused all too often by its own global economic domination.
- The North continually betrays its human rights commitments, especially through promotion of regimes of indebtedness and policies of 'structural adjustment'.[30]
- In the arena of sustainable development policies, the North has failed to assume burdens commensurate with its self-assumed leadership role.[31]
- Human rights diplomacy of the North has been complicit with the worst violations of human rights of the peoples of the South both during the Cold War and in the present post Cold War era.[32]

The politics *of* human rights in the South, naturally, seeks to use this commonality between itself and its Other—the politics *for* human rights—towards its own ends. Rights wariness in this context has to combat on the side of activist thought and praxis the extraordinarily rights-denying political appropriation by unscrupulous national regimes of their critiques of global 'order'. The mode of negotiation of this constant and fearful appropriation has much to do with the future of human rights.

(3) *Wariness of the Violated*

Human rights wariness is also increasingly an attribute of the consciousness of the violated, who find that the perpetrators of the gravest violation all too readily summon the ethic of human rights to serve their own ends with impunity. The 'originary' habitats of Euro-American cultures provide to the worst perpetrators of human rights violation a safe haven—from an Obote to a Pinochet. The violated feel mystified with the see-saw of judicial process and power. They weep one day when they hear that the Lord Chief Justice of the United Kingdom

---

[30] Susan George, *A Fate Worse Than Debt* (1994).

[31] *See*, generally, 'Report of International Commission on Peace and Food', *Uncommon Opportunities: An Agenda for Peace and Equitable Development* (1994; unsurprisingly chaired by M.S. Swaminathan, the 'father' of the Indian Green Revolution!)

[32] Noam Chomsky, *World Orders: Old and New* (1994).

not merely quashes the arrest of Pinochet on the ground that a 'former sovereign' is entitled to human rights respect but also at the award of exorbitant legal costs. They also however weep, this time with joy, the following day when a narrow majority of the House of Lords carefully reverses[33] that decision. The very day after they weep in consternation at the nullification by the House of Lords of their own judgment on the ground that one of their own was 'biased'! The day after that they begin to celebrate small judicial mercies that allow prosecution for 'alleged' acts of torture committed after the United Kingdom brought into legal being for itself an international convention prohibiting torture and cruel, inhuman, and degrading treatment or punishment.

In their exultant and depressed moods the violated find it difficult to understand the idea that five decades after the Nuremberg and Tokyo trials, learned justices should waver in locating in international law a rights-disciplined reading of sovereign immunity (as if the order of sovereignty was the order of impunity!). All this reinforces their belief that all rights-talk is just the *ruse* of governance. They know, at the end of the day, that what power gives today as rights can be taken away with equal felicity tomorrow. Their rejoicing is authentic when a judicial verdict disfavouring the powerful happens. They are also, however, aware that, structures of repressive power are also legitimated even by 'progressive' judicial discourse, which still preserves the autonomy and immunity of heads of governments and states, in the title of sovereignty of incumbency, to commit the worst possible human violation. The victims know that protection of their human rights under the auspices of the politics *of* human rights is a contingent feat; and they join, if at all, with great and grave caution, the heralding of rare triumphs as historic events for the politics *for* human rights.

V. Dialogism

Increasingly, everyone is asked to believe that the best way forward is the dialogue between the violated and the perpetrator. However, the production of the 'best way' differs, depending on its location within the politics *of*, as well as *for*, human rights. My distinction is also severely tested on this terrain.

In the model of politics *of* human rights, Truth Commissions, and their poor cousins called international hearings,[34] embody this tendency

---

[33] *Regina v. Bartle and the Commissioner of Police for the Metropolis and other: Ex Parte Pinochet* (1999, yet to be officially reported).

[34] Launched, mostly by concerned NGOs, at the site of various UN Summits in recent years.

towards dialogism. It will take this work far afield to explore, even in bare outline, the history of recent Truth Commissions, their functions and dysfunctions.[35] Clearly, Truth Commissions recover narratives of suffering seeking to impart the edge of human suffering to human rights discursivity. Because of their national, regional, or global auspices, Truth Commissions often marshal a range of authoritative data, often denied to human rights NGOs' fact-finding reportage activities. More important, the former carry some potential of policy action that the latter unevenly command. NGO reportage may primarily expose; it may not compensate victims or rehabilitate them or exercise the prerogatives of punishment or pardon. These still remain tasks of sovereign state power, regardless of how one may prophecy the end of the nation-state.

All this is well-known, as are the large questions that surround the processes and outcomes of Truth Commissions. These relate to issues of ways in which such devices result in the promotion and protection of human rights. Clearly, when the outcomes are outright grants of amnesty to the most heinous violators of human rights, it stretches the imagination to assert that internationally binding human rights treaties and customary law are protected thereby.[36] It is at least arguable that regimes of amnesty and future violations of human rights are positively corelated.[37] Truth Commissions, paradoxically, often construct a politics of memory only in order to enhance the practices of the politics of organized oblivion, at least for the communities of perpetrators. It is unlikely in the extreme that victims ever feel redressed by high moral summons of forgiveness and letting bygones be bygones. Those who have experienced genocidal rape[38] may in turn be 'forgiven' by the

---

[35] *See*, Priscilla B. Hayner, 'Fifteen Truth Commissions—1974 to 1994: A Comparative Study' in 1, *Transitional Justice: How Emerging Democracies Reckon with Former Regimes*, 225 (1995), N. Kirtz (ed.); *United Nations Commission on Human Rights, Sub-Commission on Compensation and Rehabilitation for Victims of Gross Violation of Human Rights and Fundamental Freedoms*, UN Doc.E/CN.4/SUB.2/1990/10, 26 July, 1990 [Theo van Boven, Special Rapporteur]; and related materials cited in Note 36, Chapter One. *See also*, Geoffrey Robertson, *Crimes Against Humanity: The Struggle for Global Justice* (1999).

[36] General amnesty (as in Haiti, El Salvador) or selective practices of amnesty (as probably in the case of South Africa) carry a tendency to undermine the new human rights *jus cogens* embodied, for example, genocide, torture, discrimination, and anti-apartheid conventions.

[37] *See*, *United Nations Commission on Human Rights: Report on the Consequences of Impunity*, UN Doc.E/CN.4/1990/13.

[38] *See*, Alexander Stiglmalyer, 'The Rapes in Bosnia-Herzegovnia', in *Mass Rape: The War Against Women in Bosnia-Herzegovina* (1992), A. Stiglmayer (ed.), 82–169.

community of human rights policy activists if they refuse to be persuaded to take such counsel seriously.

Another responsible form of dialogism occurs with the emphasis on the notion not of universality but of *pluriversality*, a discourse that adopts radical and moderate perspectives on human rights. The former anchors itself in the truth of grassroots experience and vision that enables us to perceive that we do not live in a universe, but in a pluriuniverse; that the universality in the human condition claimed by human rights propagators exists only in their minority world-view.[39] This perspective summons exploration of 'intercultural hospitality' based on 'a respectful and loving dialogue, a dialogue which changes its own terms'.[40]

In contrast, 'moderate' forms of dialogism insist on construction of the 'essential' patterns of 'universal cultural legitimacy' for the standards and norms of international human rights.[41] Put another way, dialogism recognizes the mutuality of human rights responsibilities in the re-invention of traditions such that no cultural or civilizational tradition be ever thought of as devoid of crucial ideals of human 'dignity', 'integrity', and equality of esteem or self and social worth. An-Naim's dialogism is based on what he calls 'constructive methodology' (for the reform of Islamic law in ways that makes it compatible with human rights norms and standards) that places in constant and creative interaction and negotiation of value inheritances in the narrative paths of 'tradition', 'modernity', and the common future of a constantly self-differentiating and diverse humanity. Whatever be the fate of the implicit 'theory', the explicit dialogical tasks it summons for critics and evangelists of human rights remain profoundly important from the point of view of those violated by formations of power in civil society and state in the circumstance of globality. With all their disagreements, the radical 'grassroots post-modernists' do not seem to me to offer much by way of praxis after the ghosts of universality have been finally slain or laid to rest.

Other forms of human rights dialogism need not detain us here. The idea that a handful of NGOs can dialogue with a handful of CEOs of multinationals to produce implementation of human rights results is simply Quixotic. The latter must inevitably deploy such dialogue as an elaborate public relations investment exercise aimed at strengthening

---

[39] *See*, note 26 *supra* at 127.

[40] Ibid., at 129.

[41] Abdullahi Ahmed An-Naim, *Human Rights in Cross-Cultural Perspectives* (1992), 431.

their global business competitiveness. This may seem harsh to those human rights friends who devote their energies and talents to producing voluntary codes of conduct and organize effective consumer resistance. I applaud these efforts with the caveat that such dialogism may not always perform intergenerationally enduring human rights attainment, especially when ethical investment becomes, at the end of the day, no more than a market practice devoted to enhancing the competitive edge in global markets. I do not wish to seem to deny, still less to gainsay, *episodic* human rights windfalls that matter a great deal to consumer–victims of unfair trade/market practice.[42] Nor do I wish to underestimate the contributions that Naderite and post-Naderite consumer movement cultures have made to the growing corpus of human-rights based practices of resistance. These have, undoubtedly, opened the locked doors of corporate wrongdoing, and at times in ways that *do* matter to here-and-now violated peoples. However, this having been acknowledged in all its fullness, it also needs to be noted that the structures of global capital remain human rights responsive only in terms of market/industry competitive advantage. Should you doubt this proposition, you only need to *read*, over and over again, the genre of literature exemplified by *A Civil Action*.[43]

Towards the end of the twentieth Christian century world, profound human rights violations are no longer the sole estate of sovereign states or histories of rebellion and order (so typical of 'civil' war or strife.) The massive formations of global capitalism, whether manifested by transnational/multinational corporations or international financial institutions *and* their normative cohorts, have also shown a remarkable resilience to legitimate grave and continuing violations of human rights of people: victims in Ogoniland and Bhopal, among myriad others, know and tell us. Undoubtedly, devices of peoples' tribunals (such as the Permanent Peoples' Tribunal, a successor to the Bertrand Russell Stockholm Tribunal on War Crimes in Vietnam) offer innovative ways of exposé. These fall far short of even a preliminary orientation to the articulation of transition to a human rights regime that articulate 'the right to bring historical capitalism to trial in a world tribunal'.[44] For those victimized by the processes of globalization, nothing seems more insistent today than such a venture.

---

[42] *See*, for a vivid account, Leslie Sklar, *The Sociology of the Global System* (1995).
[43] Jonathan Harr, *A Civil Action* (1997).
[44] *See*, Boaventura de Sousa Santos, *Towards a New Commonsense* (1995), 359–60. The fear of 'feasibility' should not rule out this important *programschrift*, although Santos' agendum requires participative development.

Dialogism in the experience, and anticipation of innovation, presents its own dangers. To give equal dignity of discourse to perpetrators and the violated of the most heinous kind (Pol Pot, Idi Amin, Mohammed Aidid, and the 'ethnic cleansers' in former Yugoslavia or Rwanda, for example) is to accord 'due process' to those who accomplished wholesale liquidation of that very notion. Accomplishing this, however, runs a grave risk of delegitimation amongst the violated of the very idea of human rights. Those who quite consciously deployed their political power to its fullest genocidal potential at least 'merit' an abbreviated due process so generously extended to people struggling against such power-formation.[45] The due process of fetishism and the valorization of 'even-handedness' (exemplified by the South African Truth and Reconciliation Commission in a 'both-to-blame' type moralism) does raise grave issues concerning the mode of production of belief in the idea of 'human rights among the growing communities of misfortune and injustice'.[46] For the violated, such forms of dialogism appear to serve more as a shield than as a sword against the perpetration of terror as a mode of governance.

VI. Human Rights Evangelism

The emergence of human rights faith communities is a notable feature of the worldwide promotion and protection of human rights. The inter-national bill of human rights is their sacred text; human rights education is their mission; and the peoples of the world their congregation. The evangelists believe in the power of the mantra: 'Human rights are inalienable, indivisible, interdependent and universal'.

They aim at a kind of moral, even spiritual, regeneration through creation of human rights cultures in which every single human struggle will be converted into human rights struggle. In their endeavour, some human rights NGOs practice robust dialogism with the worlds of power and communities of perpetrators; they believe that human rights aspirations and values can be made to permeate structures of

---

[45] Even the International Covenant on Civil and Political Rights recognizes the legitimacy of suspension of human rights in times of emergency where the 'emergency' incarnates itself as a justified regime of curtailment of 'basic' human rights.

[46] *See*, the agonizing judgement by Mr Justice Ismail Mahomed in *Azanian Peoples' Organization (Azapo) v. President of the South Africa* 1996 (4) SALR 671; and the critique, from an international law perspective, by Johan Duggard, 'Reconciliation and Justice: The South African Experience', 8, *Transnational Law and Contemporary Problems* (1998), 277–312.

state and global corporate power. For the evangelists, then, human rights constitute a new civic religion.

Of course, communities of religion have been notable precursors and companions to the secular missionaries of human rights. The former have incorporated aspects of the human rights faith as an integral aspect of their belief and practice. Most notable has been the historic work of church groups who have not merely reworked their dogma (as in the case of liberation theology) but have been actually engaged in human rights struggles from apartheid South Africa to East Timor. The Church associations have also funded the activities of human rights groups worldwide.

Together, the secular and religious evangelists promote a powerful moral vision. The fact that it is highly susceptible to political appropriation (as was the case during the Cold War and may even be said to some extent an aspect of post-Cold War politics) does not gainsay its authenticity. The history of human rights evangelism is yet to be written, but when it is written, the role of evangelists in shaping initiatives at human rights education and even norm-creation will find a prominent place.

To be sure, the overall impact of patterns of evangelism (which is not one phenomenon but many) must remain debatable. Some may question the very notion of human rights as a civic religion. Others may subject this notion to the same withering criticism that Marx visited upon the notion of religion, although it is difficult to see human rights becoming the 'opiate' of the masses, while still constituting the 'sigh of the oppressed'. It may also be said to profane the very idea of the sacred to endow iconic status to what are after all messy political trade offs and power calculi entailed in global diplomacy responsible for human rights norm-creation. Also those who would elevate all discourses and struggles to a human rights mantra remain justly liable to the indictment of creating a master metadiscourse, betraying in the process creativity, diversity, and solidarity in human resistance to violation.

VII. Human Rights Romanticism

A singular feature of 'contemporary' human rights lies in the populous presence of NGOs at the site of norm-creation in global conferences and summits from Rio to Istanbul, and the inevitable reviews styled 'Plus Five' conferences. The UN conferences and summits have provided an unparalleled opportunity to bring the world's burgeoning NGO communities together around issues such as biodiversity, population planning, development, women's rights as human rights, habitat human rights. Each of these events is marked by a series of 'prepcoms' (preparatory committee meetings) followed by 'review' of progress meetings (nowadays more stylishly called 'plus-five meetings') allowing for participatory stocktaking of the review of 'commitments' made by the state parties or by heads of governments. Accredited human rights groups enjoy observer status in the diplomatic conferences, where they seek to lobby governments to incorporate what they think to be more progressive texts or formulations.

This summation does not do justice to the rich diversity of the process, a task for another treatise. Anyone who has the privilege of participation or has followed events closely knows about great alliances, coalitions, caucuses, friendships, and enmities, networks of power and influence characterizing the enormity of NGO interaction among themselves and their governmental others. I address here only the aspect of human rights romanticism that such processes generate.

By 'romanticism', I designate the processes of politics of sheer hope and goodwill, abundantly present at these events, which give NGO participants a sense of achievement disproportionate to 'real' accomplishment. Constructivism teaches us all to take with caution the notion of the 'real'. To be sure, many summit-going NGOs feel truly empowered by the participation. At the same time, most actual, tangible outcomes occur in forms of carefully guarded texts of declarations and programmes of action. These raise the battle over brackets. The drafting process invariably entails a large number of parenthetical formulations, from which a final choice has to be made. The NGO participants seek to influence, as protagonists or antagonists, the various bracketed formulations. The best and the brightest NGOs dedicate singular energies to this task. Successful lobbying outcomes are usually experienced or presented as historic achievements of NGO communities.

Decentralization of international human rights norm-creation is of course a creative innovation of the last quarter century of the Age of Human Rights. There are however costs too,[47] and by 'costs' I do not

[47] In delineating costs, I rely on my close observer-involvement with some NGO participants in the Copenhagen Social Summit on Development, the Beijing World Conference on Women, and the Istanbul Summit on Habitat and my participation in the Vienna World Conference on Human Rights. I remain aware that the observations I offer remain 'pre-scientific' (based as they are on personal experience rather than empirical analysis) but I hope they help to open up to contestation the notion of human rights romanticism.

draw attention to the astronomical investment of resources entailed in these events, facilitating NGO–state interaction, though this when put together may exceed several times the national budgets of many a less developed and developing country, singly or in combination. I refer rather to the high costs involved in the pursuit of the politics of hope.

Summarly presented, these costs include

- creeping transformation of intensely involved NGOs in the image of international civil servants;
- displacement of the agenda of *equitable redistribution* towards an agenda of global *governance*;[48]
- enfeeblement of the potential of forms of creative antagonism into hurried and harried postures of compromise and cooperation;[49]
- construction of future horizons for NGO activity, through programmes of action that influence the allocation of resources;[50]
- a considerable loss of reflexivity among NGO communities concerning these costs.

Romanticism at times ill-serves the constituencies legitimating the NGO communities.

VIII. 'Free Choice' Politics For Human Rights

In this form of NGO praxis, the emphasis is on firmly opposing emergent global politics that directly impacts on human rights of large numbers of peoples. Sometimes (as in the World Bank Narmada or Sardar Sarovar Project in India) success is registered by affecting the practices and politics of the agency.[51] Sometimes the aggregation of uncoordinated peoples' protests has an impact on global formulation

---

[48] Upendra Baxi, 'Global Neighborhood and the Universal "Otherhood": Notes on the Report of the Commission on Global Governance', 21 *Alternatives* (1996), 525–49.

[49] Time-constraints for the production of negotiating texts and final declarations and programmes press heavily, necessitating the emergence of a statement of concerns that dissipate the urgency of concerted action as, for example, with the FAO Right to Food Declaration and Programme of Action. The Right to Food becomes the right to *food security*, the latter now installing itself as a food security system, in turn generating hybrid forms of social activism in which a Grameen Bank could even *think* of entering into an agreement with a Monsanto!

[50] The project applications for NGO funding have a better prospect of success if they can relate these to some paragraph in declarations and programmes of action.

[51] *See*, for a recent account, Catherine Caulfield, *Masters of Illusion: The World Bank and the Poverty of Nations* (1966).

of policy: the most shining example of this being provided by peoples' movements on the GATT/WTO enunciatory processes. Practices of cyber-solidarity in opposition to the draft MAI illustrate (as this work goes to press) a remarkable affirmation of 'free choice' politics for human rights.

In contrast to 'romanticism' this form of NGO action maintains a fairly robust 'Nay-saying' people's power. Its thrust is on anticipating and preventing potential future human rights violations. The order of activist integrity here is that of *participation by opposition*, rather than that manifesting through forms of diplomatic collaboration by human rights groups in the production of normativity of human rights standards. These forms of intervention are sometimes mass-based and often élite-led. This makes a difference. However, perhaps what counts, at the end of the day, is the escalated potential for abortion of globally planned human rights violations.

IX. The Bureaucratization of Human Rights

By this rather curious expression, I wish to signify the diminishing distance among forms of action constituting the orders of promotion and protection of human rights at the governmental and inter-governmental levels, and on the plane of the jural creativity of peoples' solidary action.

Increasingly, NGOs seem to believe that proliferation of human rights agencies within state structures is perhaps the best hope there is for human rights fulfilment. The story then is almost everywhere the same: more and more state agencies whose creation and expansion is justified as a creative response to peoples' aspiration for a secure future for human rights. Large agencies with ample funding and high governmental visibility flourish everywhere. Their capacity for significant action varies enormously depending on specific political, including mass media, cultures. In the absence of significant public participation in constituting these agencies, their personnel are both regime-favoured and dependent, as is their performance. The logics of 'institutional trap' become increasingly and painfully obvious as their agenda grows and tasks, with commensurate resources, multiply.

Except when these agencies assume adjudicatory forms, these tend to become yet another prison-house for aspirations of human rights attainment,[52] and even when they assume an adjudicatory form,

---

[52] These intuitive generalizations are not wholly devoid of empirical content, as anyone who sails against the wind is well aware. My colleagues in the Indian

moments of anguish at their feats overwhelm moments of celebration.

Prescinding all this, it remains the case that such agencies bureaucratize human rights and human suffering.

The reform of governance is scarcely fashioned by human rights communities by indwelling the habitus of the state ideology and apparatuses. These regularly confiscate people's jural innovation and inventiveness. The future of human rights, if any, lies in *inventing forms of participatory governance.*

X. Human Rights Realism

This then leads us to the inescapable problem of ways in which we may fashion narratives of human rights origin. By 'realism' I do not wish to refer to thought-formations that culminate in a Samuel Huntington, who conceived of order in politics as ways of *managing* people's needs, rights, and aspirations that seldom achieves their fulfilment. Rather, I wish to draw attention to people's praxes in the creation of human rights. After all, it was a man called Tilak, who at the birth of the twentieth Christian century, proclaimed that '*Swaraj* [decolonization] *is my birthright*' an assertion that earned him savage solitary confinement in British India but eventually made it incoherent. There was also a man called Gandhi who composed the first essay of refusal of early forms of South African apartheid. Generations of legendary women confronted patriarchal politics in the West that found 'liberal democracy' compatible with the civil and political dis-enfranchisement of women.

Human rights realism, in my sense of it, is the precursor of 'contemporary' human rights. To realize this, we need only to ask: would decolonization have become the international norm without Tilak and his followers? Would apartheid have become a scandal but for Gandhi and his followers? Would the motto 'Women's Rights are Human Rights' have been conceivable in the absence of the heroic suffragette and labour movements? Not merely this. The UDHR, the

---

national women's movement exiled me for a while for opposing the kind of legislation that now establishes the Indian Women's Commission. So did my human rights friends for my opposition to the way in which the Indian Human Rights Commission was structured. My opposition was based on the very premise they negated: that is, at times, *something is far worse than nothing*! It is no solace for me to have these very friends complain that these agencies in their pro-regime composition, now present another hurdle in the human rights activism!

There have, to be sure, occurred instances where the presence of these agencies have been marginally useful, but, overall their existence and functioning have also complicated rights and people's movements.

two Covenants, all the conventions on gender and racial discrimination summate the triumph of human rights movements; movements that eventually transformed the 'modern' into the 'contemporary' human rights paradigm.

The originary narratives that trace the birth of human rights in the Declarations of the Rights of Man need replacement by a history of non Eurocentric human struggles for human rights futures.

XI. 'Freedom's Children' and 'Midnight's Children'

The practices of contemporary human rights thus remain enormously varied and conflicted. These practices embody diverse interests and value-orientations, all under the banner of 'human rights'. Additionally, they enable the flourishing of different forms of politics *of* and *for* human rights, imparting both a measure of cogency and incoherence to the field of human rights as a whole. This rich diversity may in itself constitute some sort of human rights accomplishment, insofar as the many ways of rights-talk and related forms of social action tend to create (to borrow Ulrich Beck's felicitous phrase) 'something like a *co-operative or altruistic individualism*'.[53]

In another sense, however, the human rights wariness and weariness, especially of the violated, may pose substantial setbacks to future developments in the promotion and protection of human rights.

'Wretched of the earth unite, you have nothing to lose but the chains of human rights' may well become the slogan of tomorrow. When the violated feel that like previous languages (of distributive justice, revolutionary transformation, and the like) 'human rights' languages, too, interpellate or insert them merely as discursive objects in the politics *of* rights, the future of human rights must become radically insecure. Beck's type of communitarian individualism, howsoever satisfying to 'Freedom's Children' (as he prefers to term the project of the youth in Europe, now undergoing a 'second modernity') may transform the world *for them*. However, it may leave almost wholly intact the structures of global oppression for (to generalize Salman Rusdhie's metaphor) Midnight's Children everywhere in the Fourth World. As and when future practices of human rights resistance and solidarity build bridges of communicative hope between the two, the future of human rights may well be born.

---

[53] Ulrich Beck, *Democracy, Without Enemies* (1998), 9.

4

Too Many or Too Few Human Rights?

I. Overproduction of Human Rights?

Is it the case that the late Christian twentieth century 'suffers' from an overproduction of human rights standards and norms, in that it entails a policy and resource overload which no government or regime, howsoever conscientious, can bear? Does 'overproduction' entail a belief that every single major human/social problem can be best defined and solved in terms of human rights, through the talismanic property of human rights enunciations? Should concentrations of economic power be allowed to harness these talismanic properties?[1]

In addressing the notion of 'overproduction' one, of course, makes many ideological assumptions. For example, one assumes a distinction (which Braudillard draws our attention to) between *production* and *seduction*, the former making the invisible visible and the latter making the visible invisible. Anyone familiar with the ways in which the United Nations human rights discursivity is produced needs no instruction in how the final texts render invisible the original, and often lofty, aspiration. There is also the dimension of producer narcissism, be these the authors of international human rights, the makers of

---

[1] As is the case with the assorted interest groups of international airlines, hotels, travel agents who assiduously lobby the UN to proclaim a universal human right of tourism and when a group of predator investment organizations produce a Draft Multilateral Agreement on Investment.

May the aggregations of capital and technology (the propriteriat) be disabled always from acting upon the capitalist belief that protection of its rights as human rights is the best assurance there is for the amelioration of the life-condition of the proletariat?

modern constitutions, or NGOs who shape (or think they shape) many a new enunciation. In a sense, then, often human rights production also entails patterns of seduction; a loss of orders of reflexivity of what is being produced at whose *cost* and for whose gain, indeed to the point of being *alienated* production.

Similarly, the 'overproduction' metaphor conceals from view the *authorship of the violated*. When production of human rights normativity is seen primarily, or even wholly, as an act of the collective labour of bleary-eyed draftspersons and negotiators who must somehow marshal in the early moments of morning the eleventh hour consensus on a phrase-regime, one is looking at the process of enunciation as an aspect of heroic enterprise by international career bureaucrates and diplomats and privileged professional NGOs. The cosmopolitan labour thus invested makes possible human rights instruments. However, often a prerequisite for those forms of performative labours, are the lives of those exposed to suffering caused by human violation, who do not often exist in public memory. Their labour of suffering becomes embodied, often through heavily 'bracketed' texts, ripe for linguistic resolution experienced by the community of the heroic rights-producers. When we grasp the contradictory contexts in this manner, we may even begin to speak of *informal* but vital sectors of international human rights production. The formal sector of the norm-creative political economy of human rights needs to reproduce this vast informal sector of existential human suffering. Unkind, even 'post-Marxian', people may say that continual innovation in forms of human and social suffering is a prerequisite for the production of human rights normativity. A future social theory of human rights may archive different modes of production. In the meantime, the diversity of modes of suffering may continue to provide the raw materials for the production or overproduction of human rights normativity and discursivity.

Further, one usually associates 'production' with markets. I explore, in Chapter Seven, the notion of markets for, and of, human rights. Human rights enunciations are, of course, symbolic goods, and services that seek to sustain certain modes of production of belief. The production of the 'cultural software' of contemporary human rights is a complex, contradictory, and multi-layered process, an understanding of which is crucial to any notion of 'overproduction' to be at all sensible.

In the absence, or the nascence, of a comparative social theory of human rights, I address here only the issue of overproduction as a conflicted site. Overproduction implies a relatively (in)efficient business practice; one capable of redemption by planned dumping policies, for example manifest (cruelly for captive markets) of rights-oriented good governance policies of the World Bank. 'Overproduction' carries with it the management overload typically associated with the management of excess. Ideally, production of goods and services should be marked by efficiency, constructed as production not just in terms of the *quantity* but *quality*. In global markets, the costs of overproduction of goods and services are passed on to captive consumer constituencies of the Third World. Shockingly, this holds true even of the production of contemporary human rights norms and standards. For example, not just the White House and Capitol Hill but distinguished American scholars maintain that the United States' disinclination to ratify human rights instruments is justified, by the existence of a flourishing tradition of constitutional rights and judicial review.[2] In plain words, this means that overproduction of human rights is an altruistic exercise for the benighted Third World societies in their historic tryst with democratic self-governance. The 'logic' is similar to that deployed by the captains of shoddy pharmaceutical products in justifying export of hazardous drugs prohibited at home!

At the site of production, namely the United Nations system, efficiency in the production of contemporary human rights standards raises new and difficult issues[3] as does the notion of quality.[4]

[2] The doyen of the American human rights community, Professor Louis Henkin, for example, has maintained this view fairly consistently. At a recent meeting to celebrate the fifteenth year of the Harvard Human Rights Program, 16–17 September 1999, he reiterated his view that adopting international human rights norms and standards may not be necessary, or even desirable, for the United States, given her bicentennial strong tradition of judicial review.

[3] Efficiency may stand for cost-effective production of human rights standards and norms. This is a matter, but not only in part, of available budgetary outlays within the United Nations system and additional costs internalized by the member states, relative to other priorites in the field of promotion and protection of human rights. If the overall cost of production of human rights norms and standards is so substantial that meeting other rights-related priorities becomes difficult, then one may adjudge the enunciative process as inefficient, provided we assume that such processes aim at attainment of human rights.

Judgements about the efficiency of human rights production remain complex and contested, as frequently symbolized by jibes about first and business class frequent flyers debating in five-star hotel comforts strategies concerning poverty alleviation or the right to food. The question of unproductive expenditure in the production of human rights relates to ways in which resources could be channelled to programmes for the promotion and protection of human rights.

[4] The problem of *quality* suggests at least the following areas:
(1) efficiency of the deliberative process leading to production of draft movements, efficiency here measured by considerations of equitable representation and participation as well as levels of expertise or insight;

The notions of efficiency and clarity are further complicated by an insistence on the rhetoric of universality, interdependence, indivisibility, and inalienability of human rights. Eminently desirable according to the prevailing hegemonic models of human rights enunciations, these four mantras introduce imponderables in the markets for the manufacture of human rights. Judgements on the efficiency and quality of enunciation of human rights standards and norms are indeed very difficult and at times even impossible. This becomes clear when we attend to a redefinition of the scope of human rights, which now extends to addressing material and non-material needs. This constant endeavour to convert needs into rights, howsoever problematic, is the hallmark of contemporary human rights. This, however, makes difficult any serious judgement on efficiency and quality. To take a large example: when certain sets of rights entail duties of here and now enforcement (as with the Covenant on Civil and Political Rights) and certain others are subject only to the regime of 'progressive' realization (as with the Covenant on Social, Economic, and Cultural Rights) how does one apply the four mantras in evaluation of the effectiveness of rights-regimes?

The constant endeavour to convert needs into rights results in waves of rights enunciations: at times described as 'generations' of rights; at times delineated by a colour scheme as 'blue', 'red', and 'green' rights.[5] Being, as it were, 'colour-blind', I do not know which colour may best signify the emerging recognition of the collective rights of the foreign investor, global corporations, and international financial capital; in short, global capitalism. This much is however compellingly clear: the emergent collective human rights of global capital present a formidable challenge to the paradigm inaugurated by the UDHR.

---

(2) clarity and communicability (or translatability) of textual outcomes;

(3) levels of consensus reached (on individual formulations and the text as a whole; consensus levels measured, partly, by the extent of reservations, derogations, declarations, and statements of understanding when a rights enunciation takes the form of an international treaty and by patterns of voting power when it assumes forms of declarations or resolutions);

(4) specificity or diffuseness of definitions of violative behaviours and levels of accountability monitoring or implementation;

(5) mechanisms or processes for promotion and protection, including strategies for human rights education;

(6) procedures for collective review and reformulation.

[5] *See*, Johan Galtung, *Human Rights in Another Key* (1994), at 151–6.

The astonishing *quantity* of human rights production generates varieties of experiences of scepticism and faith, which I have explored in the preceding chapter. These experiences form ways of reading human rights, particularly in term of their over-, or under-, production. I refer, rather cursorily, to four principal ways of reading.

II. Quality Control in International Human Rights Production

The question of how the production of human rights may best be organized within the United Nations system, has been with us since the UDHR. The First World states questioned, in the middle phase of the Cold War, the unprecedented normative leadership role assumed by the Second and the Third World member-states in the modes of production of human rights standards and norms. This interrogation periodically raised the issue of legitimacy and quality control of the norms thus sought to be created. When these states failed to abort or amend these enunciative moves, they abstained or voted against these. All this led to some unusual doctrinal disputations and emergences. For example, some espoused the notion that the General Assembly resolutions and declarations on human rights produce 'soft' law (a euphemism for saying that these were devoid of any political or actual human rights creationit, effect). Some others maintained that this 'soft' law, when frequently reiterated in subsequent textual practice, did, indeed, become 'hard', that is it acquired some sort of customary status.[6] The notion that frequent textual reiteration of that which was originally not 'law', converts aspirational statements into an order of obligations, has been an important resource for the development of an international law of human rights. The narratives of origins and career of this notion remain an important aspect of any comparative social theory of human rights, a task I cannot pursue here.

If however, this early anxiety concerning the organizational way of production of human rights normativity raises, within the United Nations system, questions about hierarchic control over rights production that still remain relevant in the post-Cold War epoch. Increasing agency autonomy within the system is seen as a hazard that

[6] By this anti-footnote, I wish to indicate the deliberate absence of citations! The 1960s and 1970s generated a literature of contention, which will fill several floors of library collection! I invite interested readers to follow this discourse on their own, unled by the conventional mode of a footnote citation, which would be several pages long!

ought to be contained, as illustrated by the debate over the Right to Development.[7] Similarly, the manner in which treaty bodies formulate, through the distinctive device of General Comments, somewhat unanticipated treaty obligations upon state parties now begins to emerge as a contested site. For example, the Convention on Elimination of Discrimination Against Women (CEDAW), in its textual formulation, barring the solitary exception of Article 6 relating to outlawry of sex-trafficking, was concerned in original intention with *discrimination,* not *violence*, against women. Even when the CEDAW Articles 14 and 16 seek to obligate state parties to eliminate, or at least to combat, gender discriminatory practices in family relations and arrangements, they do not address these as the *orders of innate and sustained violation of, and violence against, women*. Through the device of the General Comment, the CEDAW Committee has unevenly sought to redress this lack by erasing the distinction between *discrimination* and *violence*. The reports, which the state parties are required to submit to the Committee (under Article 28), will now have to furnish information on policy measures on both counts. While this is welcome, issues concerning the transformation of treaty obligations thus entailed will remain contested.

In terms of TQM (Total Quality Management, a hierarchical management science notion that, one hopes, will *never* inflict into discourse on the multifarious and anarchic human rights creation!), however, the issues that arise do need a brief mention. First, aside from the issues of cybernetic control within the UN hierarchy on the production of human rights norms, there is the question of *management of proliferation*, vital to the credibility of the enterprise of rights entrepreneurship, especially in the conversion of human needs into human rights. May all human needs be translated *necessarily* into human rights languages? To quote Milan Kundera:

> The world has become man's right and everything has to become a right: the desire for love the right to love; the desire for rest the right to rest; the desire for friendship the right to friendship; the desire to exceed the speed limit the right to exceed the speed limit; the desire for happiness the right to happiness; the desire to publish a book a right to publish a book; the

[7] *See*, Jack Donnelly, *In Search of a Unicorn: The Jurisprudence and Politics of the Right to Development*', 15, *California Western International Law Journal* (1985), 473; Philip Alston, 'Revitalizing United Nations Work on Human Rights and Development', 18, *Melbourne University Law Review* (1991), 216; *but see* Upendra Baxi, 'The Development of the Right to Development' in *Human Rights: New Dimensions and Challenges* (1998), 99–116.

desire to shout in the street in the middle of the night a right to shout in the middle of the night.[8]

While Kundera perhaps ignores the *need* to translate certain human needs into human rights,[9] he does bring home the mindlessness of the enterprise of conversion of every single human desire, need, or want into a regime of human rights governed by the four mantras!

Second, the constant conversion of needs into rights assumes that the rights-regime is the principal mechanism for arranging human well-being. Normative renderings of human needs into rights, it is true, create a space empowering people's movements to expose contradictions between political rhetoric and structures of inequity. Occasionally, activist adjudicatory power and process may also, besides sharpening the contradiction, deliver some *real* results, as the experience of the Indian social action litigation suggests. At the end of the day, however, the rights languages enhance the power of the state against formations of violation in civil society. For example, the right to health must in some measure empower state action on medical education and profession; the right to housing must empower the state to regulate markets in real property and at times even empower it to confiscate large urban estates in ways deeply violative of the human right to property; the right to education and literacy must empower the state to regulate the free market in the provision of educational services. In the process, the bureaucratization of human rights occurs in ways that are inimical to rights-attainment. This in turn contributes to a culture of despair concerning human rights among the ostensible beneficiaries.

III. The Costs of Human Rights Inflation

Some readings question the value and the utility of inflation of human rights. The question of 'costs' of overproduction raises several considerations. First, there is the issue of resources allocated, within the United Nations system, to the production, promotion, and protection of human rights. On an expansive view of these phrases, almost all the resources would, in one way or the other, appear to be dedicated to the production, promotion and protection of human rights, while on agency-specific count the human rights allocation

---

[8] Milan Kundera, *Immortality* (1991), 153.

[9] *See*, Galtung, note 4 *supra*, who addresses the lacunae in contemporary human rights standards in non-recognition of the right to sleep or defecate which matter in circumstances of repressive torture.

would appear constantly in need of augmentation. Additional protocols to human rights treaties (as is the case with the recent welcome Protocol for CEDAW) entail an immediate here and now budgetary allocation. Pleas for increased allocation for human rights promotion activity have been intensified with, and since, the Vienna Conference on Human Rights. Whatever be the ad hoc resolution of the matter, the larger issue of costs relative to benefits from investment on human rights will always excite contention among the member states, agencies, and accredited NGO communities.

Second, the issue of socialization of costs for human rights activities of the United Nations system has led to a critical exchange between the NGOs and the system. The recent controversy concerning the UNDP favouring ways of mainstreaming human rights that justify raising resources from global corporations which have been indicted, in various fora, with the worst violations of human rights is symptomatic of 'costs' of collatrative strategies. Third, acute questions arise concerning this endless normativity of human rights enunciations: does this perform any useful function in the 'real' world? Is there an effective communication (to invoke Galtung's trichotomy) among the norm-senders (the UN system), norm-receivers (sovereign states) and norm-objects (those for whose benefit the rights enunciations are said to have been made? Who stands to benefit the most by the overproduction of human rights norms and standards? Or is it merely a symptom of growing democratic deficit, sought to be redressed by legitimation of traffic between norm-senders and norm-receivers?

IV. Over-Politicization?

A third reading, from the standpoint of high moral theory, warns us against the danger of assuming that the languages of human rights are the only, or the very best, moral languages we have. Rights languages are after all languages of contestation of claims that necessarily entail mediation through authoritative state instrumentalities, including contingent feats of adjudicatory activism. Overproduction of rights locates social movements on the grid of power, depriving human communities of their potential for reflexive ethical action. Being ultimately state-bound, even the best of all rights performances typically professionalize, atomize, and de-collectivize energies for social resistance, and do not always energize social policy, state responsiveness, civic empathy, and political mobilization. Not altogether denying the creativity of rights languages, this reading minimizes its role, stressing instead the historic role of lived relations of sacrifice, support, and solidarity in the midst of suffering in which rights languages play a historically contingent, not any foundational, role.

V. Participation as a Value

A fourth reading views the production of human rights as, perhaps, the best hope there is for a participative creation of human futures. It assumes a world historic moment in which neither the institutions of governance nor the processes of market, singly or in combination, are equipped to fashion just futures. It thrives on the potential of peoples' politics (not as a system but as chaos) which may only emerge by an ensemble of singular energies of dedicated NGOs (local, national, regional, and global). No other understanding of the women's movements celebrating the motto 'Women's Rights are Human Rights' is, for example, possible except that which regards as historically necessary and feasible the overthrow, by global praxis, of universal patriarchy, in all its vested and invested sites. This reading seeks to combat patriarchy persistent even in the making of human rights and to explore ways of overcoming the limits of human rights languages, which very frequently constitute the limits of human rights action.

VI. Interrogating Overproduction Thesis

A fifth reading questions the very notion of overproduction of human rights norms and standards. Not merely does the global enunciation of rights entail a long, often elephantine, gestation period but also much normative activity produces only 'soft' human rights law (exhortative resolutions, declarations, codes of conduct, etc.) which do not reach, or even at times aspire, to the status of operative norms of conduct. The 'hard law' enunciations of human rights, which become enforceable norms, it may be argued, are very few and low in intensity of application. Contemporary human rights production remains both sub-optimal (whatever may be said in comparison with the 'modern' period) and inadequate. The task is, on this view, to achieve an optimal productivity of internationally enforceable human rights.

VII. Too Many Rights, or Too Few?

These ways of reading carry within them all kinds of impacts on the nature and future of human rights. A fuller understanding of these impacts is an important aspect of the social theory of human rights.

Clearly, those inclined to believe the overproduction thesis would marshal abundant support for the view that we have too many rights enunciations. With equal cogency, those inclined to 'put human rights to work' may maintain that 'real' human rights are too few. Those who feel excluded from the contemporary human rights regime (in particular, the protagonists of the human right to sexual orientation or more generally to a non-homophobic dominant culture of governance) may with considerable justification maintain that the tasks of human rights enunciation have just barely begun. Indeed, the agents and managers of globalization insist that there is a greater scope and need to protect the human rights of global capital in its great March to Progress through digitalization and biotechnology. Equally, those concerned with the rights of 'nature' and sentient beings (other than human beings) lament the paucity of human rights standards and norms.

This riot of perceptions concerning over- or under-production of human rights normativity arises due to the titanic clash of two cultures of human rights: the cultures of the politics *of* human rights and those of politics *for* human rights. The latter combats as overproduction the regimes of protection of the rights of global capital, while celebrating the newly emergent rights of peoples. The former seeks parsimony in production of new human rights standards and norms while being hospitable to the proliferation of the rights of global capital enunciations (witness the draft proposals on Multilateral Agreement on Investment, the demise of which stands too hastily prognosticated by the practitioners of the politics for human rights.)

No reasoned judgment on the mode of production of human rights is thus possible. I would go so far as to say that none is desirable. It will be, in my view, a sad moment in the future history of human rights when the production of belief in the overproduction of human rights becomes universal, despite the heavy questions thus far raised in this analysis.

5
Politics of Identity and Difference

I. Approaches to a Critique of Contemporary Human Rights

Deriving from the postmodernist mood, method and messages, critiques of 'contemporary' human rights remain anxious about the re-emergence of the idea of Universal Reason, a legacy of the Age of Enlightenment, which helped perfect justifications for classical colonialism, racism, and universal patriarchy.[1]

The notion of universality is said to enact not merely new versions of essentialism about human nature but also to invoke the notion of metanarratives: global stories about power and struggle against power. This not merely denies difference but also monopolizes the 'authentic' narrative voice. Instead of being empowering, human rights discursivity is then seen, in one way or another, to be disempowering its ostensible beneficiaries. In both these tropes, do we return to modes of 'totalization' of thought and practice?

Critics of human rights essentialism remind us that the notion 'human' is not pre-given (if indeed, anything is) but constructed. This social construction of that 'human' is not necessarily human rights friendly. It often occurs with profound rights-denying impacts, as was clearly the case in the formative practices of the 'modern' human rights paradigm. Even as regards the 'contemporary' human rights discursive practices, postmodernist critiques now guide us to the idea that the idiom of the universality of human rights may also have a similar impact.

---

[1] As regards patriarchy, see Sally Sedgwick, 'Can Kant's Ethics Survive the Feminist Critique?' in *Feminist Interpretations of Immanuel Kant* (1997), 77–110. *See also*, *Feminists Read Habermas: Gendering the Subject of Discourse* (1995).

For example, the motto 'women's rights are human rights' often masks, with grave costs, the heterogeneity of women in their civilizational and class positions.[2] So does the appellation 'indigenous' in the quest for a commonly agreed declaration of indigenous people's rights.[3] Similarly the human rights protection instruments on child rights ignore the diversity of children's subject positions. In many societies the passage between the first and second childhood or the distinction between 'child' and 'adult' is brutally cut short. The hegemons of human rights allow little or no play for radical plurality.

Indeed, it has been recently suggested that the 'monoculture' of human rights[4] 'continues the cultural imperialism of colonialism', perpetuating the belief that the 'underdeveloped' cultures are too poor or primitive to promote the good of their people, while imposing the dominant cultures' notions of human well-being.[5] On this view, grassroots groups and initiatives that 'do not fall victims to this Trojan Horse of recolonization' deserve celebration, for, through their liberation from the 'Global Project' of universal human rights these

> open our eyes and 'gaze', open our hearts and minds to the diverse cultural ways of thinking about the 'good life'; to the radical pluralism with which the well-being of women, men and animals is understood and promoted in different local spaces of this world. Cultural diversity means not giving one culture's moral concept—that of human/women's rights—pre-eminence over others; bringing human rights down from its pedestal, placing it amidst other significant cultural concepts which define the 'good life' in a pluriverse.[6]

De-pedestalizing human rights is a nice polemical motif; and the contrast between 'monocultures' and 'pluriverse' is indeed striking. Beyond this, the rhetoric of diversity of conceptions of good life is persuasive only for those pre-committed to the notion that attributes

---

[2] *See*, Elizabeth V. Spelman, *Inessential Woman: Problems of Exclusion in Feminist Thought* (1988), p.x, who, maintains that the endeavours at defining 'women as women' or 'sisterhood across boundaries' is the 'Trojan-horse of western feminist ethnocentrism'. *See also*, for a sustained problematization, Judith Butler, *Gender Trouble: Feminism and the Subversion of Identity* (1990).

[3] *See*, Stephen Marqaurdt, 'International Law and Indigenous Peoples', 3, *International Journal of Group Rights*, 47 (1995); Russel Barsh, 'Indigenous Peoples in 1990s: From Object to Subject of International Law?', 7, *Harvard Human Rights Journal* (1994), 33.

[4] Gustavo Esteva and Madhu Suri Prakash, *Grassroots Postmodernism: Remaking the Soil Cultures* (1998), 124.

[5] Ibid. at 119.

[6] Ibid. at 118, 119.

the exclusive authorship of human rights only to the communities of North and its clones elsewhere.

Be that as it may, these important criticisms do not guide us to any serious construction of the notion of 'essentialism' in contemporary human rights theory and practice. I know of *no* contemporary subject-specific human rights instrument that by, and in itself, normatively denies radical diversity or plurality. A minimal human rights literacy will educate us about the obvious: when, for example, human rights declarations and treaties enunciate the rights of 'women', 'minorities', 'indigenous peoples', 'labour', 'migrant workers', and 'children', these do not enact any abstract, ahistorical universal categories with an unchanging and unchangeable 'essence'. Rather, they direct attention to a variety of subject positions of individuals and groups for whom rights have been enunciated. One may contest the adequacy, even poverty, of these designations or the actual forms and contents of rights thus enshrined. One may also contest the politics of the universality of human rights. Important as such criticisms may be, it is simply unwarranted to ascribe to contemporary human rights any sort of 'essentialism' that reduces the conception of being human to any predetermined attributes, properties, or essences. Indeed, the radical difference between the 'modern' and 'contemporary' human rights discursivity lies precisely in the fact that the latter is not founded upon any predetermined conception of what constitutes a human 'essence'.

A deeper aspect of such criticism may, however, have to do not so much with the texts of international or constitutional affirmation of human rights but with the presuppositions that animate such normativity: presuppositions that reduce all humanity to the Euro-American images of what it means to be human. It is often said that these basic presuppositions emanate from the 'Western' notions of Enlightenment that constituted the word 'human', essentially in the image of a male white individual bourgeois colonizer. While this is certainly true of the paradigm of 'modern' human rights, is it correct to extend the same indictment to the animating presuppositions of contemporary human rights? There of course remain open several ways of reading contemporary human rights. But it appears to me that, the 'contemporary' paradigm of rights postulates, and progressively recognizes, that the notion 'human' being, and being human, is itself a process of continual redefinition. In maintaining that slavery, racism, colonization, genocide, patriarchy, and violent social exclusion are per se illegitimate, the 'contemporary' paradigm not merely delegitimates the old ways of dehumanization but also enables articulation of new forms of human identity through critical engagement with structures of social, political and economic domination.

It is true that rights languages and logics complicate the construction of identities. Insofar as the contemporary human rights paradigm accentuates the individual as a 'sovereign individual',[7] it promotes visions of a 'good society', and of global justice, at the unconscionable expense of genuinely communitarian values.[8] Insofar as this paradigm promotes a culture of justice indifferent to an *ethic of caring*, it does, rightly appear, from a feminist point of view 'as frightening,... in its potential justification of indifference and unconcern'.[9] Also insofar as it raises the sceptre of denial of group rights,[10] the contemporary rights discourse may seem to re-enact the old logics of exclusion. To this extent it might be said with some justification that this essentialization of rights emerges in turn as an essentialist construction of human being, and of being human. However, just as the logics and languages of human rights complicate identity, constructions of logics and languages of identity complicate human rights. It is to this interesting intersection that we now turn.

II. The Politics of Identity

Do identities then get universalized all over again in positing a *universal* bearer of human rights, obscuring the fact that identities may themselves be vehicles of power, all too often inscribed or imposed? Also, do the benign intentions underlying such performative acts of power advance the cause of human rights as well as they serve the ends of power?

Students of international law need no immersion into the pools of postmodernisms. They are well aware of the problematic of identity as vehicle of power, from the Kelsenite 'constitutive' theory of recognition of states (under which new states may not be said to exist under

---

[7] *See*, James Dale Davidson and William Ress-Mogg, *The Sovereign Individual* (1997). In somewhat instructively irritating ways these messiahs of globalization predict the transformation of citizens into customers, where only those customers (sovereign individuals contrasted with other rational individuals) will be winners in a 'winners take all world'.

[8] *See*, for example, Charles Taylor, 'Atomism' in his *Philosophical Papers* (1985); Annette Baier, 'The Need for More than Justice', in *Science, Morality and Feminist Theory* (1987), 47.

[9] Carol Gilligan, *In a Different Voice* (1982), 22.

[10] Chandran Kukathas, 'Are There any Cultural Rights', in *The Rights of Minority Cultures* (1995), 228–55.

international law unless 'recognized' by the community of pre-existing states) to the travails of the right to self-determination. They know how that 'self' is constructed, deconstructed, and reconstructed by the play of global power,[11] with the attendant legitimation of enormous amounts of human misery. The evolution of the right to self-determination of states and peoples signifies no more than the power of hegemonic or dominant states to determine the 'self', which has then the right to self-determination. In sum, that right is only a right to an access to a 'self' already predetermined by the play of hegemonic global powers.

Is it any longer true that outside the contexts of 'self-determination', the shackles of state sovereignty determine, even when they do condition, bounds of identity? Increasingly, de-territorialization of identity, at the end of the century, is said to be a *global* social fact or human condition.[12] Identities tend to become fluid, multiple, contingent, perhaps even to a point when an individual or the subject is viewed as 'the articulation of an ensemble of subject positions, constructed within specific discourses and always precariously sutured at the intersection of subject positions'.[13] Also, the community appears as 'a discursive surface of inscriptions.'[14] There is a great appeal in Chantal Mouffe's notion of a 'non-individualistic conception of the individual'. The notion rejects, as concerns human rights the idea of the individual in terms of 'possessive individualism', but it implies more. The individual is conceived by Mouffe as 'the intersection of a multiplicity of identifications and collective identities that constantly subvert each other.'[15]

---

[11] *See*, Hurst Hannum, 'Rethinking Self-Determination', 34, *Virginia Journal of International Law* (1993), 1. He effectively contrasts the reservation by India confining the right to self-determination in Article 1, of the International Covenant on Civil and Political Rights 'only to peoples under foreign rule' with the German objection to it insisting on the availability of this right to 'all peoples'.

The zeal with which the developed countries have sought to expand the range of self-determination rights arises from their unique capacity to organize collective amnesia and ruthless prowess in supressing (not too long ago) even the softest voice urging freedom from the colonial yoke.

This having been said, it must be added that India's reservation based on 'national integrity', creatively mimes the very same order of enclosure of the politics of identity and difference in vastly different post-colonial conditions.

[12] For a vivid account of the processes, *see*, Arjun Appadurai, *Modernity at Large: Cultural Dimensions of Modernity* (1997), 27–65.

[13] Chantal Mouffe, 'Democratic Citizenship and the Political Community', in *Dimensions of Radical Democracy* (1992) at 237.

[14] Chantal Mouffe, 'Democratic Politics Today' in ibid., at 14.

[15] Chantal Mouffe, *The Return of the Political* (1992) at 97, 100.

This way of thinking does enable us to revisit the problematic of conflict of rights. In the famous *Shah Bano* case[16], for example, the Supreme Court of India constructed the Quranic texts to provide a right of maintenance to divorced Muslim wives; the Indian Parliament restored what was thought to be the orthodox reading of the Quran.[17] Progressive women's organizations and movements, across the religious divide, sought a judicial review of the Act, still pending before the Supreme Court of India.[18] When some of us gained access to Shah Bano (a woman in her sixties, who had been married for over three decades) she reminded us, at the height of impassioned national controversy, that she was not *just* a woman but that she was a *Muslim* woman. She was not a *na-pak*; as a woman she belonged, and stood constituted, by the lived tradition of the shari'a. In other words, she claimed gender equality *within* her tradition and was loathe to surrender it to the power of secularized interpretive communities.

Shah Bano's response provides a striking example of a 'multiplicity of identifications and collective identities' that 'constantly subvert each other.' Her identification as an Indian citizen led her to activate judicial power for vindication of her rights; but the rights she sought were within the shari'a, not indwelling in the much vaunted secularity of high judicial discourse. The recourse to judicial power was creatively communitarian, not a subscription to the 'Global Project' of universal human rights.

---

[16] *Mohd Ahmed Khan v. Shah Bano Begum* AIR 1985 SC 946. *See also* Zia Pathak and Rajeswari Sunder Rajan, 'Shah Bano' 14, *Signs* (Spring, 1989) 558–88.

[17] Indeed, the Muslim Women's Protection of Rights Act innovates the shari'a. In providing that any relative who has the prospect (*spec successionis*) of inheriting from her has a duty to maintain the divorced woman and that pious trusts (*wakfs*) have a duty to provide maintenance to divorced women, the Indian Parliament exercises legislative power to amend the shari'a in ways that even the most progressive reformers of Muslim law could never have anticipated! However, the politics of the situation on all sides prevented any acknowledgement (and it still does!) of this daring assertion of legislative power.

[18] The petition was filed in 1985 by Tara Ali Baig, Madhu Mehta, Lotika Sarkar, and myself. The first two petitioners have since demised, and the last two are at the edge of mortality! Obviously, the Court in its *administrative* powers has silenced the petition. The only good reason for this judicial abdication is provided by the considerations of the institutional integrity of the Court as well as political accommodation between the supreme executive and supreme judicial power the in face of a coup against the Constitution: *see* Upendra Baxi, 'The Shah Bano Reversal: Coup Against Constitution', in *Inhuman Wrongs and Human Rights: Unconventional Essays* (1994), 88–94; Flavia Agnes, *Law and Gender Inequality: The Politics of Women's Rights in India* (1999) 94–126.

Many similar examples abound. Algerian women living in France claiming the right to veil their face in schools are claiming *a right to be different* or *a right to difference;* their deployment of the logic and paralogics of human rights seeks to subvert the 'monological' view of human rights through a pluri-universalistic praxis. Here we are confronted by some of the most intractable problems of conflict of rights where self-chosen sedimentation of identity within a religious tradition is at odds with universalistic mode of de-traditionalization of the politics of difference demanding gender equality and justice. What is crucial, in my view, is the fact that this conflict of human rights (right to free choice of religious belief and practice and right to gender equality and justice) becomes socially visible when a paradigm of universal human rights is securely in place. It is this *happening* that makes legible the play of subaltern power in a constant subversion of identities.

III. Questions Raised by the Diaspora of Identity Thesis for the Politics of, and for, Human Rights

To move the discourse from a situation of agency and deliberative rationality, to the assertion that the bearer of human rights, individual or collective, does not exist as a 'unified' discursive or semiotic object, raises a different order of interlocution altogether. In a post-structuralist, postmodern world, we are all *'contingent persons'*.[19] Contingent persons may claim, if at all and with great difficulty, 'universal' human rights! The dissipation of the 'human' into an ensemble of 'subject positions', raises the question as to how these are to be constructed from stand-points of power (politics *of* human rights) and of resistance (politics *for* human rights). In other words, how may we construct a variety of subject-positions (human agency within social structures) in ways that *theorize repression*[20] which in turn enable deployment of the regime of human rights phrases to perform labours of liberation?

This kind of analysis raises several questions from the point of view of those engaged in actual human rights struggles. First, are all identities 'fluid', 'multiple', and 'contingent'? If, however, you can place yourself in the (non-Rawlsian) original position of a person belonging to an untouchable community (say, in a remote area of Bihar, India) would you find it possible to agree that caste and patriarchal identity

[19] *See,* Agnes Heller, 'The Contingent Person and Existential Choice', in *Hermeneutics: Critical Theory in Ethics and Politics* (1990), 52–69.

[20] *See,* Iris Marion Young, *Justice and the Politics of Difference* (1990), 39–66.

has become fluid, multiple, contingent? As an untouchable, no matter how you perceive your identity (as a mother, wife, and daughter) you are still liable to be raped. You will be denied access to water from a high caste village well and subjected to all kinds of forced and obnoxious labour; your huts set ablaze; your adult franchise regularly confiscated at elections by caste Hindu militia.[21]

Human rights logic and rhetoric, fashioned by historic struggles, simply and starkly assert that such imposition of primordial identities is morally wrong and legally prohibited. Discrimination on the grounds of birth, sex, domicile, ethnicity, disability, sexual orientation, for example, counts as a violation of internationally proclaimed human rights. It is the mission of human rights logics and paralogics to dislodge primordial identities that legitimate orders imposed suffering, to the point not just of its total social invisibility some times even to the repressed.

This mission is fraught with grave difficulties. When enforcement of primordial identities by forces occurs in civil society, human rights cast responsibilities upon the state to combat it, raising liberal anxiety levels concerning augmenting the New Leviathan. In addition, the state and the law can oppose such enforcement only by a reconstruction of that collective identity. The 'untouchables' in India, constitutionally christened the 'scheduled castes', will have to be burdened by this reconstitution: in law and society they would be either untouchables or ex-untouchables. Justifications of affirmative action programmes worldwide, for example, depend on the maintenance of the narrative integrity of the millennial histories of collective hurt. It is true that these essentialize historic identities as new sites of injury, but is there a way out of embattled histories undoubtedly shaped by the dialectics of human rights?

Second, what is there to subvert if identities are multiple, contingent, and fluid; if the individual or collective self may no longer exist as a 'unified' discursive or semiotic object that can be said to be a bearer of human rights? If the subject is no more and only subject positions exist, how may we construct or pursue the politics *for* human rights? Put in another way, how may one theorize repression and violation? We need to sharpen these questions, attend to their genealogy, and salvage the possibility of conversation about human rights from the debris post-identity discourse.[22]

---

[21] *See*, the devastatingly accurate account in Rohinton Mistry's novel, *A Fine Balance* (1995).

[22] These difficult and complex questions require exhaustive analysis which is beyond the scope of the present work. These entail:

Third, how does this diaspora of identities narratives empower those haunted by practices of flagrant, massive, and ongoing violations of human rights? For the gurus of postmodern ethics this is not a seriously engaged concern as is the preoccupation with defining and contesting all that is wrong with liberalism and socialism.[23]

Fourth, is this human rights path (entailing the necessity to internalize a primordial identity) counter-productive, specially when it casts state and law 'as neutral arbiters of injury rather than themselves invested with the power to injure?[24] Emancipatory in origin, human rights, in the course of enunciation and administration, may become 'regulatory discourse, a means of obstructing or co-opting more radical political demands, or simply the most hollow of empty promises'. It is ironic

---

First, ways of telling stories (*not* laboured analytic morphologies) of what constitutes a concrete history of *human suffering* both as *discursive* and *non-discursive* order of lived reality, i.e. a 'history' of human misery/immiseration in ways that the grand social theory (whether in *its originary* narrative modes or postmodern revivals) obscures.

Second, ways of narrating the histories of structures of torture and terror aimed at destroying, or subjugating, human agency in resistance to the worst forms of inhuman domination.

Third, recovery of the senses of human history in which the practices of human resistance to domination were constructed in the pre-human rights and post-human rights experience.

[23] Jacques Derrida rightly assails the heady optimism of Fukuyama, asking, rightly, whether it is credible to think that, 'all these cataclysms (terror, oppression, repression, extermination, genocide *and so on*)' constitute 'contingent or insignificant limitations' for the messianic and triumphant post-cold war moment of liberalism. Note the gesture of exhaustion in the words italicized here!

At the same time he asserts, 'Our aporia here stem from the fact that there is no longer any name or teleology for determining the Marxist *coup* and its subject.' *What follows*? Derrida, after a fascinating detour on the work of mourning and narcissism, enjoins us as follows:

One must constantly remember that the impossible ... is, alas, always possible. One must constantly remember that this absolute evil ... can take place. One must constantly, remember that even on the basis of this terrible possibility of impossible that justice is desirable ...

though beyond what he calls 'right and law'. *See*, his *Specters of Marx: The State of Debt, The Work of Mourning and The New International* (1994) respectively at pp. 57, 98, 175 (emphasis added).

Who is this 'one' addressed by Derrida? The avant-garde theorist or the being of those subjected continually to the absolute order of evil? No doubt, to sensitize theoretical fellow travellers to the dangers of amnesia is important, but what does it, or should it, mean to the victims of orders of absolute evil?

[24] Wendy Brown, *States of Injury: Power and Freedom in Late Modernity* (1995), 27.

that 'rights sought by a politically defined *group are* conferred upon depoliticized *individuals;* at the moment a particular 'we' succeeds in obtaining rights, it loses 'we-ness' and dissolves into individuals'.[25]

Indeed, in certain moments, human rights development yields itself to tricks of governance; the 'pillar of emancipation' turns out to be the 'pillar of regulation'[26] as we see in some striking detail in the next section. Were this the only moment of human rights, every triumphal attainment would also be its funerary oration. But does not a regulatory discourse at one moment also become at times an arena of struggle?

If international human rights lawyers and the movement people need to attend to the type of interrogation thus raised, postmodernist ethical thinkers need to wrestle with the recent history of the politics of cruelty, which has constructed, as it were, *new primordial communities.* These are communities of the tortured and tormented, and the prisoners of conscience across the world, espoused with poignancy and unequalled moral heroism by Amnesty International. Would it be true to say that their identity as victims is random, contingent, multiple, rather than caused by the play of global politics? Until this interrogation is seriously pursed, can it be said that human rights enunciations and movements commit the mortal sin of essentialism or foundationalism in insisting on a universal norm that de-legitimates this invention?

Nor, despite this welter of constructivism, does post-essentialism, that achieves many a rhetorical tour de force for a Derrida, respond to the problematic posed by archetypal Aung San Su Kyi. She embodies human rights *essentialism*; so do the Afghan women, under dire straits, who protest the Taliban regime. So also do the UNICEF and the Save the Children movements, which (thanks to the globalized media) seek at times to achieve the impossible. That impossible feat is moving the atrophied conscience of the globalized middle classes to an occasional act of charity, and even of genuine compassion, through excruciating CNN depictions of cruelly starved children in Sudan in the midst of their well-earned aperitif or the first course of their dinner.[27] No matter how flawed to the Parisian and neo-Parisian cognitive fashions,

---

[25] Ibid., at 98.

[26] I adapt here Santos' analysis of the dialectic of regulation and emancipation: Bouvaventura de Sousa Santos, *Towards a New Commonsense: Law, Science and Politics in the Paradigmatic Transition* (1995), 7–55.

[27] However, perhaps, suffering as a spectacle can do no more, for, the very act of mass media production of the spectacle of suffering needs to divest it of any structural understanding of the production of suffering itself. In a way, the community of gaze can only be instantly constructed by the erasure of the slightest awareness of complicity.

human rights discourse furnishes potential for struggle which postmodernist discourse on the politics of identity as yet does *not*. These cognitive fashion parades may not be allowed to drain emergent solidarities in struggle unless the postmodernist anti-essentialist critique demonstrates that *human rights are a mistake*.

Indeed, engaged human rights discourse makes possible a deeper understanding of the politics of difference insofar as it is in acts of *suffering*, rather than sanitized, thought. It insists that the Other is *not* dispensable. It sensitizes us to the fact that the politics of Otherhood is not ethically sensible outside the urgency of the maxim: 'Ask not for whom the bell tolls; it tolls for thee.' It insists with Rabbi Israeli Salanter that the '*the material needs of my neighbour are my spiritual needs.*'[28] Critically engaged human rights discourse obdurately refuses the need to de-essentialize human suffering even under the banner of the diaspora of identities.

IV. The Summons for the Destruction of Narrative Monopolies

The critique of human rights may further maintain that relating large *global* stories ('metanarratives') is not so much a function of any. emancipative project as of the politics of intergovernmental desire that ingests the politics of resistance. Put another way, these only serve to co-opt into processes and mechanisms of governance the languages of human rights such that bills of rights may adorn with impunity many a military constitutionalism and the so-called human rights commissions that thrive upon state/regime sponsored violation.

Unsurprisingly, the more severe the violation of human rights, the more the orders of power declare their loyalty to the regime of human rights. The near-universality of ratification of the CEDAW, for example, betokens no human liberation of women; it only endows the state with the power to tell more Nietzschean lies.[29]

Thus, the mass media must obscure the fact that 'all those weapons used to make far-away homelands into killing fields have been supplied by our own arms factories, jealous of their order-books and proud of their productivity and competitiveness—the life-blood of our own cherished prosperity', Zygmunt Bauman, *Globalization: The Human Consequences* (1998), 75.

[28] Cited in Emmanuel Levinas, *Nine Talmudic Readings* (1990), at 99 emphasis added.

[29] 'State is the name of the coldest of all cold monsters. Coldly, it tells lies, too; and this lie grows out of its mouth. "I, the state, am the people".' *The Portable Nietzsche* (1954), 160–1.

All too often, human rights languages become stratagems of imperialistic foreign policy through military invasions as well as global economic diplomacy.[30] Superpower diplomacy at the United Nations is not averse to causing untold suffering to human beings through sanctions whose manifest aim is to serve the future of human rights.[31] The solitary superpower, at the end of the millennium, has made the regime of sanctions for the promotion of human rights abroad a gourmet cuisine at the White House and Capitol Hill.

What is more, the critique may, rightly, insist that the paradigm of universal human rights contains contradictory elements. The UDHR provides for protection of the right to property,[32] making possible its conversion, in these halcyon days of globalization, into a paradigm of *trade—related, market-friendly human rights* (beginning its career with the WTO, maturing in an obscene progression in the draft OECD Multilateral Agreement on Investment).

Global trade relations now stand invested with the resonance of the rhetoric of the moral language of human rights (witness, for example, the discourse on the 'social clauses' in WTO as well as sundry bilateral/regional economic/trade arrangements). More to the point, many Southern NGOs who had inaugurated a critique of globalization now look upon international financial institutions as the instrumentalities of deliverance from the pathologies of the 'nation-state'.

The range and depth of many strands in the postmodernist critique of human rights is not dissimilar to Karl Marx's critique, *On the Jewish Question*,[33] though the unique idiom of postmodernism was not as abundantly available to him!

The summons for the destruction of 'narrative monopolies'[34] in human rights theory and practice is of enormous importance, as it

---

[30] *See*, Noam Chomsky, 'Great Powers and Human Rights: The Case of East Timor' in his *Powers and Prospects: Reflections on Human Nature and The Social Order* (1996), 169–93. *See also*, Chandra Muzaffar, *Human Rights and the World Order* (1993).

[31] American Association for World Health, *Denial of Food and Medicine: The Impact of the US Embargo on Health and Nutrition in Cuba*, http://www. Usaengage.org/studies/cuba.html.

[32] Article 17 protects individual as well as associational rights to property, a provision which for all practical purposes negates the radical looking assurances in Articles 23–6. Not surprisingly, intellectual property rights are fully recognized in Article 27(2).

[33] For a postmodernist revisitation, *see*, Wendy Brown, note 24 *supra* at 97–114.

[34] Lyotard insists: 'Destroy all narrative monopolies ... Take away the privileges the narrator has granted himself'. *See*, *The Lyotard Reader* (1989), 153.

enables us to recognize that the authorship of human rights rests with communities in the struggle against illegitimate power formations and the politics of cruelty. The local, not the global, it needs to be emphasized, remains the crucial site of struggle for the enunciation, implementation, enjoyment, and exercise of human rights. The prehistory of each and every global institutionalization of human rights is furnished everywhere by the local.[35]

From this perspective, the originary claims of 'Western' authorship of human rights become sensible only within a metanarrative tradition which in the past served the dominance ends of colonial/imperial power formations and now serve these ends for the Euro–Atlantic community or the Triadic states (USA, EC, and Japan). In this dominant discourse, both 'modern' and 'contemporary' notions of human rights emerge, though in different modes, as a 'vision of a *novus ordo selcorum* in the world as a whole'.[36] This discourse prevents recognition that communities in struggle against human violation are the primary authors of human rights. No task is more important, as the golden dust of Universal Declaration festivities settles, than to trace the history of human rights from the point of view of communities united in their struggle amidst unconscionable human suffering.

Various feminists have rightly contested the thematic of destruction of metanarratives as inimical to the politics of difference.[37] At the same time, they also maintain that telling of stories of everyday violation and

---

[35] To quote myself immodestly:
After all it was a man called Lokmanya Tilak who in the second decade of this century gave a call to India: *swaraj* (independence) *is my birthright and I shall have it*, long before international human rights law proclaimed a right to self-determination. It was a man called Gandhi who challenged early in this century racial discrimination in South Africa, which laid several decades later the foundations for international treaties and declarations on the elimination of all forms of racial discrimination and apartheid. Compared with these male figures, generations of legendary women martyred themselves in prolonged struggles against patriarchy and for gender equality. The current campaigns based on the motto 'Women's Rights *Are* Human Rights' are inspired by a massive history of local struggles all around. The historic birthplaces of all human rights struggles are the hearth and the home, the church and the castle, the prison and the police precinct, the factory and the farm. Upendra Baxi, 'The Reason for Human Rights and the Unreason of Globalization: The First A.R. Desai Memorial Lecture' (mimeo), 1996.

[36] David Jacobson, *Rights Without Borders: Immigration and the Decline of American Citizenship* (1996), 1.

[37] *See*, Christine Di Stefano, 'Dilemmas of Difference', in *Feminism/Postmodernism* (1990), 76.

resistance which recognizes the role of women as authors of human rights is more empowering in terms of creating solidarity than weaving narratives of universal patriarchy or theorizing repression only as a discursive relation.[38] Feminization of human rights cultures begins only when one negotiates this conflict between meta- and micro-narratives of women in struggle. One may even term the task or the mission as one of *humanizing human rights*, going beyond rarefied discourse on the variety of postmodernisms and post-structuralisms to histories of individual and collective hurt. Narratives of concrete ways in which women's bodies are held in *terroram*[39] do not pre-eminently feature or figure in human rights theory. Theorizing repression does not, to my mind, best happen by contesting Lacan, Derrida, or Foucault; it happens when the theorist shares both the nightmares and dreams of the oppressed. To give language to pain, to experience the pain of the Other inside you, remains the task, always, of human rights narratology. If the varieties of postmodernisms help us to accomplish this, they herald a better future for human rights; if not, they constitute a dance of death for all human rights.

---

[38] Ernesto Laclau and Chantal Mouffe, *Hegemony and Socialist Strategy: Towards A Radical Democratic Politics* (1985), 87–8, 115–6.

[39] Mary Jo Frug, A Postmodern Feminist Legal Manifesto, in *After Identity: A Reader in Law and Culture* (1995), 7–23. The lived reality of sex-trafficking, sweat, labour, agrestic serfdom, workplace discrimination, sexual harassment, dowry murders, rape in peace time as well as war as a means of doing 'politics', torture of women and experimental medicalization of their bodies, all these and related devices of state and society, present problems of routinization of terror. While feminist scholarship has demonstrated the power of story-telling, the social theory of human rights has yet to conceive of ways and means of investing individual biographies of the violated with the power of social texts. *See also*, Upendra Baxi, 'From Human Rights to the Rights to be a Woman', in *Engendering Law: Essays in Honour of Lotika Sarkar* (1999), 275–90.

6

What is Living and Dead in Relativism?

I. The Universality Thesis

The 'historical forms in which the relationship between universality and particularity has been thought' are many and diverse.[1] it would take this work far afield to survey the discursive scene, even from the standpoint of Western metaphysics. Yet the thesis that 'contemporary' human rights are 'universal', remains firmly imbricated within this discursive field.

If human rights are said to be universal in the very same sense as a property or a relation that may be instantiated by a whole variety of particular things, phenomena, or state of affairs, may one say that to be 'human' is to be possessed of certain kinds of rights? If 'universality' is said to exist independently of things, states of affairs, or phenomena, is it conceivable that human rights exist independently of political things, states of affairs, or phenomena, that is, rights 'manifest' themselves outside these? Or are universals nominal: just a matter of naming these under one linguistic practice? Or are these ultimately justifiable capable of being grounded, in comprehensive ethical feats of theorizing?[2] Or is the construction of the universal human rights no more than an exercise in reification; the ideological praxis of converting the multitude of diversity under the totalizing banner of a unity? Or is the expression 'human rights' merely an 'empty signifier'; a 'signifier without a signified'?[3]

---

[1] Ernesto Laclau, *Emancipations* (1996), 22.

[2] Of which Allan Gewirth is the foremost exemplar. *See, The Community of Rights* (1996).

[3] Note 1, *supra* at 36–46. I derive some of the questions here raised, though not their formulation in relation to human rights, from the older anthropological

The questions are compounded by the different constructions of 'human rights'. Quite clearly, thinkers within the Enlightenment traditions of discourse were preoccupied with the problematic of 'natural rights'.[4] Leading contemporary ethical thinkers construct 'human rights' either in social contractarian or communitarian terms; terms that relate to ways of thinking about rights that make 'just' the basic structure of a society.[5] The context of rights-principles thus articulated is that of justice through rights within individual societies or cultures even when this notion is presented as universalizable. 'Contemporary' human rights discursivity addresses, however, the problematic of a *just international order*, that is, a world order based on promotion and protection of 'human rights' *within* and *across* human societies, traditions, and cultures. Respect for 'human rights' or the right to be and remain human, entails a complex, interlocking network of meanings that have to be sustained, renovated, and replenished, at *all* levels: individuals, associations, markets, states, regional organizations of the states, and international agencies and organizations constitute a new totality that now stands addressed by the logics and paralogics of human rights. This difference raises its own distinctive problems when we address the issue of 'universality'.

Indeed, the universality of contemporary human rights marks a break, a radical discontinuity with previous Enlightenment modes of thought.[6] The epistemological break is of the same order as that which occurred in the seventeenth century European tradition. If prior to the seventeenth century, governments made no reference to rights as a standard of legitimacy,[7] prior to the mid-twentieth century, the world international order did not regard respect for human rights as a

---

discourse and the current postmodernist one. *See*, as to the former, John Ladd (ed.) *Ethical Relativism* (1973) and as to the latter, Laclau, note 1, *supra* and Ernesto Laclau and Lilian Zac, 'Minding the Gap: The Subject of Politics', in *The Making of Political Identities* (1994), 11–39.

[4] *See*, for a most recent exposition, Steven B. Smith, *Hegel's Critique of Liberalism: Rights in Context* (1989); hereinafter referred to as Smith.

[5] *See*, e.g., John Rawls, *A Theory of Justice* (1971); Michael Walzer, *Spheres of Justice: A Defence of Pluralism and Equality* (1983); Alasdair MacIntyre, *After Virtue* (1981); Michael Sandel, *Liberalism and the Limits of Justice* (1982).

[6] Thus, for example, when Hegel maintained that the 'the right to recognition', that is, 'respect for the person or "free personality" as such', is the 'core of the modern state' (Smith at 112), he was neither critiquing colonialism or imperialism, patriarchy or racism.

[7] Smith, at 61 confines his observation to the period prior to the seventeenth century.

'standard for legitimacy' of international relations or affairs. This epistemological break complicates recourse to the Enlightenment discursivity on human rights as natural rights, for, as we have seen, the notion of being 'human' was all along constructed on Eurocentric or racist, lines.

The notion of the 'universality' of 'human rights' raises heavy and complex questions that may seem distant from the real world of human rights praxis. However, these erupt constantly in that 'real' world where the lack of approaches to a response complicates the enterprise of promoting and protecting human rights.

In a sense, these issues relate to how one may construct the 'universal' in the proclaimed 'universality' and which interpretive community, if any, may feel privileged to so do. The ways in which universality of the rights is constructed and contested, as we see later, matters a great deal. But Hegel states with finality (if such things can be!) the modes of construction when he distinguishes between three 'moments': *abstract universality*, *abstract particularity*, and *concrete universality*.[8] The first moment stands for 'undifferentiated identity'; the second for 'the differentiation of identity and difference'; and the third for 'concrete universality, which is the full realization of individuality'.[9]

The claim of universality of human rights may be constructed through these three moments. Its abstract *universality* addresses the undifferentiated identity of all bearers of human rights, regardless of history or the future.[10] The second moment of abstract *universality* occurs when the identity of the bearers of human rights cognizes that bearer by *gender, indigeneity, vulnerability, or persecution attributes*. The third moment of *concrete universality* becomes possible to attain when the first two moments prevail: the moment of identity of all beings as 'fully' human and the moment of internal differentiation of that 'human'.

Should we choose to distinguish these three moments, many of the objections or difficulties with the 'universality' of human rights recede or need to be recast. The UDHR proceeded on the basis of abstract universality through its enunciatory referents: 'all human beings',

---

[8] Mark C. Taylor, *Altarity* (1987), 16–17.

[9] Ibid.

[10] '... the mutual recognition of one another's rights', according to Hegel, 'must take place at the expense of nature, by abstracting or denying all the individual differences between us until we arrive at a pure *I*, the free will or "universal consciousness" which is at the root of these differences,' (Smith, at 124).

'everyone', 'all', and 'noone'. All these entities have human rights; the only occasion when the moment of *abstract particularity*, is comprehensively cognized is in its very last article.[11] Subsequent rights-enunciations increasingly address *abstract particularities*: for example, women's rights as human rights, the rights of indigenous peoples, the rights of children and migrants, including migrant labour. These are particularities because they differentiate the *abstract human* in the Universal Declaration. These are *abstract* because the identities they constitute so far do not address the specificity of subject position/ locations of the human rights/obligations constituencies. This, however, is what must be addressed in the third moment of *concrete universality* where rights come home, as it were, in the lived and embodied circumstance of being human in time and place under the mark of finititude of individual existence. In the moment of the *concrete universality*, while structures of domination and power emerge as cross-generational (though liable to disruption and collapse), individual life spans emerge as not merely finite in the abstract but governed by the vagaries and whims of practices of the politics of cruelty and of *catastrophic politics*.

The relation between the first two and the third forms of universality of human rights remains deeply problematic. The moment of concrete universality appears, on one reading of human rights, contingent on the performative acts of the first two moments. *Concrete universality*, of human rights presupposes the movement of both abstract *universality* and *abstract particularity*. On the other hand, the moments are *reversible*, *entailing no logic of a hierarchy or progression of moments*, in the sense that often enough (as explained earlier) it is the here-and-now assertion of human rights that lack a *being in the world* that in turn creates the other two moments. The *concrete universality* of human rights often consists of the acts of a prefigurative praxis. No theory of moments of human rights guided struggles for decolonization or Mohandas Gandhi's protests against the incipient, but still vicious, forms of an early regime of apartheid. Much the same may be truly said of the civil rights movements led by Martin Luther King Jr., or women's or environmental rights movements.

This suggests the possibility of two types of distinctions: first, between the *universality* of human rights and their *universalizability*;

---

[11] Article 30: 'Nothing in this Declaration may be interpreted as implying for any state, *group* or *person* any rights to engage in any activity, or to perform any act aimed at the destruction of any of the rights and freedom set forth herein' (emphasis added) I take the reference to persons as symbolizing *corporate person* (in addition to natural persons, that is, individual human beings).

and second, between *globalization* and the 'universality' of human rights as a mode of instantiating *preferred* conceptions. The first distinction concerns the dialectic among the three moments; the second concerns the power of the play of hegemons.

As to the first, the interplay between the moments of abstract, particular, and concrete universality shapes the history, past, and future, of human rights. Each marks some kind of progress, or at least a movement, toward the universality of human rights. Without the notion, howsoever deeply anthropomorphic, that each human being is by the fact of being human entitled to 'dignity' or 'equal worth', the discourse of human rights becomes wholly insensible. So do all further attempts at extending the notion to other sentient beings (as in the animal rights movements) or to 'nature' (the notion that trees, rivers, mountains, fragile ecological systems, are bearers of certain orders of rights). Human beings are, however, both biological and social constructs. The moment of abstract particularity identifies human beings across various grids of powers of classification on the lines of race, gender, nationality, and class. Abstract particularity helps proclaim/ enunciate orders of collective/group/association identities, attaching to them configurations of distinctive vertical rights, additionally to the horizontal rights of these as human beings. Concrete universality constitutes the realm of struggle both for enunciation and enjoyment of rights in lived existence that the two moments bring to historic play. It is at this plane that decisive struggles between *rights-denying* formations of power and *rights-demanding* formations of counter power enact forms of death and rebirth of social consciousness and social organization. The struggle is inherently violent, moving along the axis of the violence of law and law of violence.[12] Not usually acknowledged, practices of violence constitute, whether of the incumbents or insurgents, or hegemonic or counter hegemonic practices of violence, the matrix of the concrete universality of human rights.[13] The moment of concrete universality is constituted both by the violence of the oppressed and that of the oppressors through distinctive histories of *pseudo-speciation* (which I allude to later in this Chapter (Section II).

In contrast, the hegemon may *globalize* human rights without *universalizing* them. Globalization of human rights consists in those

[12] Upendra Baxi, 'The State's Emissary: The Place of Law in Subaltern Studies', in *Subaltern Studies*, VII, 247–64, (1992).
[13] Upendra Baxi, 'From Human Rights to Rights to be Human', in *The Right to be Human* (1989); 'From Human Rights to the Right to be a Woman', in *Engendering Law: Essays in Honour of Professor Lotika Sarkar*, 275 (1999).

practices of governance by the dominant states that selectively target the enforcement of certain sets of rights or sets of interpretation of rights upon the 'subaltern' state members of the world system. Such practices need no ethic of 'universality' of human rights; these constitute an amoral exercise of dominant hegemonic power because the hegemon does not accept as a universal norm that its sovereign sphere, rife with human and human rights violations, ought to be equally liable to similarly based intrusion. Even when construed as ultimately designed to 'serve' without their consent and against their will the human rights of the peoples, the unilateral and ultimately unaccountable use of military force (as the recent strikes against Iraq or the United States' armed covert and overt Cold War operations in Chile and Nicaragua illustrate) remains an instance of globalization of human rights. Sometimes, globalization of human rights proceeds on moral maxims as yet not enunciated, because not acceptable to hegemons themselves. The public discourse concerning the removal of President Saddam Hussein (reiteratively explicit in statements by the US President and the British Prime Minister in December 1999), for example, seems based on the notion of justified tyrannicide, a notion as yet not articulated by 'contemporary' human rights enunciations. Globalization of human rights is also marked by moral duplicity. People in struggle are denied the same order of impunity for committing tyrannicide as the incumbent heads of states seek to 'enjoy' in relation to the commission of genocide. The first constitutes 'treason' at home and 'terrorism' abroad; the second is thought essential to preserve structures of global power against themselves.

Much the same has to be said concerning aid conditionalities, whether under the auspices of the international financial institutions or trade sanctions for violation of labour, and associated, human rights norms and standards. The hegemon insists that these standards may be enforced selectively against vulnerable and dependent states, denying that the same justification may extend to its promotion of the right of global capital to exploit workers at home and abroad. In contrast, the logics/paralogics of 'universal' human rights are deeply ethical, tormented by reflexivity *all the way*.

These summary observations commend the distinction I make between two orders of discursivity: *globalization* and the *universality* of human rights. Globalization of human rights necessarily fragments their vaunted universality; universality makes problematic practices of production of the politics *of* human rights. The discourse concerning 'relativism' remains deeply diversionary when this distinction gets overlooked in theoretical and activist critique about the 'universality' of human rights.

II. Antifoundationalism

The *universality* of human rights is also subject to a variety of antifoundational critiques. The idea that human rights are universal relies on some higher or meta-justification, drawing upon the power of ethical theory and moral reason. Alan Gewirth in *The Community of Rights* (1996) provides the most sustained account of 'objective' moral foundations for universal human rights.[14] Normative ethical theory, of course, subjects human rights discourse to strict logical scrutiny and different thinkers provide diverse foundational justifications. It, however, agrees that the idea of the universality of human rights has validity only when it is grounded on some justifiable moral or ethical foundation, and that the construction of a universal theory of rights is indeed feasible and desirable. Without such anchoring, there would be no way of distinguishing between interests, policies, and goals, on the one hand, and rights on the other.

In contrast, antifoundationalists deny the need, and question the desirability, of moral reason furnishing universal bases for human rights. It is maintained by many, and in various ways, that there is no 'ahistorical power which makes for righteousness—a power called truth, or rationality', nor indeed are there forces that may bring the powerful, unjust, and brutal people amidst us to a sense of universal human vengeful rights, 'if not a vengeful God, a vengeful aroused proletariat, or at least a vengeful superego, or, at the very least the offended majesty of Kant's tribunal of pure practical reason...'[15] It is also argued that universal human rights are simply impossible because what counts as 'human' and as rights belonging to humans, are context-bound and tradition-dependent. There is no transcultural fact or being that may be called 'human' to which universal human rights may be attached. Eduardo Rabossi (an Argentine jurist) has recently urged that the 'human rights phenomenon has rendered human rights foundationalism outmoded and irrelevant'.[16]

By human rights phenomenon Rabossi means the fact of the enunciative explosion of human rights. For him that fact is all that

[14] *See also*, his *Reason and Morality* (1978).

[15] Richard Rorty, 'Human Rights, Rationality, and Reason', in *On Human Rights: The Oxford Amnesty Lectures* (1993), 112 at 122, 130.

[16] Quoted by Richard Rorty (without citation) *supra* note 15, 112 at 116.

matters. It is unnecessary to revisit the philosophical grounds on which human rights may be based.

Anti-foundationalism is a close postmodernist cousin of relativism; each urges us to pay heed to contexts of culture and power. Both insist, though in somewhat different ways that do matter, that whatever may be the agenda of human rights is best performed without the labours of grounding rights in any transcultural fact or 'essence' named 'human being'. The claim here is that such labours of theoretical practice are either futile or dangerous. They are futile because who or what counts, as being 'human' is always being socially deconstructed and reconstructed, and cannot be legislated by any ethical imperative, no matter how hard and long one may try to so do. They are dangerous because under the banner of the universality of 'human nature', regimes of human violation actually thrive and prosper. The danger for human rights is constituted by the very construction of 'human' that then allows the power of (what Erick Erickson termed) 'pseudospeciation', a process by which the different regimes of psychopathic practices of the politics of cruelty may erect a dichotomy between 'humans' and 'nonhumans', 'people' and 'nonpeople'.[17] My own critique of what I term the 'modern' human rights paradigm commits me to an acknowledgement of the power of this very danger.

The danger is compounded when we attend the mission of the Dead White Males, or what was earlier called the White Man's Burden, drawing sustenance from the mission of universality of human rights. The American Anthropological Association, in its critique of the draft declaration of Universal Declaration of Human Rights stated, memorably in 1947, that doctrines of 'the white man's burden'

> have been employed to implement economic exploitation, and to deny the right to control their own affairs to millions of peoples over the world, where the expansion of Europe and America has not [sic] meant the literal extermination of the whole populations. Rationalized in terms of ascribing cultural inferiority to these peoples, or in conceptions of backwardness in development of their 'primitive mentality,' that justified their being held in the tutelage of their superiors, the history of expansion of the western world has been marked by demoralization of human personality and the disintegration of human rights among the people over whom hegemony has been established.[18]

[17] Tu Wei-Ming, 'Maoism as a Source of Suffering in China', in *Social Suffering* (1996), 149 at 166–7.
[18] The Executive Board, American Anthropological Association, *Statement on Human Rights*, 49, *American Anthropologist* (1947), 539.

This was stated with elegant clarity in the pre-postmodern era! And even today critiques of the universality of human rights enact only variations on this theme. Clearly, the alarm was justified at that moment. Concern with the dark side of the Enlightenment generated profound doubts about the future history of progressive 'Eurocentrism'. The concern continues in the contemporary postmodern critiques of the universality of rights. However, as we see in this chapter, the sounding of the alarm in the same mode is simply dysfunctional.

The issues involved here relate to ways in which human rights logics and paralogics have been deployed for the ends of historic forms of domination and ways through which practices of governance everywhere legitimate themselves through recourse to the languages of 'human' rights'. The language game of human rights is also a power game; a phenomenon I term the politics *of* human rights. That politics is marked by ethnocentrism, 'the point of view that one's own way of life is to be preferred to all others'.[19] which becomes particularly pernicious when it is 'rationalized and made the basis of programmes of action detrimental to the well being of other peoples...'[20]

Antifoundational critiques of human rights refer us to the moment of concrete universality and its infinite openness to violent forms of pseudospeciation. This is a valuable lesson; one that unfortunately we need to learn over and over again. At the same time, in denying, for that and related reasons, the very notion of being human, these critiques result in justificatory politics of the worst possible forms of human and human rights violation. To take a civilizational example, rather than a merely historical one, it becomes difficult, if not impossible, for Indian 'untouchables' to claim dignity and rights against the dominant and violent structure of social exclusion justified, cosmologically by some varieties of classical Hinduisms, were their claims to be held vitiated as being 'foundational'. Not all antifoundational critiques realize that the subaltern struggles remain inconceivable, or at any rate unintelligible, outside frameworks that invoke a universal conception about the meaning of being 'human'. If foundational beliefs 'justify' practices of violent social exclusion, these also ground an ethic of inclusion.

Professor Richard Rorty would, of course, disagree. This disagreement is worth noting as exemplifying the hazard of postmodern philosophical anthropology. He says:

[19] Melville J. Herskovits, *Cultural Anthropology* (1955), ch. 19; excerpted in *Ethical Relativism*; note 3, *supra* 58 at 66.

[20] Ibid. Herskovits here specifically refers to such rationalization in 'Euro-American culture'.

Most people—especially people relatively untouched by the European Enlightenment—simply *do not think of themselves as, first and foremost a human being*. Instead they think of themselves as being a *good* sort of human being—a sort defined by explicit opposition to a particularly bad sort. It is crucial for their sense of who they are that they are *not* an infidel, *not* a queer, *not* a woman, *not* an untouchable. Just insofar as they are impoverished, and as their lives are perpetually at risk, they have little else than pride in being what they are not to sustain their self-respect.[21]

This brief passage raises a whole variety of questions. First, who are the people 'relatively untouched by the Enlightenment', when almost everyone in the Third World has been deeply affected by its dark side, whether through colonization, the Cold War, or contemporary economic globalization? Second, is it true that 'most people' who value their ethical worth by their notions of good and bad do not consider themselves to be individual human beings? Third, what about people who think and act otherwise: for example women and untouchables who resist caste and patriarchy, and in the process think of themselves as human beings first and foremost? Fourth, do the impoverished and the insecure have no other ways of sustaining self-respect than to take 'pride' in social identities shaped by violent social exclusion? Fifth, how does one account for the changes in beliefs and practices of 'most people' when they either change their notions about the good sort of humans or alter their toleration of the bad ones? It is pointless to enlarge this catalogue of questions. It however needs at least to be said that if such interludes at philosophical anthropology is all we have by way of antifoundationalism, the case for foundational theorizing is adequately reinforced! An essay extolling sentiment rather than reason, or changes in transformation of sensibility, to make room for pragmatic solidarity, fails to persuade when it begins with such large-scale generalization about being human and 'good' and 'bad' human beings.

III. The 'Histories' of Universality

It is at this juncture that one may raise the issue of how the histories of 'universality' of human rights may be narrated. I have endeavoured to demonstrate, through the distinction between 'modern' and 'contemporary' human rights paradigms, the ways in which the 'universality' notions get constructed in radically different ways. Apart from the unfoldment of the politics *of* human rights, there also arises

[21] Rorty, note 15, *supra* at 126 (emphasis added).

the need to trace the interaction between two forms of human rights politics: the politics *of* and *for* human rights. From this perspective, whatever may have been the case with the UDHR, the argument concerning 'relativism' is curious in terms of the actual history of making contemporary international human rights standards and norms.

If we were to accept the view that 'contemporary' human rights authorship lies with the communities of states, no recourse to a grand theory, or to a gourmet diet of a whole variety of post-isms or endologies,[22] is required to maintain a just anxiety about universality of human rights. Any international human rights lawyer worth her calling knows the riot of reservations understandings, declarations that parody the text of universalistic declarations.[23] The *fine print* of reservations usually cancels the *capital font* of universality. In this sense, the contestation concerning universality of human rights enunciations is diversionary, embodying the politics *of*, rather than *for*, human rights.

What is 'universal' about human rights is that these become binding on sovereign states when (and to the extent) they consent to treaty obligations or demonstrate by their belief and practice that certain enunciations are obligatory as international customary law. Also, in the making of these 'universal' norms states do articulate a measure of cultural and civilizational diversity. Even in regard to such 'universal' human rights norms, the universality abides in the purported logic of aspiration, not always in the reality of attainment. Obviously, this petty detail concerning the making of internationally binding human rights gets wholly ignored in the high discourse of relativism, anti-foundationalism, and 'postmodernisms'.

If, on the other hand, we were to entertain a more 'radical' view of authorship of human rights (which I have elaborated thus far) where peoples and communities are the primary authors of human rights, the argument from relativism falls. This is because, on this view, resistance to power has a creationist role in the making of 'contemporary' human rights, which then at a second order level, get translated into standards and norms adopted by a community of states. In the making of human rights it is the local that translates into global languages the reality of

[22] Upendra Baxi, 'The Reason of Human Rights and the Unreason of Globalization: The First A.R. Desai Memorial Lecture' 1996, University of Bombay (mimeo).

[23] Upendra Baxi, '"A Work in Progress?", Reflections on the United States Report to the United Nations Human Rights Committee', 36, *Indian Journal of International Law*, 34–53 (1996); Ann Elizabeth Meyer, 'Reflections on the Proposed United States Reservations to CEDAW: Should the Constitution be an Obstacle to Human Rights?' 23, *Hastings Constitutional Law Quarterly* (1996), 727–823.

their aspiration for a just world. However, the dominant discourse wishes us to believe that the anticolonial struggles relied upon, and wholly mimed, the typical human rights discourse of the 'West'. This mode of thought invokes the notion of *catachresis*, signifying the lack of an 'adequate historical referent' in the cultures of the Other.[24]

The context bears a moment's reflection, too, upon the *world without rights*. I refer to 'modern' human rights enunciations that enacted, cruelly, an infinite variety of exclusionary 'theory'/practices. The 'modern' epoch of human rights enunciation was unabashedly relativistic; it claimed individual and collective rights for some peoples and regimes and denied these wholesale to others. These latter were denied rights either because they were thought not fully human or the task of making them fully human required a denial of rights to them. Do not the colonial practices of power provide a full repository for practices of relativism?

Human rights universalism *somehow*, begins to become problematic at the very time of the beginning of the end of colonialism and the value of self-determination proclaimed in the UDHR! True, the Declaration also occurs at the onset of the Cold War: true too that it also embodies exceptional regard for the right to property (Article 17, 27(2)). It, however, also contains vital social rights (education, work, and health) that can be, and have been used, to impose an array of reasonable restrictions on the rights to property. The values repressed by the Empire, by the doctrines of the White Man's Burden, are no longer considered legitimate. Were not the anti-colonial struggles partly about the realization of the right to a just 'international and social order' respectful of the dignity and human rights of all people (Article 28)? Or about rights to freedom of opinion and expression (Article 19)? Or about the right to peaceful assembly and association (Article 20) and a right to democracy (Article 21)?

If these were typically 'Western' values, how may we explain their resonance in the later regional human rights instruments, for example, the American Declaration of the Rights and Duties of Man (adopted at Bogota, 2 May 1948, followed by the Pact of Jan Jose, the American Convention on Human Rights, 1969), the 1988 Protocol of San Salvador amplifying the Convention? Or the African Charter on Human Rights and Peoples' Rights, 1981, the Cairo Declaration of Human Rights in Islam, 1990? Undoubtedly, these instruments innovate human rights enunciations (by their emphasis on the rights of peoples

---

[24] Gayatri Chakravorty Spivak, 'Constitutions and Culture Studies', in *Legal Studies as Cultural Studies: A Reader in Post(Modern) Critical Theory* (1995), 155.

or on human duties). However, a close comparison with the UDHR would also show that they converge on many a crucial human rights value.

Indeed, this disregard of the history of *normative* consensus over the universality of some human rights norms and standards becomes all the more striking when we become aware of the fact that the discourse on relativism scarcely pauses to notice the subsequent developments. These occur, undoubtedly, under the auspices of the Third World leadership (in the 1960s and 1970s) crystallizing its distinctive conceptions of global justice and human rights. Human rights norms and standards proliferate, extending to the collective rights of decolonized states and peoples, from the Declaration on Permanent Sovereignty Over Natural Wealth and Resources (to take a long leap!) to the Declaration of Rights of States and Peoples to Development. I suggest that the discourse on 'relativism' remains afflicted by its very own (to borrow Fredrik Jameson's fecund notion)[25] political unconscious.

That political unconscious, in relation to human rights discursivity, assumes many forms of historic, cultural, civilizational, and even epistemic racial arrogance toward the Other of the Enlightenment, and even post-Enlightenment, thought and political action. That arrogance which regards all human rights imagination as the estate of the West, which others can at best only mime, prevents recognition of authorship of human rights by states and peoples of the Third World. Must all that the latter history be reduced to the thesis that 'universality' of human rights is the pervasive syndrome of Western hegemony? Does not, after all, this 'cultural' or 'ethical' relativism talk ostensibly directed to the recognition of diversity perform, in reality, the labours of reinstalling the Myth of Origins about human rights?

What is of interest here is the fact that the practices of politics *of* human rights converge here with those of the politics *for* human rights. The very regimes and cliques that deny freedom and dignity, and canons of political accountability, denounce human rights 'universality' as a sinister imperial conspiracy find support from intellectual and social activists critiquing the 'universality' in the same prose. Undoubtedly, the United States, and her normative cohorts, have conspicuously consumed human rights rhetoric, most brutally in moves to make the 'world safe for democracy' (read global capital) during the Cold War and beyond. An exposé of this horrible practice

---

[25] Fredric Jameson, *The Political Unconscious: Narrative as a Socially Symbolic Act* (1981).

of the politics *of* human rights is continually necessary and desirable. It is only natural that peoples and states that believe in 'manifest destiny' to lead the world deploy all available normative resources, including the languages of human rights, to pursue it. Does that, however, necessarily constitute an indictment of the very notion of universal human rights? Should this ineluctable critique of the politics *of* human rights also become the *norm* of politics *for* human rights?

Free-floating historians of ideas keep telling us that Asian, African, or other 'non-Western' traditions had no analogue to the expression 'human rights',[26] but neither had the 'Western traditions' even the phrase 'rights' till the 'mid-nineteenth century'.[27] Indeed, the invention of the phrase 'human rights' is very recent. Apart from the sociolinguistic discovery of novelty, nothing much follows! Undoubtedly, words and phrases carry burdens of histories, but histories also give rise to regimes of phrases that mould the future. Surely, the discourse on human struggles and movements that empower human beings in time, place, and circumstance to resist oppression (whether in East Timor or Myanmar) is also entitled to the same order of privilege that historians of ideas of cultural anthropologists claim for themselves!

This work does not address the daunting tasks of tracing these scattered hegemonies of 'relativists', desires, a task crucial for a social theory of human rights. But as a preliminary step towards it I undertake a critical overview of the agendum of relativism in relation to contemporary human rights discursive formation. In doing so, I transgress simple logic. A logical way, exposing the faultline of relativism, is to present it as an axiom that maintains that there are no truths save the truth that all truths are relative! You may substitute 'truth' in this axiom for 'values', 'human rights', notions of being 'human' (or whatever the context requires). It is well known by now that logically such a position is simply incoherent.

IV. Absolute Versus Universal

Foremost among the many anxieties that surround the notion of the universality of human rights is confusion between universality and

---

[26] Interested readers may pursue the citation to relevant literature in the massive footnote 3 in Stephen P. Marks, 'From the "Single Confused Page" to the "Declaration for Six Billion Persons"': The Roots of the Universal Declaration of Human Rights in the French Revolution', 20, *Human Rights Quarterly* (1998), 459 at 460, and an equally massive footnote in Burns Weston, 'The Universality of Human Rights in a Multicultural World', in *The Future of International Rights* (1999), 65 at 69–70.

[27] Alasdair MacIntyre, *After Virtue* (1981), 69.

absoluteness of rights. However, nothing about the logics of universality renders human rights absolute for at least two reasons. First, as Herskovits has reminded us:

> *Absolutes* are fixed, and as far as convention is concerned, are not admitted to the variation, to differ from culture to culture, from epoch to epoch. *Universals,* on the other hand, are those least common denominators to be extracted from the range of phenomena the natural or cultural world manifests.[28]

Second, it is clear that my right to do or have or be *x* (or be immune from *y*) is also limited by similar, and corresponding, rights[29] of others. If human rights release individual energies, talents, and endowments to pursue individual or collective life projects, they also set bounds to these. Human rights thus make sense only within the texture of human responsibilities. The logics of universality entail *interdependence* of human rights: every human person or being is entitled to an order of rights because every other person or being is so entitled to it. If this were not so, human rights would cease to have any ethical justification whatsoever.

It is true that this was not always the case. 'Modern' human rights logics were *absolutist*, not *universal*. 'Contemporary' human rights are, in contrast, *universal* precisely because they deny the absoluteness of *any* positing of rights, although some human rights are said to be *near absolute*, as is the case with a handful of, and often contested, *jus cogens*. Also, the logic of universality is constantly bedevilled by 'utilitarianism of rights', that is, by arguments from consequences. The universality of human rights symbolizes the *universality of the collective human aspiration to make power increasingly accountable, governance progressively just, and the state incrementally more ethical*. I know of no 'relativist' strand of thought that contests this desideratum.

V. 'Multiculturalism'?

'Multiculturalism', as this relates to the discourse on the future of human rights, needs to be grasped in at least three distinct ways. First, we need to ask: are expressions of 'contemporary' human rights standards and norms merely variations on the Euro-American themes and traditions? Second, given the processes of globalization, as well as the earlier histories of the formation of 'minorities', what conceptual

---

[28] Herskovits, note 19, *supra* at 74.
[29] Allan Gewirth, *The Community of Rights* (1996), 47–8.

resources exist to make human rights standards and norms relevant to situations of voluntary and imposed migration of human beings across national frontiers? Third, we need to ask, more profoundly with Žižeck, whether 'multiculturalism' is, after all, a species of postmodern racialism?

(1) *Variations on the Liberal Thematic?*

In complete disregard of the fact that contemporary human rights norms and standards are not monologically but dialogically produced and enacted (and are brokered and mediated by global diplomacy, including that of the NGOs), it is still maintained that these ignore cultural and civilizational diversity. This is bad, indeed even wicked, sociology. The pro-choice women's groups at the UN Beijing Conference, for example, confronted by His Holiness the Pope's Open Letter to the Conference, or the participants at the Cairo UN summit on population planning know this well.

The enactment of human rights into national social policies is even more heavily mediated by the multiplicity of cultural, religious, and even civilizational traditions. The American feminists on the anniversary of *Roe v Wade* know this, as does the African sisterhood modulating public policy on female genital cutting, and indeed the Indian sisterhood in its moves to effectively outlaw dowry murders. No engaged human rights theory or practice, to the best of my knowledge, enacts, in real life, the pursuit of universal human rights without any regard for cultural or religious traditions, nor do these completely succumb to the virtues and values of 'theoretical' ethical relativism.

In ways the arguments from relativism do not, the logics of universality of rights do open up for interrogation the settled habits of representation of 'culture' and 'civilization'. These make problematic that which was regarded as self-evident, natural, and true, and make it possible to practise human rights friendly reading of the tradition or scripture[30] and even to claim that some contemporary human rights were anticipated by these.

---

[30] Readings of scriptural traditions yield repressive as well as emancipative consequences. As is well-known (or ought to be) long before the advent of contemporary feminisms, the Koranic verse on polygamy generated a two century old debate, before the doors of *itjehad* were declared to be closed in tenth century AD on the verse on polygamy which was construed to *prohibit* the practice of polygamy which it, on the established reading, permitted. Similarly, the right to sexual orientation-friendly readings have been discovered in the major religious texts of the world by the hermeneutic labours.

Of course, as is well known, conflicts over interpretation of tradition are conflicts not just over values, but also about power. In turn, both the 'fundamentalists' and human rights evangelists become prisoners of a new demonology. Both tend to be portrayed in the not always rhetorical warfare[31] that follows, as *fiends*, not fully human and therefore unworthy of the dignity of discourse. Practices of the politics of intolerance begin to thrive all around. Practices of solidarity among human rights activists, national and transnational, begin to be matched by powerful networks of power and influence at home and abroad. The politics of the universality of human rights becomes increasingly belligerent, and the martyrdom count of human rights activists registers an unconscionable increase.

At this level, the universality of human rights ceases to be an abstract idea, with its history of doctrinal disputations. It becomes a living practice; a form of struggle, a practice of transformative vision. Its truths of resistance, in constant collision with the truths of power, seek to universalize themselves, and its truths are formed not in the comfort of contemplative life but in and through the gulags.

In this sense, the claim to universality of human rights signifies an aspiration, and a movement, to bring new civility to power in society of states and all human societies. That civility consists in making power increasingly accountable. Does the dialogue over the relativity of values matter much *when so much is at stake*?

(2) *Human Rights and the Challenge of 'Multiculturalism'*

Most societies are multicultural and most states are multinational.[32] That any rate, is one truth that requires, at the close of the second millennium, no labour of demonstration. The recognition of diversity, and respect for it, is aptly writ large in 'contemporary' human rights enunciations and movements. However, deference to diversity remains a complex and contradictory affair. Put another way, the *concrete universality* of recognition of, and respect for, diversity is culture and history bound, and that culture and history entails not just feats of high

---

[31] Those who proselytize radical readings of the scriptural traditions, though no longer burnt at the stake, are relentlessly subjected to territorial, and even extra-territorial, repression and punishment.

[32] Obviously, a single country may be both multinational (as a result of the colonizing, conquest, or confederation of national communities) and polyethnic (as a result of individual and familial migration)', Will Kymlicka, *Multicultural Citizenship: A Liberal Theory of Minority Rights*, (1995). (Henceforth, referred to as Kymlicka).

social theory but also forms of both human rights generative[33] and destructive practices of power of state as well as of the violence of insurrection.[34]

Despite the history of the radical logic of the right to self-determination, it is clear that both the extant international legal regime and the regime of multinational states, do not recognize the human rights of 'nationalities' to secede from the existing 'nation'-state frameworks and frontiers.[35] In this zodiac, any practice of the 'right' to secession involves forms of both state and insurgent 'terrorism', a site where human rights have no presence 'whatever may be said about their future. Understandably, then, 'contemporary human rights discourse focuses on the rights of 'minorities', 'indigenous people', 'migrants' and 'refugees', and 'displaced' peoples in terms and vocabularies of the stability, more or less, of a global order that valorizes the actually existing imagined communities (I use this phrase with apologies to Benedict Anderson) of the 'nation-states'.

Then what we are left with (and this is important) is the problematic of minority rights. The problematic is acute everywhere but I take, for the present purposes, the theoretic feat offered by Professor Will Kymlicka. He, rightly, insists that 'an adequate theory of rights must ... be compatible with the just demands of disadvantaged social groups'.[36] It must recognize three broad forms of 'group-differentiated' rights of the minorities: self-government rights, polytechnic rights, and special representation rights.[37] While the first and third forms of rights are integral to the international law of human rights, the second form is of interest to us here in terms of liberal tradition specific relativism.

'Polytechnic rights' are

> intended to help ethnic groups and religious minorities express their cultural particularity and pride without it hampering their success in the economic and political institutions of the dominant society.[38]

---

[33] *See*, Robert Cover, 'Foreward: Nomos and Narrative', *Harvard Law Review* 62 (1987), 97.

[34] *See*, E. Valentine Daniel, *Chapters in an Anthropology of Violence: Sri Lankans, Sinhalas and Tamils* (1997).

[35] *See*, the interesting account analysis by Allen Buchanan, *Secession: The Morality of Political Divorce* (1991).

[36] Kymlicka, at 19.

[37] Ibid. at 10–34.

[38] Ibid. at 31.

These rights are justified because the 'dominant society' may not 'adequately support [those] through the market',[39] or minority may be disadvantaged '(often unintentionally) by existing legislation'.[40] These rights typically accrue to immigrants and refugees.[41]

The recognition of polyethnic rights is, of course, instrumentalist; it enables both the dominant society and subservient cultures to coexist in a functional mode. The preservation of some cultural identity is important for the immigrant and refugee groups; and the dominant society benefits, in the long run, from the protection of 'narcissism of minor differences'.[42] More importantly, care has always to be taken to ensure that such recognition does not hamper 'their success in the economic and political institutions of the dominant society'. In other words, subaltern cultures need to be contained by strategies of polyethnic rights, the justification of the conferral of which is that they internalize the values of the economic and political institutions of the dominant society.[43]

'Multiculturalism' conceived through the prism of polyethnic rights is, at the end of the day, an adaptation by liberal cultural traditions of universal human rights and standards. Such adaptations flourish outside Euro-American cultures too. In each the abstract universality and abstract particularity of human rights remain in tension with the concrete universality. What remains important is the fact that the universal human rights culture makes problematic the project of concrete universality. National definitions of minority rights become contested fields from the standpoint of the abstract universal and the abstract particular.

(3) *Multiculturalism as Postmodern Racism*

Slavoj Žižek has recently commented on the obvious contemporary 'paradox of colonization, in which there are only colonies, no colonizing

---

[39] Ibid. at 38. The examples here are: 'funding immigrant language programs or arts groups'.

[40] Ibid. The examples here are: 'exemptions from Sunday closing legislation or dress codes that conflict with religious beliefs'.

[41] Kymlicka, at 98–9.

[42] This phrase comes from Michael Ignatieff, *Blood and Belonging* (1993), 21, quoted by Kymlicka at 88.

[43] I do considerable violence to Kymlicka's finely nuanced reworking of the 'liberal' tradition, yet some such reading will be plausible from the point of view of a beneficiary of many polyethnic rights. Indeed, she would agree with Kymlicka, that the 'only long term solution is to remedy the unjust international distribution of

countries—the colonizing power is no longer the nation-state but the global company itself.' The ideology of contemporary capitalism generates varieties of 'autocolonization', and foremost among this is 'multiculturalism'. Its paradox parallels that of new colonialism:

> the relationship between traditional imperial colonization and global capitalist self-colonization is exactly the same as the relationship between Western cultural imperialism and multiculturalism—just as global capitalism involves the paradox of colonization without the colonizing nation state metropolis, multiculturalism involves a patronizing Eurocentric distance and/or respect for local cultures without roots in one's own particular culture.[44]

As concerns human rights, multiculturalism concedes both '*too much* and *not enough*'. It tolerates the Other not as a real Other 'but the ascetic Other ...' This much is clear from the notion of the polyethnic rights of immigrants from the South to the North. Zizek's point however cuts deeper. The multiculturalists advance and applaud the progressive abolition of capital punishment as a kind of (Parsonian) evolutionary universal of human rights; on the other hand, they remain 'tolerant of the most brutal violations of human rights' lest they be accused of preferred (White) value imposition.[45] The Other needs fuller recognition: on the one hand, in terms of 'cultural *jouissance* that even a "victim" can find in a practice of another culture that appears cruel and barbaric to us' (here, of course, Talal Asad, to whom I refer later, is a more insightful guide than Žižek), and on the other hand, in terms of the split in the Other (a point I have been making under different phrase-regime so far). In the latter situation, reference to human rights (presumably defined by the West, and on this point Žižek is still Eurocentric as concerns the site of the origins of human rights!), as a catalyst which sets in motion an authentic protest against the constraints of one's own culture.[46]

---

resources' (Kymlicka, at 99), a problem that existing reworking of 'liberal' traditions scarcely ponder.

Incidentally, an immensely useful account of how, outside the logic of polyethnic rights, strategic identity formation offers moments of resistance (till the unjust distribution of world resources is remedied, is provided by Anna Marie Smith, 'Rastafari as Resistance and the Ambiguities of Essentialism in the "New Social Movements" ', in *The Making of Political Identities* (1994), 17.

[44] Slavoj Žižeck, *The Ticklish Subject: The Absent Centre of Political Ontology* (1999), 215–6.

[45] Ibid. at 219.

[46] Ibid. at 220.

Žižek brings valuable correctives to the current conceptions of multiculturalism generally, and their implications on human rights in particular. Neither takes seriously new modes of social reproduction of globalized coloniality nor alerts us so fully to the empty potential of multiculturalism as a culture of no cultures. A reminder of epistemic racism always renders great service to the futures of human rights.

Yet the examples that guide Žižek remain problematic, whether progressive abolition of capital punishment as merely constituting a 'Western' evolutionary indicator (*as if* traditions such as Hinduism, Buddhism, Confucianism, or indigenous religions had no space in the denial of retribution of this magnitude) or clitoridectomy as a pathway to 'feminine dignity', even as a form of 'victim' cultural *jouissance*. Traditions, as well as critiques, of multi-cultural theory and practice that so justify these practices will cause anxiety across the North–South divide on the universality of human rights.

The point, from a human rights perspective, is simply that extremes of *too much* and *not enough* remain constructed, in the final analysis, from the perspective of progressive Eurocentrism with all its contradictions. Were the subaltern ever to speak, its Other will be the split Euro-american postmodern 'absent' subject!

V. Westoxification

The complex history of the notion of westoxification cannot be pursued here[47] but its interlinked, epistemological and political dimensions that concern the future of human rights warrant some attention. The project of Islamic revival contests the notion that it is '*only* Western civilization which is universal' making the discourse of modernity (and postmodernity) a 'discourse the centre of which is occupied by a particular identity'.[48] On this view, 'Muslims who use Islamic metaphors' interrogate the 'dominant language games of the last two hundred years'[49] and contribute, in ways very different from the postmodern, the 'de-centring of the West'.[50] The contrast between that which is *globalized* and that which one may describe as 'universal' comes alive

---

[47] *See*, for a rich account of the history of origins, John L. Esposito, *The Islamic Threat: Myth or Reality?* (new edn. 1995), 188–253. *See also* the provocative analysis by Bobby Sayyid, 'Sign O' Times: Kaffirs and Infidels Fighting the Ninth Crusade', in Laclau, note, *supra* at 233.

[48] Sayyid, note 47, 43, *supra* at 277.

[49] Ibid. at 265.

[50] Ibid. at 276.

in the distinction between the "'politics of difference" at the centre' and a "'politics of authenticity" at the periphery'.[51] In sum, here are different ways of *knowing* and *being* that Islamization, taken seriously, brings to the world of theory and praxis that represent 'a *continuation and radicalization of the process of decolonization*'.[52]

The westoxification critique insists that human rights enunciations and cultures represent secular versions of the Divine Right to Rule the 'Unenlightened'. It demonstrates that the West seeks to impose standards of right and justice which it has all along violated in its conduct towards Islamic societies and states.[53] It rejects the notion that the outpourings and actions of the United States State Department, and their normative cohorts, are exhaustive of the totality of contemporary human rights discourse. It seeks to locate the politics of human rights within the tradition of the shari'a.[54] As Muhammad Shykh Fadalla eloquently stated:

> As Moslems, we consider politics to be part of our whole life, because the Koran emphasizes the establishment of Justice as a divine mission... *In this sense, the politics of the faithful is a kind of prayer.*[55]

At the heart of the critique lies the epochal politics of difference, which, of course, does not regard Islam in the image of 'the recurrent Western myth' as a 'monolithic' tradition.[56]

Responsible 'westoxification' notions seek to bring an element of *piety* within the logics and paralogics of construction of human rights. If the politics *for* human rights is a kind of 'prayer of the faithful' for pious Muslims, so it is for the secular congregation of a civic religion named human rights.

The contribution that this kind of understanding brings for the future of human rights (of a very different order than that provided by postmodernisms or recrudescent forms of relativism) calls for inter-faith dialogue. A dialogue that will yield a sense of justice to the worlds of power provides invaluable resource for the universalization of human rights.

---

[51] Ibid. at 279.

[52] Ibid at 281.

[53] *See*, Chandra Muzaffar, *Human Rights and the New World Order* (1993).

[54] *See*, the recent 'Cairo Declaration on Human Rights in Islam', in *Human Rights: A Compilation of International Instruments, Volume 11: Regional Instruments* (1997), 478–84.

[55] Quoted in Esposito, *supra* note 47 at 149 (emphasis added).

[56] Esposito, *supra* note 147 at 201.

VI. Types of Relativism

Relativism, a coat of many colours,[57] indicts the logic of the universality of human rights (as noted) on the ground that different cultures and civilizations have diverse notions of what it means to be human and for humans to have rights. While this is true, it is also trivial[58] and does not make impossible cross-or inter- or trans-cultural understandings.

If, on the other hand, relativism is a claim that 'what people believe to be right or wrong determines what is wrong or right for them',[59] then universal standards of human rights (such as the prohibition of genocide, torture, racial discrimination, and violence against women) remain 'universal' only for the groups of people who so believe. The insistence on universality is mistaken when it erects the notion that moral judgements apply not just to 'a particular action but to a class of actions', that these judgments apply to everybody, and that 'others besides the speakers are assumed to share' these.[60]

---

[57] *See*, the superb analysis in Christopher Norris, *Reclaiming Truth: Contribution to a Critique of Cultural Relativism* (1996).

Of course, 'relativism' is a vacuous word. We need to distinguish between several types of relativism. *See* the useful effort by Fernando R. Teńson, 'International Human Rights and Cultural Relativism', 25, *Virginia Journal of International Law* (1985), 869; Adamantia Polis, 'Cultural Relativism Revisted: Through a State Prism', 18, *Human Rights Quarterly* (1996), 316.

A more sustained analysis of relativism offered by R.G. Peffer, *Marxism, Morality and Social Justice* (1990), 268–316, (henceforth referred to as Peffer) who distinguishes between four types of relativism:

'[d]escriptive ethical relativism ... the doctrine that what people believe to be right or wrong differs from individual to individual, society to society, or culture to culture;'

'[n]ormative ethical relativism ... the doctrine that what *is* right or wrong differs from individual to individual, society to society, culture to culture (because what people believe to be right or wrong determines what is right or wrong for them);'

'[m]etaethical relativism ... the doctrine that there is no sure way to prove (to everyone's satisfaction) what is right or wrong ...'

'[m]etaevaluative relativism ... The doctrine that ensures agreement on 'one *unique* set of *normative* principles as correct ...'

[58] Because what people may believe is an important social datum, nothing follows from this on the issue of what they ought to believe. *Cf.* Peffer at 272–3.

[59] For an elaboration of the notion of 'normative ethical relativism' as entailing two distinct positions, *see* Peffer at 273–4 and the literature cited there. Does normative ethical relativistic position refer to an individual's criteria of moral rightness or does it refer to criteria accepted by a society or culture as a whole?

[60] Bernard R. Mayo, *Ethics and Moral Life* (1958), 91–2, quoted in Peffer at 276.

That this form of relativism turns out to be logically or analytically flawed is fortunately good news that does not travel fast! The fatal flaw lies in the fact that even when those who believe it to be 'good' or moral to kill, torture and rape, may not claim a duty on the part of others (who believe otherwise) not to interfere with their practices of 'virtue' (as seen, I must add, by them).[61] The bad news is that even a gifted philosopher like Richard Rorty could base his entire meditation on human rights at the Oxford–Amnesty Lectures with the following initial statement:

> ...Serbian murderers and rapists do not think of themselves as violating human rights. For they are not doing these things to fellow human beings but to *Muslims*. They are not being inhuman, but rather are discriminating between the true humans and pseudo-humans. They are making the same sorts of distinction as the Crusaders made between humans and infidel dogs, and Black Muslims make between humans and blue-eyed devils. The founder of my university was able both to own slaves and to think it evident that all men were created equal... Like the Serbs, Mr Jefferson did not think of himself as violating *human rights*.[62]

What follows? Does it follow that the 'murderers and rapists' are justified? From the relativist position so far canvassed they could so maintain. Professor Rorty, however, suggests that the way out of all this lies in 'making our own culture—the human rights culture—more self-conscious and powerful', not in 'demonstrating its superiority to other cultures by an appeal to something transcultural'.[63] By 'our culture', 'the culture of human rights', Rorty means primarily the United States culture (and more broadly the Euro–Atlantic culture.) The Other has to be educated in human rights sensibility, not by any allegiance to the UDHR values (since these are transcultural invoking a transcendent human nature). The acknowledgement about Jefferson, and the Crusaders, suggests heavily that there has been progress in moral sentiments in the United States (and allied Northern cultures), which has yet to reach the benighted Serbs.[64]

---

[61] *See* the logical demonstration of this in Peffer, at 275.

[62] Richard Rorty, 'Human Rights, Rationality, and Sentimentality', in *On Human Rights: The Oxford Amnesty Lectures 1993* (1993), 111 at 112.

[63] Ibid at 117.

[64] It is remarkable that Rorty collapses the 'pre-modern' (Crusades), the 'modern' (colonial/imperial) and 'contemporary' (human rights era) into one master narrative! On the paradigm offered in this text, Jefferson was consistent with the logics and paralogics of the 'modern' human rights practices of exclusion. Rorty's Serbs are, however, located in a world which invented human rights, including perhaps the basic human right against (to invoke Eric Erickson's term again) 'pseudospeciation'.

Probably, what Rorty exemplifies is not so much a variety of normative ethical relativism but either or even both 'metaethical' and 'metaevaluative' forms of relativism. Probably, there are no 'sure' or 'objective' ways of proving to everyone's satisfaction that something is morally right or wrong or just that something is 'simply' right or wrong. Who, however, is that 'everyone'? This is apparently a vexed question for ethical theorists[65] and may well remain so for the better part of the next millennium. However, both these forms of relativism rely on, or at any rate invoke, the possibility of 'intrasubjective consensus' on at least the prima facie validity of certain moral norms. Neither prevents us from claiming that 'a certain moral principle (e.g. slaughtering of defenceless infants) is *prima facie* wrong'.[66] If so, 'human rights' constitute at least the burden of ethical justification on those who engage in practices of 'pseudospeciation' or indulge in catastrophic practices of the politics of cruelty.

Also, if serious-minded relativism suggests that construction of such an *onus probandi* is itself a complex moral affair, and accordingly requires great *care* in the enunciation of human rights norms and standards, this message is of considerable importance for those who would steer the future of human rights.

Anyone familiar with the Asian, Arab, African, and Latin American charters or conventions on human rights (and at the spawning NGO rearticulation of the Universal Declaration on its golden jubilee) surely knows that human rights enunciations are marked by such moral agonizing, though not always in languages that comfort moral philosophers. Arguments from relativism that remain wilfully ignorant or dismissive of the histories of construction of the 'universality' of human rights are altogether unhelpful. From the perspectives of the sociology of knowledge, they may even appear to some as exercises in unconscious Realpolitik, which it is the task of 'contemporary' human rights to render problematic.

VII. Human Suffering

What is, perhaps, helpful in the discourse on relativism in relation to the contemporary human rights movement is the notion that human suffering may not be wholly legible outside cultural scripts. Since

---

[65] *See*, William K. Frankena, *Ethics* (1963); Kurt Baier, *The Moral Point of View* (1965), and the discussion in Peffer at 281–5, 305–13.

[66] Peffer at 273.

suffering, whether defined as individual pain or as social suffering is egregious, different religions and cultural traditions enact divergent hierarchies of 'justification' of experience and imposition of suffering, providing at times, and denying at others, language to pain and suffering.

The universality of human rights, it has been argued recently by Talal Asad, extravagantly forfeits cultural understanding of social suffering[67] and alienates human rights discourse from the lived experience of culturally/civilizationally constituted humanness. Professor Asad highlights the fact that the Western colonial discourses on suffering valorized '[P]ain endured in the movement of becoming "fully human"'... was seen as necessary because social or moral reasons justified why it must be suffered'.[68] He shows the ways by which the very idea of cruelty and degradation becomes and remains 'unstable, mainly because the aspirations and practices to which it is attached are themselves contradictory, ambiguous, or changing'.[69] This instability, he argues, is remedied neither by the 'attempt by the Euro–Americans to impose their standards by force on others nor the willing invocation of these standards by the weaker peoples in the Third World'.[70] He alerts us to the fact that 'cruelty can be experienced and addressed *in ways other than violation of rights*—for example, as a failure of specific virtues or as an expression of particular vices'.[71]

This is a responsible practice of cultural relativism indeed because, while maintaining scepticism regarding the 'universalistic discourses' around the UN enunciatious concerning torture, cruel, degrading, inhuman treatment marking punishment, it does not attack its legitimacy on any ethical grounds. Rather, it shows us how ethnographies of cruelty may assist progressive promotion and protection of human rights there enshrined, in ways that respect discursive traditions other than those of human rights.

Ethnography of suffering summons us to focus on the difficult relationship between violence and rights. The protection and promotion of rights has always entailed regimes of practices of *justified* or legitimate violence, although rights-talk habituates us to the idea that violence is the very antithesis of rights. Moreover, human rights discursivity

---

[67] Talal Asad, 'On Torture, or Cruel, Inhuman and Degrading Treatment', in *Social Suffering* (1997), 285.

[68] Ibid. at 295.

[69] Ibid. at 304.

[70] Ibid.

[71] Ibid. (emphasis added).

rarely concedes that the violence of the oppressed can often be rights-generative even when dreadfully destructive.

Veena Das addresses the latter in her pioneering exploration. Her construction of violence brings to us the 'unnameable' phenomenon, when the horrors of the partition of India inscribed on the bodies of women led to the birth of citizen–monsters: 'If men emerged from colonial subjugation as autonomous citizens of an independent nation, they emerged simultaneously as monsters'.[72] Her precious, anguished insights invite us to consider what Walter Benjamin termed the *foundational violence of the law*[73] and, one may add, of historic practices of human right to self-determination. The citizen–monster dialectic is writ large too in the everyday life of women suffering despite law, policy, and administration, even when human rights oriented.

The enormous challenge that this genre of writing, which exposes law as violence, poses for human rights logics and paralogics, cannot be captured by the unfeeling and dense prose of relativism. It directs attention to ways in which human rights languages lie at the surface (and not in any Foucaldian sense that treats *depth* as a mere fold on the surface) of lived, and embodied, human anguish and suffering. It interrogates distinctions between forms of suffering as an aspect of state-imposed and 'people/civil society' inflicted or even self-chosen and imposed suffering, and hierarchies or 'transactions in construction of suffering'.

The practices of protection and promotion of universal human rights entail the construction of moral or ethical hierarchies of suffering.[74] Such construction takes place when certain rights (such as civil and political rights) stand prioritized over other human rights (such as social, economic and cultural rights). It occurs when even the former set of rights are subjected to the reason of the state (as when their suspension stands legitimated in 'time of public emergency in the life of the nation'.[75] It occurs when solemn treaties prohibiting genocide and torture, cruel and degrading treatment or punishment allow scope

[72] Veena Das, 'Language and Body: Transactions in Construction of Pain' in *Social Suffering* (1997), 67 at 86. *See also* Stanley Cavell, 'Comments on Veena Das...' in the same volume at 93.

[73] Jacques Derrida, 'The Force of Law: The Mystical Foundation of Authority', in *Deconstruction and the Possibility of Justice* (1992), 3 at 29–67.

[74] I derive this notion from Veena Das. *See*, her 'Moral Orientations to Suffering', in *Health and Social Change* (1994), 139.

[75] Article 4, International Covenant on Civil and Political Rights (ICCPR).

for reservations and derogations that eat out the very heart of remedies otherwise declared available for the violated.

Not merely does the community of states construct such transactional hierarchies, but even human rights praxis *does so*.[76] This makes human rights praxis at best *global* but not *universal*, with deep implications for the future of human rights.

[76] The ways in which human rights mandates are fashioned or formed within the United Nations agencies and across the NGOs illustrate this problem quite strikingly.

As concerns the former, it is often argued that specialized agencies claim a version of human rights for themselves rather than for the violated. Katarina Tomasevski has shown recently that much discourse of the UNHCR has been focused on the right of access by intergovernmental agencies to victims of wars of hunger, rather than of the human rights of access by the violated to ameliorative agencies. Katerina Tomasevski, 'Human Rights and Wars of Starvation', in *War and Hunger: Rethinking International Response to Complex Emergencies* (1994), 70–91.

As concerns the sculpting of human rights mandates, activist grapevine all too often condemns Amnesty International for focusing too heavily on violations of civil and political rights, in the process failing to fully understand the importance of the protection of economic, social, and cultural rights.

Human rights NGOs who adopt a special mandate for themselves (e.g. 'sustainable development', 'population planning') are often charged for neglecting other bodies of crucial human rights.

It is pointless to multiply instances. In each such situation, the criticism is only justified from the standpoint of different constructions of the hierarchy of suffering or evil, rarely made theoretically explicit.

7

Human Rights Movements and Human Rights Markets

I. Human Rights Movements as Social Movements

Human rights struggles are among the most defining characteristics of the second half of the Christian twentieth century; indeed more often than not, we think of human rights praxis in terms of social movements. The notion of social movement raises many perplexing issues concerning how one may define, classify, and evaluate them and these questions remain apposite to a social theory of human rights as yet in its infancy. Among the first necessary steps is a fuller grasp of the potential benefits and costs of exploring human rights movements as social movements. How the former define their identity, their antagonists, and teleology (visions of transformation)[1] shape the future of human rights as a whole.

Social theory about social movements stresses the importance of either Weberian value neutrality or the postmodern suspicion of 'predetermined directionality': thus writes Manuel Castells:

> Social movements may be socially conservative, socially revolutionary, or both, or none. After all, we now have concluded (I hope for ever) that there is no predetermined directionality in social evolution, that the only sense of history is the history we sense. Therefore, from an analytical perspective, there are no 'bad' and 'good' social movements. They are all symptoms of our societies and all impact social structures, with variable intensities and outcomes that must be established by research.[2]

[1] Manuel Castells, *The Power of Identity* (1977), 71.
[2] Ibid. at 70 (emphasis added).

Human rights movements demand such research.[3] However social theory of human rights may have considerable difficulty with the perspective, that even the manifestly rights-denying or rights-diminishing social or human rights movements should await moral evaluation pending social research. A willing suspension of ethical beliefs deferring human rights action to sustained social science research can have impacts on the power of human rights movements to name an evil and to create public concern and capability to contain or eliminate it. For example, some social movements may defend as just traditions confining women to the home and hearth, or may find justifications for reinventing apartheid and genocide. Indeed, they may claim the protection of extant human rights regimes to do so. Hate speech missionaries seek to 'justify' racism as an aspect of freedom of speech and expression. Some protagonists of human life invoke, in the United States, the fetal human right to life even to justify aggression on abortion clinics and professionals. The recent Rawlsian notion valorizing the defence of 'well-ordered societies' is eminently suitable to justify regimes of military intervention or superpower sanction against the less well-ordered societies.[4]

Such movements enfeeble the very power of human rights logics and rhetoric. The power of human rights discourse to name an order of evil is used to name human rights as the very order of evil! Perhaps this standpoint emerges as a 'symptom' of our societies. Undoubtedly, as Castells says, these symptoms 'impact social structures, with variable intensities and outcomes', inviting prolific growth of cognitive social science knowledge industries to empower us with some understanding. At the same time, human rights praxis (whether through movement or markets) may generate scientific knowledge , rather than await it; the history of human rights praxis, from a Mohandas Gandhi to a Nelson Mandela, from a Joan of Arc to a Petra Kelly, is truly pre-figurative of future knowledges about freedom and fulfilment.

The social theory of human rights, of necessity, has to find bases for ethical judgement concerning 'good' and 'bad' social movements; howsoever contestable, human rights movements cannot take as axiomatic the notion that 'the only sense of history is the history we

[3] Upendra Baxi, 'The State and Human Rights Movements in India', in *People's Rights: Social Movements and the State in the Third World* (1998), 335–52; Upendra Baxi, 'Human Rights between Suffering and Markets', in *Global Social Movements* (2000), 33.

[4] John Rawls, 'The Law of the Peoples', in *On Human Rights: The Oxford Amnesty Lectures* (1993), 41.

sense'. It does seek to provide a 'predetermined directionality' in human social development by articulating an ethic of power, whether in state, civil society, or the market. It contests the notion that certain human transactionalities constitute moral free zones.[5] It is then perhaps understandable that most contemporary social theory and history of new social movements does not focus on human rights movements as social movements.[6]

II. From 'Movements' to 'Markets'

Increasingly, human rights movements organize themselves in the image of markets if we use that notion intuitively to denote competition among individuals and groups for scarce or limited resources. NGOs of various kinds and at various levels emerge as economic actors insofar as these seek to mobilize resources for their work; and as such many of them compete *inter se*. Funding agencies (whether national, regional, or global, private, governmental, inter-governmental or international) are economic actors that allocate resources. Some NGOs also seek to generate resources additionally through private individual or citizen contributions. Human rights markets thus comprise a series of transactions across a range of economic actors that pursue competition within a framework of collaboration. This signifies at least that both types of economic actors seek to shape each other's agenda, or the sum total of human rights goods and services thus produced, circulated, and 'consumed'. This process of social production, however, raises many problems that actors in human rights markets have to necessarily negotiate, giving rise in turn to what may be termed human rights market rationality.

Across time and place, there arises the formidable question of social reproduction of human rights market actors. Non-governmental economic actors, or agencies, that fund human rights NGOs (call these 'investors') remain embedded in the cultural traditions of philanthropy. These are (for reasons I cannot explore in this work) socially reproduced more readily in the North than in the South. The flow of South–South resources for promotion and protection of human rights is miniscule compared to the flow of North–South resources. The issue of social reproduction of investors is important for the future of human rights at least for two reasons. First, in terms of net flow of influence, the combined and uneven distribution of investors creates difficult, at

---

[5] David Gauthier, *Morals By Agreement* (1986), 13, 83–112.

[6] Upendra Baxi, 'Human Rights: Between Suffering and Market', in *Global Social Movements* note 3, *supra*.

times, intractable problems for South recipients in terms of autonomy, accountability, and national legitimacy: South governments find it relatively easy to come down hard on fragile NGOs in the title of regulation of foreign funding, even when their own national budgets remain heavily dependent on this very source. Second, most North investors remain tied to corporate philanthropy. Insofar as one strategic objective of the NGO movement is to combat human wrongs promoted and perpetuated by global capital, this feature often sets the bounds of the debate. The invisible hand does not quite reign, but it *does* rule.

Moreover, market rationality is quite often produced at the global level, especially in the United Nations system. Since the 1980s, the production of international agenda for human rights is increasingly marked by a dominant concern to make the 'civil society' a co-equal partner, whether through the idiom of 'sustainable development', 'global governance', or 'good governance'. The various United Nations' social summits (Copenhagen on Social Development, Beijing on Women's Rights as Human Rights, Cairo on Population, Istanbul on Habitat, Rome on the Right to Food and the UNDP programme of 'mainstreaming' human rights) stress the notion that corporations and other economic entities are equal partners to human rights realization. Given the exigencies of the United Nations budget, the call to corporations, especially global corporations, to assume this role is understandable. At the same time, this marks a process of what I have termed the *privatization of the United Nations* as well. This tendency is likely to grow, not diminish, in the first half of the twenty-first century. To a considerable extent, then, the NGO movement remains exposed to the new grammar of market rationality. The very production of human rights goods and services now entails new, often onerous, patterns of social cooperation (working together) between the efficient causes of human and human rights violation and progressive social human rights movements that still must, somehow, tackle the problem of collaboration with violators to reduce the nature and scope of violation. In the process, some degree of commoditization of human suffering and human rights becomes ineluctable.

Human rights markets consist of a network of transactions that serve the contingent and long-term interests of investors, producers, and consumers. These transactions rely upon the availability, which they in turn seek to re-inforce, of symbolic capital[7] in the form of international human rights norms, standards, doctrines, and organizational networks.

---

[7] Pierre Bourdieu, *Outline of a Theory of Practice* (1977, R. Nice trs.); *idem The Field of Cultural Production* (1993), 74–142.

Since grids of power are globalized, human rights markets also create and reinforce global networks, each of which seeks to influence the patterns of compliance and violation of human rights norms. Market rationality requires the production and reproduction of skills and competences, which enable negotiation of tolerably acceptable outcomes between and among the violators and the violated such that market failures do not erode the legitimacy of the network of overall transactions. Human rights markets thus share salient features of global service industries.

Of course, the use of terms like 'market' and 'commoditization' may cause deep offence to human rights practitioners, and the analogy with markets may turn out, on closer analysis, not to be very strong. We ought also to distinguish between the discourse of social movements and the 'social processes with which they are associated: for example, globalization, informationalization, the crisis of representational democracy, and the dominance of symbolic politics in the space of media'.[8] From this standpoint (and quite rightly so) 'movements' are analytically distinguishable from 'markets'. A reductionist analysis, which disregards the relative autonomy of movements from markets, does not advance clarity or conviction. At the same time, the idiom of the 'market' brings more sharply to view the complexity and contradiction of human rights movements; perhaps even more vividly than the alternate symbols of economic coordination such as 'networks' or 'associational governance'. While these images undoubtedly enhance our understanding of social cooperation beyond the metaphor that 'market' may ever bring to us, there is some merit in resorting at least to the notion of a *'quasi-market'*.[9]

III. The Investor and Consumer Markets in Human Rights

Human rights movements at all levels (global, regional, national, and local) have tended to become capital-intensive. The praxis of protecting and promoting human rights entails entrepreneurship in raising material resources, including funding, from a whole variety of governmental, intergovernmental, international, and philanthropic sources. These sources are organized in terms of management imperatives, both of line management and upward accountability. Any human rights NGO or NGI (nongovernmental individual) currently involved in programmes

[8] Castells, note 1 supra at 70.
[9] Gary S. Becker, *A Treatise on the Family* (1981).

for the celebration of the Golden Jubilee of the UDHR surely knows this! Protection and promotion of human rights is an enterprise that entails access to organized networks of support, consumer loyalty, efficient internal management, management of mass media and public relations, and careful crafting of mandates. A full analysis of these variables will unconscionably burden this work; but it needs to be acknowledged that both the NGOs and funding agencies compete for scarce resources; this scramble for support generates forms of investor rationality, which may be generally defined as seeking a tangible return on investment.[10] That rationality has to negotiate the Scylla of mobilization of support of governmental and corporate conscience money and community contributions, and the Charybdis of their legitimation in host societies and governments. This in turn, requires marshalling of high entrepreneurial talent suffused with a whole range of negotiating endowments. Understandably, investor rationality in human rights markets is constantly exposed to a crisis of nervous rationality. Both the inputs and outputs in the portfolio investment in human rights protection and promotion remain indeterminate; nevertheless, these have to be ledgered, packaged, sold and purchased on the most 'productive terms'.

The crisis of nervous rationality stands replicated in consumer rationality. Human rights NGOs, especially in the Third World, need to negotiate the dilemmas of legitimacy and autonomy. The ever so precarious legitimacy of human rights networks seems forever threatened by allegations of foreign funding orchestrated both by national governments and by rival NGO formations who want to do better than their 'competitors'. There exists too, competition to capture the beneficiary groups who measure the legitimacy of human rights networks not in terms of any 'cargo cult' or messianic rationality but in those of what these bring to people in terms of here-and-now accomplishments or results.

At the same time, NGOs seek a free enterprise market relative to the agenda of their semi-autonomous human rights concerns. They seek to define their markets for rights promotion and protection not merely in terms of what the markets of human rights investment will bear at any given moment but also in terms of how these markets may be reorientated in terms of consumer-power. This may, partly, explain the populous presence and participation by the brightest and the best

---

[10] *See*, David Gillies, *Between Principle and Practice: Human Rights in North-South Relations* (1996); Katarina Tomasevski, *Between Sanctions and Election: Aid Donors and Human Rights* (1997).

of NGOs and NGIs at the United Nations Summits: Vienna, Cairo, Copenhagen, Beijing, and Istanbul. By their determined participation at these (and the inevitably mandated plus–5 meetings) they seek to reorient the global investment markets in human rights. The interests of civil servants (national and global) intermesh, in this process, with those of the NGOs and the NGIs.

IV. Techniques of Commodification of Human Suffering

The raw material for investment and consumer markets is provided by here-and-now human misery and suffering. Howsoever morally deplorable, it is a social truth that the overall human capacity to develop a fellowship of human suffering is indeed awesomely limited. It is a salient truth of the contemporary human situation that individual and associational life-projects are rarely disturbed, let alone displaced, by the spectacle of human suffering or human suffering as a spectacle. In such a milieu, human rights markets, no matter whether investor or consumer, remain confronted with the problem of compassion fatigue. This is a moral problem, to be sure; but it is also a material problem. Of necessity, markets for human rights concentrate on this aspect of the problem, if only because when compassion dries out, the resources for the alleviation of human suffering through human rights languages also stand depleted.

This intersection registers the necessity for human rights entrepreneurs to commodify human suffering; to package and sell it in terms of what markets will bear. Human rights violations must be constantly commoditized to be combated. Human suffering must be packaged in ways which the mass media markets find it profitable to bear overall.

By definition, however, the mass media can commodify human suffering only on a dramatic and contingent basis. Injustice and human violations is headline news only as the pornography of power, and its voyeuristic potential lies in the reiterative packaging of violations that titillate and scandalize, for the moment at least, the dilettante sensibilities of the globalizing classes. The mass media also plays a creationist role in that they

in an important sense 'create' a disaster when they decide to recognize it ... they give institutional endorsement or attestation to bad events which otherwise will have a reality restricted to a local circle of victims.[11]

[11] Jonathan Benthall, *Disasters, Relief and the Media* (1993), at pp 3–4, quoted in Stanley Cohen, *Denial and Acknowledgement: The Impact of Information About Human Rights Violation* (1995), 90.

Such institutional endorsement poses intractable issues for the marketization of human rights. Given the worldwide patterns of mass media ownership, and the assiduously cultivated consumer cultures of 'info-entertainment', the key players in human rights markets need to manipulate the media into authentic representations of the suffering of the violated. They have to marshal the power to mould the mass media (without having access to resources that the networks of economic/political power so ever-readily command) into exemplary arenas of human solidarity, going beyond commoditization of human suffering, exploiting the markets for instant news and views.

In a germinal monograph, Professor Stanley Cohen has brought home the daunting tasks entailed in the commodification of human suffering. Cohen brings to attention an entire catalogue of perpetrator-based techniques of denial of human violation and the variety of responses that go under the banner of 'bystanderism', whether internal or external.[12] The de-commodification of human suffering has as its task (according to Cohen, with whom I agree) the conversion of the 'politics of denial' into the 'politics of acknowledgment'.

The various techniques of marketizing human suffering under the title of human rights succeed or fail, according to the viewpoint one chooses to privilege. Efficient market rationality perhaps dictates a logic of excess. The more human rights producers and consumers succeed in diffusing horror stories the better it is, on the whole, for the sustenance of global human rights market cultures. The more the accountability institutions (truth commissions, human rights commissions, commissions for human rights of women, indigenous peoples, children, urban and rural impoverished) the better commerce there is. Giving visibility and voice to human suffering is among the prime functions of human rights service markets. This is however an enterprise that must overcome compassion fatigue[13] and overall desensitization to human misery.

---

[12] These consist in (a) denial of injury; (b) denial of victims; (c) denial of responsibility; (d) condemnation of the condemners; and (e) appeal to higher loyalty. These 'neutralization' techniques are firmly in place and violators only play variations on a theme.

Professor Cohen also offers a typology of bystander passivity or effect. This ensemble consists of: (a) diffusion of responsibility; (b) inability to identify with the victim; (c) inability to conceive of an effective intervention.

See, Cohen, note 11 *supra* at 32–5. *See also* the insightful analysis in Arthur and Joan Kleinman, 'The Appeal of Experience; The Dismay of Images, Cultural Appropriations of Suffering in Our Time', in *Social Suffering* (1997).

[13] Cohen, note 11 *supra* at 89–116.

When the markets are bullish, the logic of excess does seem to provide the most resources for disadvantaged, dispossessed, and deprived human communities. However, in situations of recession serious issues arise concerning the ways in which human suffering is or should be merchandized, and when those who suffer begin to counter these ways, we witness crises in human rights market management.

Human rights markets are crowded with an assortment of actors, agencies, and agenda but appear united in their operational techniques. A standard technique is of reportage: several leading organizations specialize in services providing human rights 'watch' and 'action alerts'. A related market technique is that of lobbying, where official or popular opinion is sought to be mobilized around human rights situations, events, or catastrophes. A third technique is that of cyber-space solidarity: the spectacular uses of instant communication networks across the world. Manuel Castells has recently provided stunning examples of how cyber-technologies have made a dramatic difference in networking of solidarities; but as his analysis itself suggests, these solidarities may work for human rights advancement (as in the case of the Zapatistas) or, more importantly, against the nascent human rights cultures (as in the case of the American militia or the Japanese Aum Shinrikyo movements).[14] Apparently, the days of the pre-cyberspace creation of mass movement solidarity are numbered, even over, if one is to believe that the cyberspace markets for human rights provide the only or best creative social spaces. In any case, once we recognize the danger of ahistorical cyberspace romanticism, it remains true that cyberspace offers a useful marketing technique. A fourth technique consists in converting the reportage of violation in the idiom and grammar of judicial activism. An exemplary arena is provided by the invention of social action litigation, pursuant to which Indian appellate courts, including the Supreme Court of India, have been converted from being the sites of ideological and repressive apparatuses of the state into an institutionalized movement for the protection and promotion of human rights.[15] The resonance of this movement extends to many third world societies.

[14] *See*, Castells, note 1 *supra* at 68–109.
[15] *See*, Upendra Baxi, 'Taking Suffering Seriously: Social Action Litigation before the Supreme Court of India', in *Law and Poverty: Critical Essays* (1988); *idem*, 'The Avatars of Judicial Activism: Explorations in the Geography of (In) Justice', in *Fifty Years of the Supreme Court of India: In Grasp an Reach* (2000), 156–209; *idem*; Preface, in S.P. Sathe, *Judicial Activism in India* (2001).

A fifth technique aims to sustain the more conventional networks of solidarity, of which the facilitation of inter-NGO dialogue is a principal aspect. Usually effected through conferences, colloquia, seminars, and the facilitation of individual visits by victims or their next of kin, this technique has in recent times extended to organizing hearings/listenings of victim groups. This device seeks to bring unmediated the voice and texts of suffering to empathetic observers across the world. The various UN summits have provided an arena for a spectacular emergence of this technique, but there exist more institutionalized arrangements as well. All these bring the raw material of human suffering for further processing and packaging in the media and related human rights markets.

A sixth technique is somewhat specialized, comprising various acts of lobbying of the treaty bodies of the United Nations. This form of marketing human rights specializes in making legislative or policy inputs in the norm-creation process, with NGO entrepreneurs assuming the roles of quasi-international civil servants and quasi-diplomats for human rights, although it is the thinking and conduct of the de jure international diplomats and civil servants that they seek to influence. Through this specialized intervention, this activity runs the risks of co-optation and alienation from the community of the violated, especially when the NGO activity provides the mirror-image of inter-governmental polity. This sort of intervention does offer, when invested with integrity, substantial gains for the progressive creation of human rights norms.

A seventh, and here final, technique is that of global direct action against imminent or actual violation of human rights. Apart from the solitary, though splendid, example of Greenpeace, this technique is not considered sustainable by the leading global and regional NGOs. Of course, there are no less spectacular and sustained examples furnished in the narratives of resistance on global events such as the G–7 and APEC conferences where methods of 'citizen arrest' of global leadership are enacted or when celebrations of the golden jubilee of international financial institutions are sought to be converted into events of global embarrassment. Not to be ignored, in this context, are recourses to direct action by the Argentinian mothers against the 'disappearances' or the British women's movements against the sites of civilian or military nuclear operations.

At the end of the day, however, the dominant market cost-benefit rationality does not legitimate such recourse to direct action in the dramaturgy of human rights.

The point of this illustrative listing is to suggest the variety and complexity of human rights market initiatives, which entail high quotients of managerial and entrepreneurial talent, and the ability to boost/deflate market or investor confidence in human rights ventures. It is also partly my intention to suggest that the 'science' of risk-analysis and risk-management integral to the practices of human rights violation remains relevant to the markets for the promotion and protection of human rights.

It is true that as human suffering intensifies, markets for human rights grow. However, to say this does not entail any ethical judgement concerning commodification of human suffering, although the reader may feel justified in treating some anguished sub-texts in this chapter as warranting a wholesale moral critique of human rights markets. The future of human rights praxis is, as always, linked to the success or failure of human rights missions with their, latent or patent, capability to scandalize the conscience of humankind. The modes of scandalization will, of course, remain contested sites, among the communities of the violators and the violated. The task for those who find the commodification of human suffering unconscionable lies in contestation of ways of this accomplishment, and not in lamenting the global fact of the very existence of human rights markets.

V. The Problems of 'Regulation' of Human Rights Markets

State regulation of human rights markets is fraught with complexities. When may it be said to be invasive of human rights? How far should, if at all, states regulate the very existence or modes of operation of NGOs? Should the certificatory regime of accreditation of NGOs in the United Nations system be based on restrictive criteria? What ought to be the scope of regulation? Regulation of human rights markets in the South assumes a number of specific forms. Some Southern states provide a number of 'umbrella' laws that facilitate associational forms. The typical legislative formats are: registered societies, cooperative societies, charitable foundations and trusts, trade unions, and companies. The latter, the more frequent form in the North, is generally disfavoured by South activist associations. Each, however, empowers and enables state bureaucracy to pose an obstacle race for the NGOs, even in their foundational moments, such as the very naming of an associational activity.[16] However, routine surveillance, through devices of statutorily

---

[16] Thus, when Professor S. Dasgupta and I sought to register an association called the PIDIT(People's Institute in Development and Training) in 1975, the period of

mandated annual reporting is the norm. In addition, the requirement that NGOs may not engage in 'political' action gives a large measure of latitude to state authorities to police the extent of transgression, defined by a particular and peculiar regime style. Given the patterns of 'mediocre liberalism' (to evoke Ranajit Guha's favoured phrase from a different context) post-colonial, 'overdeveloped' state apparatus revels in tormenting NGOs for indulging in 'political' activity, as if mobilization of mass or popular action can ever be apolitical! Further, there exist regimes of foreign exchange regulation, under which all associational activity entails a home office registration and remains liable to arbitrary accounting oversight. Overall, and in complete plain words, NGOs remain more accountable to South governments than their governments remain accountable to the electorate!

To say this is not to deny the function of sovereignty. 'Destabilization' of South governance regimes is seen to be, and often is, the privileged function and role of some foreign funding auspices, and this is as true of the Cold War as of the post-Cold War practices of pursuit of human rights as an aspect of foreign, and global, economic policies pursued by nations of the North. When this sentiment is whipped into paranoia by South regime styles, regulation becomes a pattern of persecution and engine of governmental conformity. In the process a vital truth is lost to the national experience of state formation. This is that human rights praxis, under authentic or legitimate social movement, is always *context-smashing*, which as Roberto Unger says, is the defining characteristic of human rights.

The problem of regulation of human rights markets is not just state-centric. The investor, as well as the consumer, and communities, are stakeholders. The investor-based regulation takes myriad forms of channelling and controlling human rights agenda and transactions, generating a product mix that is the very essence of an audit culture (of upward accountability and line management). However, the investors themselves may be regulated, in response to which they must manufacture legitimation with the host society and government in ways wholly propitious with cross-border markets in human rights protection and promotion.

---

internal emergency during which all civil rights were suspended, the Registrar of Societies objected to the name on the specious ground that 'development' and 'training' constituted an eminent sphere of state action, not permissible to an NGO! Sex-workers in India were for a long time denied associational rights as trade unions on the ground that there existed no employer-employee relationship!

The operators of the local/global human rights markets confront related but distinct problems in devising self-regulatory and the other-oriented regulatory frameworks. Self-regulatory frameworks must address the crises of investor consumer rationalities, in a highly competitive scramble for resourcing. Other-directed regulatory approaches are no less complex. On the one hand, there is a need to maintain acceptable patterns of consumer solidarity in the global investor markets; on the other, there exists the historic need, from the standpoint of the ultimate beneficiaries, to keep a watch on sister NGOs exposed to corruption, co-optation, or subversion by the forces of global capitalism—a problem that has recently been illustrated, in the now happily aborted Bangla Desh Grameen Bank adoption of proposed 'deal' with Monsanto for terminator seed technology. If there was no peer group regulation of occasions of co-optation, human rights markets may undergo substantial downturns.

However, forms of peer-group based regulatory interventions raise difficult, if not intractable, issues. When are the NGO communities entitled to sound an alarm? Which modes of alleviation of human suffering are more progressively 'just'? What supererogatory ethics is at play here? Put another way, what standards the extant human rights instruments (addressed primarily to state prowess) furnish for the NGO's critique of sister NGOs? Are human rights markets more sensibly informed *per se* by morals than all other markets?

I hope that I have demonstrated to a degree the usefulness of the market metaphor. Just as surely human rights discourse remains abundantly ideologically permeated, its materiality is also ever present in the cross-border transactions in the symbolic capital of human rights.

8

The Emergence of an Alternate Paradigm of Human Rights

I. The Paradigm Shift

My thesis here requires a brutally frank statement. I believe that the paradigm of the Universal Declaration of Human Rights (UDHR) is being steadily, but surely, *supplanted* by that of trade-related, market-friendly human rights. This new paradigm seeks to reverse the notion that universal human rights are designed for the attainment of dignity and well-being of human beings and for enhancing the security and well-being of socially, economically and civilizationally vulnerable peoples and communities. The emergent paradigm insists upon the promotion and the protection of the collective human rights of global capital in ways that 'justify' corporate well being and dignity even when it entails gross and flagrant violation of human rights of actually existing human beings and communities.

I am aware that my way of formulation of a new paradigm raises many distinctive questions. Among these are:

- With what justification may we speak of *any* human rights paradigm? Is this, after all, not a 'false' totality?
- In what senses may we speak about *human rights* of global capital? Is it sensible to endow mere aggregation of economy and technology with human rights attributes? At best, is it not more accurate to speak of legal (and equitable) rights of business associations and multinational enterprises?
- Whatever may one mean by trade-related and market-friendly human rights? Should this be a sensible description, one may further ask: *circa* when 'human rights' were not trade-related and market friendly?

- What is unethical about trade-related, market-friendly human rights?

These questions are important and will be addressed in this chapter within the context of the globalization processes. But an extensive ethical investigation concerning morals and markets,[1] or a rigorous analysis of post-War and post-Cold War global economic development, lies well beyond the scope of the present work.[2] Still, it may be useful to provide a 'raw' sense of these very recent developments in terms of challenges posed to the very future of human rights. In this chapter I seek to situate human rights within the dominant narratives of globalization in terms of (i) the 'end of nation state' thematic (ii) the global reproduction of 'soft' states; (iii) the emergence of an alternate paradigm of human rights, and (iv) the materiality of globalization.

II. Dominant Narratives of Globalization

The 'G' word, 'Globalization!', is one word comprising diverse realities. Not merely are complex and contradictory events, processes and happenings lumped under this rubric, signifying uneven and indeterminate developments, but also theories about globalization bring to us (to use a favourite phrase of Habermas) a 'whole continent of contested conceptions'. Some maintain that the contemporary globalization process is *sui generis*, marking a radical discontinuity; others maintain, more or less, that there is 'nothing new', contemporary globalization being merely a further progression of the inter-nationalization of the state and the economy.[3] Some locate the distinctiveness of the contemporary 'globalization' processes in terms of the emergences of a global culture that encompasses us all and in ways that are nearly irreversible; others contend for the autonomy of the 'local' within the heterogeneity of the 'global'.[4]

---

[1] *See*, for example, David Gauthier, *Morals By Agreement* (1986).

[2] *See*, e.g., Robert Brenner, 'The Economy of Global Turbulence: A Special Report on the World Economy, 1950–98', 229, *New Left Review* (1998).

[3] *See*, Roland Robertson, *Globalization: Social Theory and Global Culture* (1992); Paul Hirst and Grahame Thompson, *Globalization in Question* (1996); Winfried Ruigrok and Rob van Tulder, *The Logic of International Restructuring* (1995).

[4] *See*, e.g., Arjun Appadurai, *Modernity at Large: Cultural Dimensions of Globalization* (1997); Mike Featherstone, *Undoing Culture: Globalization, Postmodernism and Identity* (1995); *Global Modernities* (1995).

Contention is also rife concerning the ways of privileging the narrative of 'globalization'. Should we narrate the march of global capital, at the end of the second Christian millennium, as monolithic and invulnerable? Or regard this in autopoietic theory terms as a 'self-dissipating structure'? Put in another way, are there any more possible ways of social and political struggle that may still ambush, both through the (Gramscian) wars of manoeuvre and position, the 'cunning' of late capital? How may the new social movements (say the feminist or the ecological) hunt and haunt the habitats of global capital[5]? Moreover, acute contentions mark the discourse on 'globalization' concerning the manifestation of its agency, whether through 'multi-' or 'trans-' national corporations, international financial institutions, regional economic arrangements, or the unique hegemon, the United States or the Euro-American domination of the rest of the world.

As discourses on ideology, or as ideological discourses, 'globalization' narratives remain tormented, when reflexive enough, by images of ending, that which I term *endology*, often assuming forms of *endolatry* and even *endomania*. The end of something or the other is being ceaselessly proclaimed; so much so that everything is at an *end* save the gifted vocation of the theoretical practice of *endology*! I have distinguished between practices of formal, eclectic, and material endology.[6] The latter direct our attention to the ways in which new forces of production (biotechnology, digitalization, third generation robotics, and information technology) mark the end of work,[7] end of the farmer[8] facilitated by new forms of total multinational enterprise control over world food production,[9] and the end of nature, which now (both as biodiversity and as *in vitro* production of new forms of genetically mutated organisms) becomes a multinational enterprise corporate resource.[10] This riot of 'endings', marks *beginnings* of the

[5] Leslie Sklair, 'Social Movements and Global Capitalism', in *The Cultures of Globalization* (1998) 291–311; J.K. Gibson-Graham, *The End of Capitalism* (*As We Know It*) (1996); Upendra Baxi 'Human Rights: Between Suffering and Market', in *Global Social Movements*, 33 (2000).

[6] Upendra Baxi, The Reason of Human Rights and the Unreason of Globalization', the First A.R. Desai Memorial Lecture, University of Bombay (1996: mimeo);

[7] *See*, H. Braverman, *Labour and Monopoly Capital* (1974); Andrew Gorz, *Farewell to the Working Class; An Essay on Post-Industrial Socialism* (1982). Gorz's thesis is far more complex than his title suggests. His concerns relate to enhancement, autonomy, efficiency, and creativity in complex knowledge-based heteronomous production.

[8] Paul Kennedy, *Preparing for the Twentieth Century* (1993), 74–5.

[9] *See*, for an account of the emergent patterns of 'food dictatorship', 28, *The Ecologist: The Monsanto Files* (Sept./Oct. 1998).

[10] Jeremy Rifkin, *The Biotech Century: The Coming Age of Genetic Commerce* (1998).

New World Order Inc. backed by the rise of economic fundamentalism.[11] This, *inter alia*, articulates a notion that not just the state and the law be global capital friendly but also the rights of global capital formations are (as we note in some detail later) to be considered *human* rights at times trumping the universal human rights of individual human beings and communities.

On the other hand, some 'globalization' theories/narratives remain obstinately optimistic. Roseate in the afterglow of 'globalization', these seek to demonstrate that the contemporary movements for human rights owe a great deal to the 'global institutionalization' of human rights,[12] in ways previously unimaginable even half a century ago. In all its *de-* and *re-*, gen(d)eration, the United Nations system, and its normative regional cohorts, seem (to them) to offer the best historical sites that *somehow* remain 'available' as discursive moment for alternate (even insurgent) normativity. Even the globally monopolistic mass media becomes, on this view, a resource for human rights as social movements for transforming a globalizing world.

The place of human rights is not of any explicit concern to theorists of contemporary globalization. Yet the state of current theorizing on reflexive globalization is not bereft of implications for the future of human rights. First, though the end of human rights is not as yet proclaimed, it must remain heavy on the agendum of endologists since, like all 'things' or states of affairs, human rights become contingent, revisable, even perishable truths of politics, lacking any 'universal' ethical foundation. Second, the end of the redistributionist 'nation-state' complicates the realization and enjoyment of social and economic rights. Third, trans-state entities (that is regional/international economic arrangements, international financial institutions, multinational enterprises, and the network of NGOs) increasingly assume significant social power over the spheres of human rights. Fourth, processes of globalization, especially digitalization and biotechnology, all over again render problematic the notion and status of that which we term 'human'. Indeed, the progress narratives of technoscience seek to convert current human hazards into future human hopes. In what follows, I explore these and related implications arising out of different modes of narrating globalization.

[11] Jane Kelsey, *The New Zealand Experiment: A World Model for Structural Adjustment?* (1995); reprinted as *Economic Fundamentalism* (1995); *Reclaiming The Future: New Zealand and the Global Economy* (1999).

[12] Roland Robertson, *supra* note 3 at 133–4, 181–2.

III. The 'End' of the 'Nation-state'

The end of the 'nation-state' (what an oxymoron!) is indeed a striking thematic of globalization, a thematic that remains extremely problematic from the standpoint of human rights. Descriptive and prescriptive factors tend to get rolled up in any discussion concerning the end of the nation state, so that this discourse on ending does not quite guide us on the normative issues, such as the norm of sovereign equality of states or the value of self-determination. Neither is the distinct observational standpoint always made clear: it is, therefore, not clear for *whom*, and *when* the 'nation-state' has 'ended'.

The territorial state, with more or less well-defined boundaries, within which duties of allegiance and powers of coercion are routinely exercised (for weal or woe) continues to exist. It stands reinforced by the critical normativity of sovereign equality of states. The territorial state has been reaffirmed, and continues to be affected, by the practices of the right to self-determination, in the sense that the value of self-determination seems best consummated through the achievement of political community through statehood.

Although its governance propensities vary, the repressive might of the territorial state is, from the standpoint of the subjugated, still awesome and its human rights-denying practices protean. So is its capacity to acquire weaponry of mass destruction and potential for 'scientific' experimentation with human subjects. The modern state is, however, increasingly interdependent in a globalizing world, which attenuates the classical notions of state sovereignty. Different descriptions of this transformation arise from distinct observational standpoints.

From a human rights standpoint, the processes of globalization of the state refer to the fantastic growth of human rights enunciations and the development of shared global cultures of human rights. Both reorient notions and practices of state sovereignty. The extent of the erosion of the traditional notions of sovereignty is a function of practices of the politics *of* and *for*, human rights. The latter challenge not only the performative acts of sovereign state power but also the bases of the legitimacy of political power. The former deploys human rights as practices of governance and strategies of global diplomacy, tending primarily to reinforce national sovereignties as well as global hegemony. Both tendencies are heavily at work in the contemporary phase of globalization.

What the gurus of globalization mean by the thematic of ending is induced by the standpoint of global capital. In that perspective, the nation-state becomes a point, perhaps, not even a nodal one, in the network of intensified international economic relations in a 'borderless world'. Most independent states, especially of the South, emerge as the managing committees (to evoke that famous phrase from Marx and Engels) for the entire bourgeoisie comprising multinational foreign investors and the international finance capitalist classes.

Also, the state in the North, too (even the solitary and capricious global hegemon that seeks to enforce its fractured values and visions of an international rule of law) is subject to the cumulative 'de-territorialization'. National sovereignties stand reconfigured by networks that comprise international financial institutions, postmodern confederations (like the European Union), global and regional human rights intergovernmental frameworks, global trade pacts (such as the WTO and the proposed order of MAI), and regional economic arrangements, with varying degrees of effective presence (from NAFTA on the one hand to APEC on the other).

If you switch perspectives, the dominant perspective that highlights the creation of a borderless world for capital emerges as marked by new and viciously violent forms of social exclusion. The so-called borderless world remains cruelly *re*-bordered for the violated victims subject to practices of the politics of cruelty, even barbaric practices of power. Myanmar is thus borderless for Unocal, though not for Aung San Su Kyi and the thousands of Burmese people she symbolizes. India is borderless for Union Carbide and Monsanto but not for the mass disaster violated Indian humanity. Ogoniland is borderless for Shell but becomes the graveyard of human rights and justice for a Ken Saro Wiwa, and the people's movement martyred alongside him.

The hollowing out of state sovereignty, we must recall, is an uneven process. As the second Christian millennium has drawn to its checkered close, the Euro-American states have maintained a surprising degree of state resilience, at least in comparison to the debt and crises ridden orders of sovereignties in the South. Also, overall, human rights confrontations with state power in the North remain less of a 'threat' to the state bourgeoisie even in the increasingly 'multicultural' North than in the South. When inherently multi-civilizational South nations aspire to forms of 'liberal democracy' in contexts of mass impoverishment, (as, for example, in India and South Africa) human rights based contestation concerning the creation of a world safe for the foreign investor assumes tormenting proportions for the managers and agents of globalization.

However, the progressive diminution, even to the point of extinction, of state sovereignty in the South, needs to be viewed too from the eye of global capital, that fantastic entity that Marx sought to demystify for us. In almost all its historic forms, capital is at best a faction-ridden coalition of competitive and strategic interests. Though it is increasingly the case that Marxian languages of class have been rendered inarticulate, any future that human rights may have, or thought worthy of having, needs to be based on his perception of the contradictory unity of the formation characterizable as 'global capital'.

From the standpoint of the oppressed everywhere, and their next of kin the human and social rights activists, this faction-ridden 'entity' appears, and is almost always best presented as, a monolithic order of multitudinous evils. This radical reductionism lives on in the embodied histories of collective hurts. For the radical next of kin (the world constituted by the possibility of vicarious suffering by the NGOs) people's power amounts to nothing at all so long as the *Fortune 500* are not driven out of global existence.

On an internal view, global capitalism is a highly complex and contradictory state of affairs though united in the vision of power and profit. While this differentiation brings little immediate solace from the viewpoint of human violation, it provides an important resource for human rights movements. The current controversies that engulf trade relations between the EU and the USA (for example, the banana dispute or the Burton-Holmes law that empowers the USA to impose retaliatory trade sanctions on European corporations that dare to do business with Cuba, or the genetically mutated foodstuff) manifest intra-global capitalist conflicts. It would be an extraordinary reading that suggests any human rights potential in these somewhat incredible developments. The EU heart does not bleed for the impoverished Caribbean or for the more than three decades old misery of the US Cuban embargo. Rather, these conflicts pulsate with the competitive edge of global trade. This is manifest in the recent trade wars between Euro-American states. Despite the outcries at the WTO dispute panel's recent rulings authorizing the United States to impose retaliatory trade sanctions against the EU for its human right to health oriented prohibition on importation of meat treated with growth hormones, the EU is *ad idem* with the US on the need for a new millennium WTO round of talks that will further release transnational corporate genius for global human welfare!

The difference between the internal and external perspectives sets the stage, as it were, for any scenarios concerning the future of human rights. For example, like, for the time being, the victorious NGO coalition that retarded the path of progress for the MAI, the NGO world, again rightly, hails the failure of the (November, 1999) Seattle WTO Millennial Round as a milestone for the might of global civil society. In contrast, Heads of States have now chosen to deploy the formidable power of collective lamentation triggered by these setbacks, a solitary exercise wholly congenial to the cunning of capital. Between the shadowy (even the Derridean 'spectral') spaces of the carnival and the dirge, and their re-enactments to follow, lies congealed both the promise and the peril for the future of human rights. These spaces take many forms.

IV. The Progress Narratives, All Over Again!

The coalition of forces that nourish the global vision of borderless international capital seeks to proselytize the end of the nation-state regulatory prowess. From this standpoint, 'globalization' means the diminishing of the state as the planner of national economic development, the owner of capital and other means of production, an active participant in the production of goods and services, and the proactive regulator of patterns of corporate behaviour. It also signifies that the state will be a willing, even enthusiastic, promoter of free market. All this in some important ways marks the end of the processes and regimes of *human rights oriented, redistributionist governance practices*, in ways that are directed to the 'progressive realization' of the social, economic, and cultural rights of the people.

The UDHR model assigned human rights responsibilities to states: it called upon the states to construct, progressively and within the community of states, a just social order, national and global, that will at least meet the basic needs of human beings. The new model denies any significant redistributive role to the state; it calls upon the state [and world order] to free as many spaces for capital as possible, initially by fully pursuing the three-Ds of contemporary globalization: deregulation, denationalization, and disinvestment. Putting an end to the national regulatory and redistributive potential is the leitmotif of present-day economic globalization, as anyone who has read several drafts of the MAI knows. Deregulation is, perhaps, best understood as selective strategic de-governmentalization of the capacity to make informed, responsible, and autonomous public choices by those democratically elected to govern. Important though the distinction between 'state' and 'government' may be, the project of globalization (to evoke Jane Kelsey's phrase) lies in 'rolling back the state'. The project of politics *for* human rights remains (in the Sol Picciotto–Theda

Stockpool phrase) 'bringing the state back in'. Strategic de-governmentalization combines the force of both *de-* and *re-* regulation. Deregulation trajectories aim at the evacuation of governmental/legislative/adjudicatory control over the free flow of goods, services, and currency movements. These simultaneously call for vigorous state action when the interests of global capital are at stake. To this extent, *deregulation* signifies not an end of the nation-state but an end to the *redistributionist state*.[13] *Re*-regulation takes the form of global/regional treaties/trade arrangements that induce, as well as coerce, state compliance (as, for example, the WTO regime's 2005 deadlines for the full TRIPS and TRIMS implementation), sculpted, of course, by special interests of global capitalism.

V. The Reproduction of a Soft State

Recent history has shown that multinational capital needs at one and the same time a soft state and a hard one. In the heyday of 'developmentalism', Gunnar Myrdal identified the crises of development in South Asia as caused by 'soft states' that could not discipline practices of politics and effectively exercise the power to rule.[14] An effete state was unable to fulfil any of its major social welfare roles, providing literacy and quality education, health services, agrarian reforms; both its practices of politics and profiles of overdeveloped bureaucracy were anomic, corruption-ridden, and marked by a conspicuous lack of discipline. Capricious and corrupt law-enforcement practices aggravated the growing lack of a civic culture, in which the new middle classes claimed rights (and abused these) but acknowledged no social responsibility for the realization and enjoyment of human rights assured to human beings everywhere. Social and economic development stood thereby redefined and reversed.

The processes of globalization, thriving upon the heavily critiqued ideologies of developmentalism and its eventual demise, seek to reproduce the soft state. That notion is, however, now reconstructed in several important ways. The 'progressive state', at least in, and for, the South, is now conceived not as a state in its internal relations with its own people but in relation to the global community of foreign

---

[13] *See also*, John Braithwaite and Peter Drahos, *Global Business Regulation* (2000).
[14] Gunnar Myrdal, *Asian Drama: An Enquiry Into the Poverty of Nations* (1963). Myrdal's concern was to portray South Asian states as lacking in social and institutional discipline that made the society and state vulnerable to both crises of development and the 'revolution' of rising expectations.

investors. A progressive state is one that is a good *host state* for global capital. A progressive state is one that protects global capital against political instability and market failures. A progressive state is one that represents accountability *not* so much directly to its peoples, but to the World Bank and International Monetary Fund. A progressive state is one that instead of promoting world visions of a just international order learns the virtues of debt repayment on schedule. Finally, a progressive state is one that gleans conceptions of good governance neither from the histories of struggles against colonization and imperialism nor from its internal social and human rights movements but from the global institutional gurus of globalization.

The construction of 'progress' is animated by a post-Fukuyama world in which there is no Other to Capitalism, writ globally large. Of course, the contradictions between democracy and capitalism are once again, recognized, but these too are reconstructed, for example, as follows:

- War against hunger gets transformed in the 1998 Rome Declaration on the Right to Food into the free market oriented state and international management of food security system;[15]
- The struggle against homelessness and for shelter, in the 1998 United Nations Social Summit at Istanbul, becomes a series of mandates for the construction industries and urban developers;
- 'Sustainable development', becomes an instrument of policy for the promotion and protection of corporate governance practices of 'greenwashing';[16]
- The UNDP inspired 'mainstreaming' of human rights 'mission' envisaging the raising of a billion dollars for the Global Sustainable Development Facility has already been subscribed to by way of seed money by some of the most egregious multinational enterprise corporate human rights offenders.

In sum, all progress towards the achievement of social, economic and cultural rights is thought best attained, by the cash-stripped United Nations system, within a cooperative framework of global capital–nation-state collaboration. This framework was fully articulated

---

[15] The shift from the right to food to an integrated management of food security systems in the Rome Declaration opens up arenas for state–multinational enterprise collaboration, rather than for human rights oriented regulation over agribusiness. *See*, for an anticipatory critique, *Twelve Misconceptions About the Right to Food as a Human Right* (1996) by FIAN.

[16] *See*, Jed Greer and Kenny Bruno, *Corporate Greenwash: The Reality Behind Corporate Environmentalism* (1996); Andrew Rowell, *Green Backlash: Global Subversion of the Environmental Movement* (1996).

recently in the United Nations' Secretary General's Davos speech, where Kofi Annan suggested a 'social compact' between global capital and the United Nations. While global corporations and foreign investors were urged to collaborate with the United Nations, there was not even the hint of a suggestion that egregious violations of human rights entailed in corporate governance were per se illegitimate and that they were bound by a regime of human rights obligations.

However this framework, assiduously promoted, and even promulgated by the various UN Summit Declarations and Programmes of Action, is by and large congenial to transnational capital and its legions of normative cohorts because it mandates an uneven partnership between global capital and 'developing states'. Unshackled by even a minimal international code of conduct, the partnership between state and civil society so abundantly emphasized in the various UN summit declarations empowers multinational enterprises to mould state policies and purposes to their own ends. Naturally, the production of soft states is its strategic high priority agendum, which craftily deploys the language of humane development and governance, and human rights and well being.

I cite as a prime example of this the continuing reports of Ms Fatima–Zohra Ksentini, the Special Rapporteur to the Commission on Human Rights, on the adverse effect of the illicit movement and dumping of toxic and dangerous wastes on the enjoyment of human rights.[17] The biggest waste exporters are, of course, the most 'developed' countries and wastes continue to be dispatched to regions lacking the political and economic power to refuse these.[18] This lack is not innate but caused, in the last instance, by the formations of global economy.

All kinds of business practices abound: the use of falsified documents, bribing of officials in the 'country of origin, the transit country or ... the country of final destination', and the existence of private contracts 'between Western companies, and African countries whereby the companies paid a pittance for the land on which to dump toxic products ...'[19] The latter scandal brought forth an anguished resolution from the Organization of African Unity a decade ago, which declared toxic dumping a 'crime against Africa and African people'.[20] The

[17] Commission on Human Rights, 'Adverse Effects of the Illicit Movement and Dumping of Toxic and Dangerous Products and Wastes on the Enjoyment of Human Rights', UN Doc. E/CN.4/1998/10 (20 January 1998).

[18] Ibid. at paras 54 and 56.

[19] Ibid. at paras.

[20] Ibid. at para 57.

Special Rapporteur has no difficulty in cataloguing the very large number of violations these practices knowingly and *criminally* entail.[21]

Soft states and regimes need to be continually produced for the benefit of global capital, benefiting a few communities of people. That this occurs at the cost of incredible human suffering of the impoverished nations[22] is irrelevant to global capital, which must measure the excellence of economic entrepreneurship by standards other than those provided by endless human rights normativity.

The contextuality of this enterprise demands a moment of reflection. Multinational corporations may not perform toxic dumping projects without the active support provided, for example, by the operations of the international financial institutions. These 'persuade' some Third World countries, ridden by 'over-indebtedness and collapse of raw material price', to view the import of hazardous wastes as 'attractive' as a last resort for improving liquidity.[23] One is talking about, in this context, of no bad business practice which international codes of conduct may rescue but rather of genocidal corporate and international financial institutional regimes of governance. These are, to coin a neologism (a barbarism in language that is sufficient to cope with the savagery of the 'free market') *righticidal* practices of management *of governance.*

Hardheaded international business practices also require the proliferation of hard states and regimes, which must be market-efficient in suppressing and delegitimating human rights-based practices of resistance or the pursuit of alternate politics. Rule of law standards and values need to be enforced by the state on behalf, and at the behest, of formations of global economy and technology. When to this end it is necessary for the 'host' state to unleash a reign of terror, it must be empowered, locally and globally, to do so. The 'host' state is now, in complete plain words, a state held hostage. It, at all times, must remain sufficiently active to ensure maximal security to the global or foreign investor, who has corresponding duties to assist the state in managing or refurbishing any democratic deficit that might thus arise. The flagrant, ongoing and massive violations of human rights thus entailed must be denied a voice by a post-Bhopal catastrophe Union Carbide

---

[21] Ibid. at paras 77–107.

[22] If you find this too metaphorical please recall children playing on irradiated nuclear waste dump sites in Marshall Islands or the victims of Bhopal still suffering from the lethal impact of catastrophic exposure to 47 tons of MIC. *See also*, Upendra Baxi, 'Mass Torts, Multinational Enterprise Liability, and Private International Law', 279, *Recueil des Cors*, 301–427 (1999).

[23] *See* note 17 *supra* at para 57.

state-of-art management of public and political opinion, nationally and globally.

VI. The Trade-Related, Market Friendly Human Rights Paradigm

(a) *Some Threshold Difficulties*

My notion of the emergent paradigm (hereafter TRMFHR), so far implicit, needs a fuller statement. If one were to signify by it the feature that corporations and business associations are claiming human rights to which they are not, or ought not to be, entitled, this would constitute an enormously inaccurate misreading of human rights norms and standards. The right to property (including intellectual property) and the right of association have been acknowledged as basic human rights since the UDHR. It is also true that contemporary human rights enunciations typically describe 'persons' as rights-bearers; this expression (as the context may require) includes 'legal persons' such as corporations and other business associations. Both these propositions may lead some to conclude that what I describe as a new paradigm is nothing more than the unfoldment of the liberal logic of the UDHR.

It may also be argued that insofar as corporations and business associations are protected by the existing regime of human rights, states have obligations relative to these rights, both under customary and conventional international law. On the other hand, unless the existing human rights regime so provides, corporations cannot be said to have human rights obligations to anyone. The deeply moving critique of multinational corporations' abuse of power thus misses the mark, it may be maintained, when formulated in terms of 'violation' of human rights and urging human rights oriented or compliant policies and practices of doing business.

However, this way of reading UDHR is in itself excessively trade-related and market-friendly. Its Article 17 endowing 'everyone' with the 'right to hold property, alone or in association with others' does not lay down what constitutes property; nor does it concretize what action will count as an 'arbitrary' deprivation of property. Closely read, Article 17 does not quite enshrine what are called intellectual and industrial property rights; it only speaks of the right to 'the protection of the moral and material interests resulting from any scientific, literary, or artistic production of which he is the author'. The UDHR neither universalized the bourgeois capitalist conceptions of corporate and individual property rights nor the Marxist–Leninist notions of social ownership. The determination of the nature and scope of the right to 'property' was left to the powers of national self determination, manifest in different modes of Cold War constitutionalism.

Whatever one may think of these provisions of the UDHR, it should be clear that the 'right to property' was among many human rights thus enshrined. As such, it was subject to inherent limitations arising from rights such as immunity from discrimination on the ground, *inter alia*, of 'property' (Article 2); ownership of human beings 'slavery or servitude' (Article 4); the 'right to work' and to leisure (Articles 23, 24); and the right to 'adequate standard of living' (Article 25). Also, it remains important to stress that while these other rights find further elaboration, the right to property does not find *any* place in the two human rights covenants. To this extent, to say that the TRMFHR paradigm is just an unfoldment of the potential of UDHR is plainly incorrect.

The argument that corporations have associational and property rights under customary and conventional international law may find support from normative regimes, such as state responsibility for injury to aliens providing the right to prompt, effective, and just compensation for taking and the law of belligerent occupation. However, these special normative regimes do not bear any family resemblance to human rights. Injuries thus suffered by corporate entities are construed as injuries to the national state and duties to recompense, if any, lie with the violating state. All this is very different from treaty provisions, such as NAFTA, that enable corporations to sue treaty party states for violation of their rights.

Finally, the objection that corporations cannot be said to have, under international law, any human rights responsibility remains unpersuasive. The Nuremberg International War Crimes Tribunal did, indeed, sentence two leading German corporations for participation in genocide and crimes against humanity. Article IV of the Convention on the Prevention of Genocide, 1948, provides for punishment of 'persons' committing genocide 'whether they are constitutionally responsible rulers, public officials or private individuals'. Arguably, this inclusive definition may extend to corporate entities. Similarly, the Convention on Discrimination against Women, 1979, at several places imposes duties of respect and compliance to women's rights declared applicable to 'any person, organization and enterprise' (Article 2(e)). Numerous United Nations Summit Declarations and Programmes of Action and provisions of environmental treaties and arrangements are open to a reading that cast certain human rights responsibility upon global corporations. Of course, such reading will initially provide exercises in subaltern construction of instruments that emplot trade-offs between human rights and the values of international social corporation.[24] It is beyond the scope of this work, for reasons of space, to develop this theme further.

However, the most overarching principles of human rights responsibility of corporations (as well as states and individuals) are enshrined in Articles 28 and 30 of the UDHR. The former declares that: 'Everyone is entitled to a social and international order in which the rights and freedoms set forth in this Declaration can be fully realized', and the latter states, memorably, that: 'Nothing in this Declaration may be interpreted as implying for any State, group or person to engage in any activity or to perform any act aimed at the destruction of any of the freedoms set forth herein'.

Article 30 clearly extends to all the beneficiaries of human rights including aggregations of economic and technological power in the shape of business association groups or corporate legal persons. They have a duty, among others, to so behave and conduct themselves as not to engage in destruction of rights and freedoms thus enshrined.

I am aware that many interpretive strategies could be marshalled against this conclusion. One that is clearly illegitimate is that which insists on the exhortative, non-binding character of the UDHR; if it is open to derive basic rights of economic associations from it, it should remain equally open to derive obligations from the same text, especially when these are so explicitly worded. Nor is the notion that corporations are not subjects of international law persuasive in the light of developments already mentioned.

(b) *Why Speak of Human Rights of Corporations?*

I have already encountered some discomfort among, and incurred reproach from, human rights activists and lawyers at what they think to be an unnecessary, and even dangerous, extension of using language that even attributes human rights to corporations. It is unnecessary because common convention only requires a reference to their legal and even constitutional rights. It may also be dangerous to allow the possibility of such attribution as such transference of logic and rhetoric to formations of capital and technology could only further enhance their formidable powers. Surely, it might be said that the course of human rights activism illustrates the strength of the denial of any claim to

[24] *See*, for an interesting account of the complex bargaining position of the industry lobby groups, corporation sponsored NGOs, and environmental NGOs, Chiara Giorgetti, 'From Rio to Kyoto: A Study of the Involvement of Non-Governmental Organizations in the Negotiations on Climate Change', 7, *New York University Environmental Law Journal* (1999), 199–244.

human rights by concentrations of economic and technological power.

These are not entirely unpersuasive positions, and it certainly is no part of my intention to further empower these enormous formations in a world rife with massive human violation. This notwithstanding, it seems essential to me that all of us, activists and theorists, need to realize that the power of human rights discourse has already been critically appropriated by global capital. A comparative sociology of human rights leaves us with no other credible option. I cite below a few examples.

First, global capital increasingly seeks to inscribe its rights through treaty regimes. The archetype of this is, of course, the WTO agreement, in particular the agreement on trade-related intellectual property rights (TRIPS). The extensive regime of basic rights has been further codified in the World Copyright Treaty, 1996, which now protects 'digital works', in particular ownership over electronic and genetic (human genome project) databases. Further rights are asserted in the arena of scientific research and experimentation (which has now become hi-tech and capital intensive, and therefore increasingly corporatized) as essential aspects of the human right to freedom of speech and expression. Corporations have also claimed and acquired the right to 'commercial free speech' as well as a right to reputation and honour, not just as a property but as a personality interest. Besides, the MAI drafts tell their own stories of dreams of an ever-increasing range of rights now sought by global capital. These rights constitute a web of Hohfeldian jural relationships: these include rights as enforceable claims, privileges, powers, and immunities, with all their specific jural correlatives.

Second, the justification typically offered for this panoply of rights thrives on the logics, paralogics, and languages of human rights. Collective orders of capital and technology must have these rights as emanations of already existing human rights of individual human beings since these are human associations, collections of individual humans pursuing in acts of social cooperation their common aims and aspirations. When severely interrogated, protagonists of these new rights justify these in terms of the legitimacy and potential of free markets to secure a better future for human rights as such. To take a few examples, it is argued, or indeed arguable, that

- human right to health is best served, in a variety of contexts, by the protection of the research and development rights of pharmaceutical and diagnostic industries;
- the right to reproductive autonomy, the right of women over their bodies, becomes possible only in a technological era, based on protection of industry rights in reproductive technologies;

- a whole variety of sustainable development rights and processes depend on technological fixes that corporate technosciences make possible in the form of new technologies inventing ways of biodegradable and other forms of recycling and treating of wastes;
- the menacing environmental problems confronting humankind as a species (depletion of biodiversity, perforations in the ozone layer, and climate change) can best be redressed by technoscience;
- the right to food (now re-conceptualized by the Rome Declaration as the right to food security systems) is best served by protection of the rights of agribusiness corporations;
- the right to public and political participation (enshrined in the Declaration on the Right to Development) is best secured by the rapid growth of information technologies which has made unanticipated forms of global solidarity of the new social movements possible, in all their resilience.

In sum, the promotion and protection of some of the most cherished contemporary human rights becomes possible only when the order of human rights for global capital is fully recognized.

Third, contemporary movements aimed at making global corporate power accountable already address it in terms of human rights; and, as we have seen, that power too has the potential to convert such human rights movements into markets.

Fourth, market competition serves, directly or indirectly, human rights, whether this occurs through 'ethical investment', fair-trading, consumer accountability, or more recently in industry-wide leadership in banning the production and distribution of genetically mutated foodstuff. Also, increasingly, many human rights activist groups seek to influence global trade policy to arrest the massive violations of human rights of the vulnerable sectors of society (child labour or gender based wage discrimination, for example).

Fifth, even though a cynical view of it is possible, perhaps we should not obliterate altogether from activist memory the remarkable Principles for South Africa developed by Reverend Leon Sullivan, a Board Member in General Motors and named after him. The Sullivan Principles were, on one estimate, adopted by 200 of 260 US corporations doing business with the South African apartheid regime. Much the same may be said concerning the MacBride Principles for Northern Ireland. Also, at long last the European Bribery Convention, 1996, marks a triumph for people's right to transparency in international business, even though beset by constructive ambiguity about the proscribed conduct[25] as it also registers the success of underlying pressures from American industry for the creation of a level playing field.

Of course, a radical reductionist position will refuse to recognize these industry initiatives as anything more than tokenism, given the dominant business ideology summed up in the maxim: 'The Social Responsibility of Business is to Increase Profits.'[26] It is also certainly true that the community of multinationals (no matter how riven with internal competition) maintains an unsurprising solidarity against the imposition of new human rights obligations on their structure and operations. This is clearly manifest in the recent successful efforts to exclude multinationals from the jurisdiction of a proposed international criminal court and since the 1970s preventing all UN-based efforts at a Code of Conduct for Transnationals. A less fundamentalist position, while recognizing failures, would maintain that global capital is already in the throes of the politics *of* human rights and the task is to seek to aggravate these by a more thoroughgoing politics *for* human rights.

(c) *The Nature and Content of TRMFHR*

Increasingly, global capital claims a new order of international rights for itself in ways that have profound destructive impacts on the human rights of human beings everywhere, as even a bare reading of the early version of MAI shows. Protection of the rights of the foreign investor is to be of such a high order as to deconstruct all traditional and newly emergent human rights as 'trade distorting' policy obstacles that need to be overcome in the very title of making the future of human rights secure.

In 1995, as befitted the occasion of the UN Copenhagen Summit on Social Development, I circulated the following Draft Charter of the Human Rights of Global Capital:[27]

---

[25] The Convention makes it an offence to bribe foreign state officials. This apparently excludes acts that comprise bribing political parties, their leaders, and cadres. The reason for this is obvious. Corporate funding for election campaigning has acquired the dimensions of the First Amendment type rights in the United States; in other Euro-American states it has proved difficult to structure limits to it as well as duties of disclosure. Such funding, legitimate at home, forbids its description as 'bribery' when practiced abroad. In any case, outlawing such practices is left to the regulatory potential of the 'soft' states!

[26] Advocated by Nobel Laureate Milton Friedman, *New York Times* (Magazine section) 13 Sept. 1970.

[27] *See*, Upendra Baxi, ' "Summit" of "Hope" in the Depths of Despair: Social Development as Realization of Human Rights', *Mainstream*, 19 April 1995. The statement is here reproduced with minor editorial variations.

Acknowledging that economic development is the quintessence of human and social development;

Realizing that the pursuit of profit, at any or all costs, is the quintessence of all economic growth and development;

Noting that throughout human history trade and commerce have laid foundations for multicultural/multi-civilizational contacts and exchanges in the naturally legitimate traditions of Social Darwinism;

Appreciating fully that all possible alternatives to capitalism have been tried and found wanting by the states and peoples of the world;

WE, the Founding Fathers of Globalization, affirm and announce the following inalienable rights of global capital as the best assurance of achieving a new world order, having the potential for progressive realization of all other subsidiary human rights:

(a)   the right to immunity from any symbolic or other significant displays or exercises of state sovereignty;

(b)   the right to cajole, corrupt and coerce, national regimes in the interest of human and social 'development';

(c)   the right to command, as required, national sovereignties to co-opt, corrupt or coerce human rights communities engaged in acts, and even thoughts and beliefs, manifestly subversive of globalization;

(d)   the right to suborn all learned professions (including law, medicine, media, science and education) to practise and propagate values serving processes of globalization;

(e)   the collective right of the capital to use democratic processes and power (and where necessary the right to subvert these) by way of special interest lobbying to enhance the factors of production;

(f)   the right to immunity against corporate confusion or incoherence arising from unsolicited, undue, and untoward exposure of management and entrepreneurial talent to the counterproductive and corrupting languages of human rights;

(g)   the right to freely create, with sustainable impunity, human, bio, eco and genetic hazards and an order of human violation commensurate to, and functional with, the development of the productive forces of globalization, without undue obligation for reparation, restitution, and rehabilitation;

(h)   the right to resist, covertly and overtly, all threats to global capital and in particular to freely organize, reorganize, and disorganize public memory concerning the so-called corporate violations of human rights, as an integral aspect of the human right of corporations to privacy, honour and the near-absolute right of commercial free speech;

(i)   the collective right of capital to invent, and put to work, international and intergovernmental organizations which are functionally superior equivalents to the protection of rights set forth herein.

Thus enunciated this Magna Carta of global capital may invoke a moment of mirth, both amongst the CEOs of multinationals and even among communities of 'human rights activism. However, once the satisfaction of the as yet unscripted, yet basic, human right to laughter is met, my point remains, and that is: the Draft Declaration reflects many elements or configurations of collective rights of global capital currently firmly in place. An exhaustive demonstration furnishes scope for another book; here a few illustrations will have to suffice.

I attend to (*g*) and (*d*) above in some detail in the section that deals with what I call the materiality of globalization. The right enshrined in (*b*) has a long history of fruition in the ways in which American global corporations, during the Cold War era, sought to depose duly elected leaders (as, for example, in Chile) and supported, and connived with human rights violative authoritarian regimes in Latin America, Africa, the Middle East, and Asia. The rights enshrined in (*i*) are already at work in the current processes of the privatization of the United Nations[28] and the formulation of powerful intergovernmental global and regional trade organizations. The rights enunciated in (*c*) have been poignantly illustrated in the now well-established patterns of multinational–host state collaboration resulting in the judicial murders of leading activists. Other examples of repressive complicity abound: industry based NGOs that exploit the freedom of association and expression, which is usually denied, or is attained after prolonged and often bloody struggles, to the oppressed and the repressed.

The recent emergence of SLAPPS (Strategic Law Suits Against Public Participation) deserves special emphasis in relation to the rights enshrined in (*h*) above. No reader of the work of the George W. Pring and Penelope Canan, who first invented this neologism, entitled *SLAPPS: Getting Sued for Speaking Out* (1996) will contest their conclusion either about the 'chilling effects' of SLAPPS or the ideology and material interest formations that these represent. As they present the heart of darkness:

[28] There is no other way of describing the state of the current initiatives at 'mainstreaming' human rights.

By filing the SLAPP, economic interests express their intolerance for and seek to stifle the expression and views of other citizens, effectively denying the equality of citizenship so fundamental to informed political decision-making. SLAPP filers justify solving political disputes non-politically on the basis of righteous economic self-interest coupled with intolerance for civic-minded public participation. This is an ideologic argument for economic interests as the superior voice in determining public policy [at p. 221.]

SLAPPS, a dominant modality of multinational endeavour at the cancellation of the rights of free speech and expression of individual human beings, is also directly violative of the value of public participation affirmed by the UN Declaration on the Right to Development.[29] It is a mistake to conceive of it as a distinctive American phenomena. South human rights activists are confronted as well by its 'chilling' potential.

VII. The Paradigms in Conflict

The new paradigm may succeed only if it can render unproblematic the voices of suffering. This occurs in many modes. One such is rationality reform, through the production of epistemologies that normalize risk (there is no escape from risk), ideologize it (some grave risks are justified for the sake of 'progress', 'development', 'security'), problematize causation (in ways that the catastrophic impacts may not be traced to the activity of global corporations), raise questions (so dear to law and economics specialists) concerning the efficiency of legal regimes of liability; interrogate even a modicum amount of judicial activism (compensating rights-violation and suffering, favouring—when risk management and damage containment strategies fail—unprincipled and arbitrary extra-judicial settlement). It is not surprising that some of the most important questions in globalization discourse relate to how we should conceptualize the 'victim'; who may authentically (on their behalf and behest) speak about victimage; and what indeed may be said to constitute 'suffering'.

The new paradigm asks us to shed the fetishism of human rights and appreciate that in the absence of economic development human rights have no future at all. Some behavioural scientists urge us to believe in a quantitative methodology that produces results, certainly for them, demonstrating a positive correlation between foreign direct investment, multinational capital, and observance of human

[29] Upendra Baxi, 'The Development of the Right to Development', in *Human Rights: New Dimesion and Challenges* (1998).

rights.[30] It is easier to combat dictatorial regimes that suspend human rights on the ground of the priority of economic development than to contest the Gospel of Economic Rationalism which is mystified by new scholasticism content with the assertion, for example, that 'meso-development' is best promoted under conditions of authoritarian governance.[31]

Faute de mieux, human rights communities must now work within the languages and imperatives of 'economic rationalism'; they must not only cover the high ground of postmodern political theory but also the new institutional economics, maintaining at the same time constant conversation with human suffering.

The paradigm of universal human rights progressively sought normative consensus on the *integrity* of human rights, expressed though in different idioms. The diverse bodies of human rights found their highest summation with the Declaration on the Right to Development insisting that the individual is a *subject of development, not its object*. The emergent paradigm reverses this trend. It seeks to make not just the human individual but *whole nations* into the *object*s of development, as defined in 'economic rationalism' of the supra-statal networks like the World Bank and the IMF, which are neither democratically composed nor accountable to any constituency save perhaps that of investors. Their prescriptions for reorientation of the economic structures and policies of the indebted and impoverished Third World societies, far from being designed to make the world order equitable, are addressed to serving the overall good of world hegemonic economies. Prescriptions of 'good governance' are viciously addressed only to states and communities outside the core Euro–Atlantic states. Even so, good governance articulates a set of arrangements, including institutional renovation, which primarily privileges and disproportionately benefits global producers and consumers.

The paradigm of universal human rights enabled the emergence of the United Nations system as a congregation of faith. Regarded as no omnipotent deity but only as a frail, crisis-ridden arena, it became the privileged historic site for cooperative practices of reshaping the world through the idiom and grammar, as well as the vision, of human rights.

[30] William H. Meyer, 'Human Rights and MNCs: Theory Versus Quantitative Analysis', 18, *Human Rights Quarterly* (1996), 368–97.

[31] World Bank, *Governance: The World Bank's Experience* (1994), xiv; *see also* Catharine Caulfield, *Masters of Illusion: The World Bank and the Poverty of Nations* (1996).

The votaries of economic globalization who proselytize free markets offer the best hope for human redemption capturing this arena. But the residue of the past cultures of universal human rights remains nonetheless, as recently manifested in a UN document that dares to speak about *perverse forms of globalization*: namely, those, which abandon *any* degree of respect for human rights standards and norms.[32]

But, of course, at the end of the day, no United Nations formulation would seriously explore 'perverse forms of globalization', given the emerging global economic realities. The Vienna Conference on Human Rights summed it all up with its poignant preambular reference to 'the spirit of our age' and 'realities of our time'.[33] The 'spirit' is human rights vision; the 'realities' are furnished by headlong and heedless processes of globalization creating in their wake cruel logics of social exclusion and abiding communities of misfortune.

Of course, the continuing appropriation by the forces of capital of hard-won human rights for its own ends is not a *sui generis* event. Long before slavery was abolished, and women got recognition for the right to contest and vote at elections, corporations had appropriated rights to *personhood*, claiming due process rights for regimes of property, denied to human beings.[34] The unfoldment of what I term 'modern' human rights is the story of near-absoluteness of the right to property as a basic human right. So too is the narrative of colonization/imperialism which began its career with the archetypal East India Company (which ruled India for a century) when *corporate sovereignty was inaugurated*. Politics was *commerce* and commerce became *politics*.

So, it might be said, this is the case now. Some would even maintain that it was the case even during the halcyon days of striking human

---

[32] *See* note 17 *supra* I also rely for this prognosis on my own startlingly solitary experience in the mid-1980s as an expert consultant to the United Nations. Requested, on behalf of the Secretary-General, I prepared a report on 'Crimes Against the Right to Development'. I was naturally pleased that the draft report contained generous excerpts from my paper. Within a month, the final draft altogether avoided any reference whatsoever to the five categorie. f crimes against the right to development that I had proposed! *See*, for the text of my submission, Upendra Baxi, *Mambrino's Helmet? Human Rights for a Changing World* (1994), 33–54.

[33] *See*, Upendra Baxi, '"The Spirit of Our Age, The Realities of Our Time": The Vienna Declaration on Human Rights', *Mambrino's Helment? Human Rights for a Changing World?* (1994), 1–18.

[34] *See*, for an analysis of this, by no means complex process, Carl J. Mayer, 'Personalizing the Impersonal: Corporations and the Bill of Rights', 41, *Hastings Law Review* (1990), 576.

rights enunciation (from the Declaration on Permanent Sovereignty over Natural Wealth and Resources to the Declaration on the Right to Development). Peel off the layers of human rights rhetoric, they would maintain, and you will find a core of historic continuity where heroic assertions of human rights remained, in reality and effect, the insignia of triumphant economic interests.

This continuity thesis deserves its moment. It directs attention to facts and feats of politics *of* human rights in ways that ought to moderate, or even cure, the celebrationist approach to human rights (whether human rights *romanticism, mysticism, triumphalism or hedonism*). It alerts us to the fact that the heart of human rights enunciations pulsate with the regular heartbeats of hegemonic interests. It directs us towards a mode of thought that relocates the authorship of human rights away from the politics of intergovernmental desire to that of multitudinous struggles of people against human violation.

If so, is there a paradigm shift or merely an extension of late capitalism, which has always moved (as the readers of *Das Kapital* surely know) across the bourgeois human rights trajectories? This is an important and difficult question. My short answer for the present is that while the appropriation by the capital of human rights logic and rhetoric is not a distinctively novel phenomenon, it is the *scale of reversal* now entailed that marks a radical discontinuity.

Global business practices cancel, for example, many normative gains of contemporary human rights movements through techniques of *dispersal of these evils*. The exploitation of child and sweated labour through free economic zones, and the accompanying sex-based discrimination in even subsistence wages, is the hallmark of contemporary economic globalization. So is the creation of a 'global risk society'[35] and the very legible scripts of 'organized irresponsibility' and 'organized impunity' for corporate offenders, of which the Bhopal catastrophe furnishes a mournful reminder.[36]

What distinguishes the paradigm shift is the doctrine of *legitimation of extraordinary imposition of human suffering* in the cause and the course of the contemporary march of the global capital. In the 'modern' epoch of human rights, such suffering was considered *per se* legitimate. Contemporary human rights logics and paralogics challenged, and at times denied, this self-evident axiom. The paradigm shift seeks to cancel the historic gains of the universal human rights movements, in

---

[35] Ulrich Beck, *The Risk Society* (1992).
[36] *See,* Upendra Baxi, 'Introduction', in *Valiant Victims and Lethal Litigation* (1990), lxix.

apparently irreversible ways. It seeks to mute the voices of suffering and, in the process, regress human rights futures.

VIII. The Materiality of Globalization

The paradigm shift cannot be understood outside the materiality of globalization. By this expression, I wish to signify the *technoscientific mode of production* and the accompanying organic ideology (in a Gramscian sense) that presents itself as redemptive of human suffering. That mode presents itself in several unfolding moments: in the civilian use of nuclear energy, the incredible growth of information technology (digitalization); and the development of new biotechnologies. Each one of these, singly and in combination, threatens us all with the prospect of rendering contemporary human rights language *obsolescent*. Each one of these stands promoted in human rights, human future fulfilling sense. Underlying each of these is the ceaseless promotion of what are conceived and spoken of as 'strategic' new industries whose competitive promotion is, and ought to remain, the be-all and end-all of the contemporary Euro-American directed notions of human progress. The creative energies of the new social-movements, of civil society groups offer resistance, often in the title of human rights, to these new formations of technoscience power. But the challenges thus posed to the universal human rights paradigm grow apace. A brief review must here suffice.

(a) *Nuclear Energy and Weaponry*

The development of nuclear weaponry and energy for civilian uses is coeval with the growth of contemporary human rights, which were born in the context of the Holocaust as well as Hiroshima and Nagasaki. These affect for better or worse, the nature, career, and the future of human rights. The struggles against proliferation, and the movement to end nuclear weapons, have been among the most impressive moments of human solidarity worldwide. They even led to a partnership of professions that initiated a functional equivalent of social action litigation before the World Court on the issue of legality of nuclear weapons.[37] It yielded some human rights gains but it would be difficult to glean as among its achievements the right to peace or even a right to a denuclearized world order.

---

[37] *See*, e.g., *International Law and World Order: A Problem Oriented Case Book* (3rd edn 1997), 1306–19.

The most profound effect on emergent human rights cultures of nuclear military technology was the construction of a security state, which readily converted itself into an order of (what E.P. Thompson described as) the *secret state*.[38] The culture and the cult of official secrecy monopolized information in a few hands and structured censorship that in turn helped promote paranoia and propaganda. The state shield also extended to civilian nuclear energy plants, whether or not state-owned. From the very beginning defence industries secretized the processes of scientific research and technological development and legitimated egregious violation of human rights: experimentation with human subjects,[39] exposure to impermissible levels of radiation to scientific, technical, and menial workers at the site, consensual or coerced exportation of nuclear wastes, escalating orders of health and environmental harm by nuclear test sites and zones, both within and outside national borders, and the development of a policy culture of environmental racism that, most crucially, confiscated indigenous peoples' lands and rights. The Secret State (network of defence establishments, industries, civilian scientists and technologists, and band of select politicians) marks a total negation of human rights. Propaganda of course maintained that the Secret State was the best assurance for the achievement of national, and global security, within which alone rights-talk makes sense. In some sense, the development of biotechnological industries was, as we notice later, to reproduce some of these very features.

Promoted assiduously as 'safe' even as relatively eco-friendly (in comparison to coal mining, and associated violations of the human right to health), the nuclear industry has silenced, everywhere and by all manner of means, issues concerning safety at the workplace, reactor accidents, disposal of toxic, long-life nuclear wastes, and decommissioning of civilian nuclear plants for which no known safe technology exists. The industry representation of exceptions (the Three Mile Island or Chernobyl) proved the rule. Its promoters, at least on Capitol Hill, capped through congressional legislation corporate liability to an order of $560 million, the rest, where required being the responsibility of the federal government, whose regulatory agencies were already captive to the strategic industry.

The amniocentesis of human rights was thus predetermined by patterns of state–industry collaboration, which *normalized* risk-analysis

---

[38] E.P. Thompson, *Writing by Candlelight* (1980), 149–80.
[39] *See*, Kelvin M. King, 'A Proposal for the Effective International Regulation of Biomedical Research Involving Human Subjects', 34, *Stanford Journal of International Law* (1998), 163.

·to the point of industry-oriented, rather than *human rights-oriented*, risk analysis and management. Movements, both social and human rights specific, were thus constrained, from the start, by the logic of this state–industry combine. Pitted against the state/technoscientific combine, social movements, including human rights movements, were reduced to confrontation over locale decisions, nuclear waste disposal, and eventual decommissioning public choice decisions. The might of the state-industry combine has proved, however, overwhelming for human rights theory and action.

The industry marshals languages of risk-analysis and risk-management to which human rights languages have yet to provide an effective response. If scientific and 'menial' workers stood exposed to radiation risks, of course these are at once presented as minimal, of no different order than those involved in conventional uses of energy. When state-of the art nuclear safe technology fails, this is said to be due only to an inefficient state management (as in Chernobyl). Nuclear technocrats surely have better answers to the safety of reactors than ill-informed, loud-mouthed, and scientifically illiterate public opinion leaders and movements. In any case, we are asked, isn't it true that more human beings perish in road accidents, drug addiction, smoking-induced ailments, premature sport fatalities and AIDS epidemiologies? What the nuclear czars ignore is the order of mutagenic risks thus entailed. Who, however, can then say in the state even of post-Hiroshima/Nagasaki discourse, what the environmental and health risks may be, given the World Court's recent determination on the impossibility of determination of the hazards of nuclear weaponry?[40] Nothing further, they maintain, needs to be said against the 'obscurantism' of human rights movements. Should we rather not accept the delightful insouciance of James Schlesinger, the Chair of the AEC, who observed an underground explosion of a nuclear device at Amchitka, Alaska, saying: '*It's fun for the kids and my wife, delighted to get away from the house for awhile!*'[41] Thus it comes to pass, in these halcyon days of globalization, that the corporate image of weekend 'fun' symbolizes a badge of nuclear safety for human beings and their environment.

Of course the rights of affected local communities in their radically altered environments are gravely jeopardized, as Chernobyl showed. The testing of nuclear weapons has the same adverse effect, as shown by the plight of affected people in Pokharan, Rajasthan; indeed the

---

[40] *See supra* note 37.
[41] James Ridgeway and Jeffrey St. Claire, *A Pocket Guide to Environmental Bad Guys* (1998), 100 (emphasis added).

Indian Prime Minister was heard to say in justification that some citizens had patriotically to bear the burden of India's pride in acquiring nuclear weapons capacity.

The post Cold War 'decommissioning' of nuclear weapons masks many an unconscionable human, and human rights violation. As many as 13,233 weapons or warheads were 'disassembled' 'in the US in 1982–92 at an average of 1300 per annum[42] and an estimated 10,000 warheads are to be dismantled in the 1990s; one does not have any information on the Russian side. The life of contaminant waste was estimated to be: 700 million years for Uranium–235; 24,000 years for Plutonium–239;[43] and six million years for Plutonium–240; similar problems, though on a lesser scale, exist for aging nuclear power plants.[44]

This somewhat summary narration, despite being judgemental, is intended to convey that nuclearization constitutes a dominant and determinant domain of the materiality of globalization. It is a force of production that suspends the ethical order. It also produces certain superstructures, among them the emergence of a New International Military Order[45] at war with the logic and rhetoric of contemporary human rights enunciations and movement[46] and war too with its own distinctive hegemonic logics by and subordination of civic cultures, legal orders, and belief systems.

Besides, the current movement towards reduction of nuclear weaponry while open to a human rights reading, is dictated more decisively by inner strategic compulsions in a post-Cold War scenario as shown by the carefully orchestrated Bush administration compaign for the re-nuclearization of the world. The future of human rights remains as fractured as it was for the past half century.

(b) *Digitalization*

Enwombed in the defence industry, the emergence of information technology is decisive transformation. The contemporary world has been

---

[42] US Office of Technology Assessment, *Dismantling the Bomb and Managing the Nuclear Materials* (1993); *see also Aging Nuclear Power Plants; Managing Plant Life and Decommissioning* (1993).

[43] *See, Dismantling the Bomb* (1993), 68.

[44] *See, Aging Nuclear Plants* (1993), 101–47.

[45] *See,* Anthony Giddens, *The Consequences of Modernity* (1990), 63–78, 183. He depicts 'globalization' as a mix of four orders, defining the cartography of the human condition: the nation state system, international division of labour, world capitalist economy, and world military order.

[46] Soaring arms expenditures and unconscionably high defence budgets have forever deferred the 'progressive realization' of social, economic and cultural rights.

transformed in several ways by the revolution in microchips and integrated circuitry. First, it enables patterns of time–space compression, a defining feature of contemporary globalization.[47] Second, it makes real the hitherto unimaginable advances in genetic sciences and strategic biotechnology industries: advances in recombinant DNA technologies depend wholly on revolutionary techniques of artificial intelligence.[48] Third, it threatens the very foundations of a secret state monopoly over weapons of mass destruction. Fourth, this development provides a driving force for the global emergence of TRMFHR. Fifth, it leads a movement towards redefinitions of impoverishment: poverty is no longer to be identified in terms of material deprivations but in terms of access to information or to cyberspace. Thus, one hears of 'dead' or 'wild' zones of the urban impoverished in terms of cyber-poverty, rather than in those of the right to food, housing, and health.[49] The new South is cyber-poor; the new North is cyber-rich. Sixth, we have the emergence of network society[50] in which political practices are heavily mediated by the time–place of privatized mass media, and one in which human and social suffering becomes heavily commoditized and fungible, to a point where it appears to lack any voice or future outside corporate media packaging. Seventh, the emergence of information technologies has facilitated widespread privatization of governance functions, whether in, education and research, health and sanitation, banking and finance, transport and telecommunications. Eighth, robotics has had enormous impacts on nations of work and leisure, and patterns of systemic underemployment.[51] Ninth, this emergence makes incoherent old approaches to regulation by means of law, policy, and administration as the current controversy over subjection of Microsoft to the US antitrust jurisprudence and over the regulation of the flows of obscene and violent traffic over the internet shows. Finally (without being exhaustive), digitalization of the world provides time-place for increased and voluminous solidarity among new social movements, nourishing as well as fatal to contemporary human rights cultures.[52] The halcyon days of mass movements tend to be replaced by performative acts in cyberspace.

These ten features symbolize many complex and interlocking challenges for human rights enunciations and movements. One thing

---

[47] Robertson, *supra* note 3 at 8–33; David Harvey, *Justice, Nature and the Geography of Difference* (1996), 207–328.

[48] *See supra* notes 8, 9, 10.

[49] Scott Lash and John Urry, *Economies of Sign and Space* (1994), 145–171.

[50] Manuel Castells, *The Rise of the Network Society* (1996).

[51] Gorz, *supra* note 7.

[52] *See* Castells, *The Power of Identity* (1997), 68–109.

is, however, clear. The patterns of global hegemony of ownership of cyber-technology, and consequent cyber-vassalage, are here to stay and grow, further enhancing the North–South inequities unless human rights movements foster new futures for the cyber-proletariat. It is also clear that instant email solidarities, while serving to arrest (as the reformation of the MAI shows), carry with them the danger of making local mass movements almost irrelevant to the making of the future human rights. Indeed, as the monumental analysis of Castells shows, Cyber Solidarity while enhancing the power of social movements in the cause of human rights may also escalate the potential of social movements that seek to name the very order of contemporary human rights as an *order of evil*.

(c) *Biotechnology*

If the early decades of the second half of the Christian twentieth century were dominated by extensive civilian and military uses of nuclear power, the latter decades have been marked by the pervasive break-throughs in the field of genetics. The advances in recombinant DNA engineering have been spectacularly wide-ranging and relate to almost every area of human life. Dependent on advances in cyber technology, a whole variety of new biotechnologies have given rise to the formation, on the one hand, of 'technosciences'[53] and strategic industries on the other.[54] Together, these constitute a genomic materiality of globalization (little noticed in social theory narratives of globalization) contributing to the formation of 'New World Order, Inc.'[55] Biotechnologies, united in the pursuit of reductionist life sciences— where 'life' is no more than information open to techno-science codification, manipulation, and diverse techniques of mutation and reproduction—fall into several domains. Each domain promises the 'greatest human good'. Agricultural biotechnology, fostered by agribusiness, promises food for all; pharmaceutical biotechnology promises health for all; industrial biotechnology promises sustainable development for the world and the human genome projects, among other things, now promise new possibilities in therapeutics and herald

[53] Donna Haraway, *Modest-Witness@ Second-Millennium. Femaleman* -*Meets*-*Oncomouse*™: *Feminism and Technoscience* (1997).

[54] Dan L. Burk and Barbara A. Boczar, 'Biotechnology and Tort Liability: A Strategic Industry at Risk', 55, *University of Pittsburgh Law Review* (1994), 791; Office of Technology Assessment, U.S.Congress, *New Developments in Biotechnology: U.S. Investment in Biotechnology* (1998) 78–9; Calestous Juma, *The Gene Hunters* (1989).

[55] Haraway, *supra* note 53 at 151–72.

the threshold of 'benign' human cloning. The belief that biotechnology provides unprecedented vistas of human progress is not just media hype; its practitioners, in all parts of the world, live by it. It is an article of faith with this community that, no matter what human rights and social movements may say about the human and social costs entailed in the processes of genetic research, experimentation, and application, the overall gain to humankind is so immense as to render any social critique counter-productive.[56]

The mode of construction of progress narrative has little use for the old paradigm of human rights, based as it is on notions that corporate technoscience now renders obsolete. The essentialist ideas animating this paradigm now seem insensible, insofar as these invoke the notion of inviolability of that which constitutes the distinctively 'human' and the 'dignity' that should invest that 'human'. Technoscience constructs the notion of being human altogether differently as hi-tech, capital-intensive sites of research and innovation, where being human is constituted by an ever so readily available and exploitable ensemble of genetic information. What is human is truly a cyborg (in Dona Haraway's inimitable conception).[57] Notions based on the integrity of the body, for example, make very little sense because the 'body' is now big business.[58] Genetic information in bodily tissues, parts, fluids, emanations, and wastes, including the DNA of 'vanishing' indigenous people,[59] has now become the common *corporate heritage of humankind*. What 'dignity' and 'integrity' may we attach, outside the considerations of management of ploughing in super-profits for billion dollar biotech strategic industries to human particulate matter, these tidbits of a gigantic genetic seesaw, is a question considered not merely unworthy of a sustained response but as a frivolous mode of interlocution.

There is no doubt that in some ways technoscience must remain accountable. This accountability is, however, owed to technocratic peer groups not to 'people' at large who are both scientifically pre-literate and at the same time avid consumers of sundry biotech Santa

---

[56] *See*, Martha Nussbaum and Cass R. Sunstein (eds), *Clones: Facts and Fantasies About Human Cloning* (1998).

[57] Donna Haraway, *Siminans, Cyborgs and Women: The Reinvention of Nature* (1991).

[58] E. Richard Gold, *Body Parts: Rights and Owonership of Human Biological Materials* (1996); Dorothy Nelkin and Lori B. Andrews, 'Homo Economicus: Commercialization of Body Tissue in the Age of Biotechnology', 28, Hastings Centre Report (1998), 14–22.

[59] Ibid. at 17.

Claus bearing r-DNA stockings, the gifts of health—the promise of cure of dreaded genetic diseases, xenotransplants, life-sustaining therapies, incredible diagnostic immunioessay toolkits, genetic enhancements, long shelf-life genetically mutated foods and beverages, and the future markets for bodily spare parts through human clones.

In a great inversion, then, the global communities of techno-scientists, not the 'duly' elected representatives of the people, become the custodians of public policy and human futures. The category of 'people', a suspect category in much of non-socialist democratic theory, to whom accountability is owed now gets replaced by the category of needy consumers. Their legitimation derives in responding to these peoples' needs, wants, and desires. Law, policy, and administration must then stand in fiduciary relationship to potential of self-regulation amongst the technoscientific peer-groups. These understand best the need for self-restraint on where to go next and how far to go. Also 'they' do not constitute a monolithic community: the dissenting academies within peer group knowledge production modes, will insure against errancy and profligacy of technoscience development. In such a situation, neither legislative policy nor judicial oversight furnish the best model for public regulation.[60] Surely, trans-science comprising questions that can be 'asked of science and yet cannot be answered by science'[61] must be best left to those who know what technoscience is, and not to outsiders who at best can only practice 'junk' science.[62]

The death of regulation, or deregulation as a form of regulation, is a defining mode of genomic culture now upon us.[63] From Asilomar to the current debates on human cloning, the progress narrative of biotechnology constructs mid reconstructs the selfsame scenario of self-regulation: proclaim technoscientific concern about new developments, declare self-imposed moratoria on some kinds of research, encourage well-managed interrogation of mega-science, promulgate regimes of hi-tech, non-transparent self-regulation, thus preempting public oversight, and allow a cascading takeover by special interests of the public arena, precluding popular constructions of risk, mayhem, and injury. A new global public of technoscientists thus constitutes the public sphere that controls discursive will-formation and public opinion

---

[60] Susanne Wright, *Molecular Politics* (1984); *see also infra* note 62.

[61] Alvin M. Weinberg, 'Science and Transcience', *Minerva* (1972), 209–22.

[62] Kenneth R. Foster and Peter W. Huber, *Judging Science: Scientific Knowledge and the Federal Courts* (1999); Peter W. Huber, *Galileo's Revenge: Junk Science in the Courtroom* (1993).

[63] *See* Wright, *supra* note 60.

making—the *sine qua non* of the production of 'legitimate law' (to invoke a phrase of Habermas) in postmodern societies.

Despite all this, this new formation nourishes itself on some old elements of the human rights paradigm, transforming it, though in Mosanto–Du Pont–Shell terms of the TRMFHR. The right to perform scientific research is presented as immanent in the model of free speech; so is the right to experiment, mostly without 'informed consent'.[64] The right to privacy, through its reincarnations as the right to publicity[65] and as a competitive right to know-how and trade secrecy, becomes paramount. All human rights become trade and investment related, empowering the Northern industrial–military complexes to further enhance the inequities of the New World Order Inc. 'Nature', and the very notion of a deep ecological self, sustaining the environmental and human rights movements, becomes corporate raw material merchandise.

(d) *The Situatedness of Movements*

Human rights and social movements are already thus situated in the new paradigm, and have begun to work within it in many complex ways. Perhaps, the most complex of these modes is oppositional, as with the full history of the surprising results obtained by a coalition of NGOs in aborting the first draft text of the MAI and in producing a more sustained framework of participation in dialogue with 'civil society'. I describe this mode as complex because the opposition to the MAI was not, in my impression, so much based on mass mobilization as in the case of the GATT/WTO proposals but was rather a conversation among 'radical' professional experts, networking the informed NGOs with growing support of kindred souls ensconed within cyberspace. The terms of discourse were set by those who saw no difficulty in putting on paper the sovereign profile of the foreign investor. It was time to be explicit on behalf of global capital, accustomed to regulatory capture in several arenas, and experience and wisdom indicated the overall gains of getting the adversary to fight within the strategically choosen terrain. How 'radical' can then the oppositional discourse be? It may not deny the importance of direct foreign investment; it may not advocate any

---

[64] *See* King, *supra* note 39, raising the issue of the woeful inadequacy of the ICCPR standards on the right to informed consent. Indeed, what is required is not so much *informed consent* (which in any case lay people can scarcely understand) but the human right to *full disclosure* of the material benefits that biotech multinationals may derive from commercial uses by pharmaceutical biotech industries.

[65] Gold, *supra* note 58, at 86–106.

more regimes of nationalization and state finance capitalism; nor may it challenge the idea that global capital, personified in several modes, may indeed share the logics and the language of human rights discourse. All that it may insist on is the rolling back the extensive derogations from the contemporary human rights normativity. At the same time, the derogations exist *de facto*. The power of the current campaigns against the MAI of course justify a degree of triumphalism; an invaluable resource after all for the morale of collectivities that seek to roll back the tide of future histories of globalization. One needs to ask, that feature amply conceded: what remains?

To such interrogation, a major answer is to say that what remains is more than the *volksgeist*, in a manner of speaking the Spirit of the Sixties; a site for romantic revival in a post-romantic era of globalization, a process of interlocution of power in all its global hiding places. Though this in itself is an important revival,[66] what matters is the way in which the rather technical, and at times esoteric, issues of world trade and finance were demystified and presented as human rights issues. The MAI campaign marks, hopefully, a beginning of a process of partnerships between activist NGOs and professional experts in the context of extraordinary assertions of rights by global capital. At the same time, the new paradigm confronts human rights movements to be more *process,* and less, *result* oriented. Human rights, in an age of new global forces of production, have a future only to the extent that dissenting academics begin to converse, on a common platform, with anti-globalization activists in ways that respect the integrity of each form: activists do not become academics and academics may not become activists.

However crudely put this distinction is, any worthwhile mode of resistance to globalization demands this. Dissenting academics require to be seen as academics in the eyes of the peer group; otherwise they lose its support and legitimation, and with it the access to resources needed to develop counter-knowledges useful to social activism. Activist groups, likewise, remain wary of specialists that move in and out of the corridors of power. Both may lay claim to relevant knowledges and

---

[66] Surely, the recovery of the histories of imagination of popular movements is far more crucial to the actual accomplishment in here-and-now struggles, because these histories enhance human solidarity. The perfection of practices of political memory, is a resource for the future of human rights. The struggle of men (and women) over power, as Milan Kundera memorably said, is the struggle of memory over 'forgetting'. To this I add a footnote: Contrary to the public adage, public memory is not short; rather it is made short or shortened by those whose pursuit of power and profit requires the organization of oblivion of human violation and injustice.

insights that the other may never have. No member of the dissenting academy can quite claim the grasp of organic knowledges that arise through everyday struggles against modes of existence and the orders of resistance; no activist can claim access to technoscientific knowledges that *do matter* for peoples' struggles. The partnership between professionals and peoples evolves a pattern of uneasy coalitions. The very materiality of globalization, and its TRMFHR superstructures, call for the invention of sustained, and sustainable, modes of partnership between the practitioners of erudite and organic knowledges.

From the point of view of the managers and agents of the processes of globalization, these forms of knowledges are commodities that can be transacted through ever growing human rights markets. Members of the dissenting academies and NGO entrepreneurs, the innovators of social action, seem constantly needed, and often in large numbers, by the United Nations agencies, international and regional financial institutions, development networks, the mass media, and leading foundations. The belief that working within these frameworks is crucial to the future of human rights, is on a high growth curve. Partnership between these commoditized niches of knowledges and social action, on the one hand, and those who work on the ground, and the field, with and for peoples and communities in struggle, is often presented as the best hope there is for the future of human rights; a partnership presented in frankly welfare dialogical terms.[67] It is my impression (and I hope that I am wrong) that these ways of foreclosing the imagination of alternatives are the ways best known, for a *very long while*, to the 'cunning of the capital'.

The phrase that so dominates practices of resistance to the TRMFHR is the 'creation of space'. However, the *places* created by the activist created *spaces* stand, to a large extent predetermined by contemporary globalization.[68] Is the contemporary human rights mode of resistance to globalization historically adequate to retrieve the human rights *movement* from the market?

[67] When some of us, leading a campaign against the UNDP's Global Sustainable Development Facility met (in May 1998) the head of the agency, he opened the meeting with an account of his own early entailment as an environmental activist now confronted with the need to evolve an agenda of partnership in the mainstreaming of human rights oriented development. Did we have any guidance to offer him? he asked. His concern for the impoverished people and countries was genuine; but so was his concern to move the agency's future forward; so, too was his belief that dialogue with multinational corporations was imperative. Dialogue however requires commonality in the pursuit of aims. How is that to be established save on the terms already preset?

[68] Harvey, *supra* note 47.

References and Bibliography

Agnes, Flavia (1999): *Law and Gender Inequality: The Politics of Women's Rights in India* (Delhi: Oxford University Press).

Alston, Philip (1991): 'Revitalizing United Nations Work on Human Rights and Development', 18, *Melbourne University Law Review*, 216.

American Anthropological Association, The Executive Board (1947): 'Statement on Human Rights', 49, *American Anthropologist*, 539.

American Association for World Health: *Denial of Food and Medicine: The Impact of U.S. Embargo on Health and Nutrition in Cuba* (visited 24 October 1998) http://www.usengage.org./studies/cuba.html.

An-Naim, Abdullahi (1992): *Human Rights in a Cross Cultural Perspective: Quest for Consensus* (Philadelphia: University of Pennsylvania Press).

An-Pyong, Jik (1979): 'Han Yougun's Liberalism: An Analysis of the Reformation of Korean Buddhism', 19, *Korea Journal*, 3–18.

Appadurai, Arjun (1997): *Modernity at Large: Cultural Dimensions of Globalization* (Delhi: Oxford University Press).

Aquinas, St. Thomas (1989): *The Literal Exposition on Job: Scriptural Commentary on Providence*, Anthony Damico (trs.) (Atlanta, Georgia: Scholar's Press).

Arendt, Hannah (1958): *The Human Condition* (Chicago: Chicago University Press).

Asad, Talal (1997): 'On Torture, or Cruel, Inhuman or Degrading Treatment', Arthur Kleinman, Veena Das, and Margaret Lock (eds), *Social Suffering*, 285 (Berkeley: University of California Press).

Baier, Anette (1987): 'The Need for More Than Science', *Science, Morality and Feminist Theory*, Marsha Haen and Kia Neilsen (eds) 47 (Calgary: University of Calgary Press).

Baier, Kurt (1965): *The Moral Point of View* (Itacha, New York: Cornell University Press).

Balkin, J.M. (1998): *Cultural Software* (New Haven: Yale University Press).

Barsh, Russel(1994) 'Indigenous Peoples in 1990s: From Object to Subject of International Law', 7, *Harvard Human Rights Journal*, 33.

Bassiouni, M. Cherif (1994): 'Enforcing Human Rights Through International Criminal Law and Through International Criminal Court', *Human Rights:*

An Agenda for the Next Century, L. Henkin and L. Hardgrave (eds) (Washington D.C.: American Society of International Law).

Bauman, Zygmunt (1998): *Globalization: The Human Consequences* (Cambridge: Polity Press).

Baxi, Upendra (2001): 'Preface', *Judicial Activism in India*, S.P. Sathe (Delhi: Oxford University Press).

——(2000): 'The Avatars of Judicial Activism: Explorations in the geography of (In) Justice', *Fifty Years of the Supreme Court of India: Its grasp and Reach*, S.K. Verma and Kusum (eds.), 156–209 (Delhi: Oxford University Press and Indian Law Institute).

——(1999): 'Voices of Suffering, Fragmented Universality and the Future of Human Rights', *The Future of International Human Rights*, Burns H. Weston and Stephen P. Marks (eds), 101–56 (New York: Ardsley, Transnational Publishers).

——(1999): 'Human Rights: Between Suffering and Market', *Global Social Movements*, 32–45, Robin Cohen and Shirin Rai (eds) (London: Altheone).

——(1999): 'From Human Rights to the Right to be a Woman', *Engendering Law: Essays in Honour of Professor Lotika Sarkar*, Amita Dhandha and Archana Prasher (eds) 275–90 (Lucknow: Eastern Book Co.).

——(1998): 'The State and the Human Rights Movements in India', *People's Rights: Social Movements and the State in the Third World*, Manoranjan Mohanty, Partha Nath Mukherji and Olle Törnquist (eds), 335–52 (New Delhi: Sage Publications).

——(1998): 'The Development of the Right to Development', *Human Rights: New Dimensions and Challenges*, Janus Symondies (ed.), 99–116 (Hants: Dartmouth).

——(1997) 'Human Rights Education: The Promise of the Twenty-First Century?', *Human Rights Education*, George Andreopoulos and Richard Pierre Claude (eds), 142–54 (Philadelphia: University of Pennsylvania Press).

——(1996) 'The "Reason" of Human Rights and the "Unreason" of Globalization', University of Bombay, The First A.R. Desai Memorial Lecture (mimeo).

——and Amita Dhanda (eds) (1990): *Valiant Victims and Lethal Litigation* (Bombay: N.M. Tripathi).

——(1996): 'Global Neighbourhood and Universal Otherhood: Notes on the Report of Commission on Global Governance', 21, *Alternatives*, 525–49.

——(1995): 'Justice as Emancipation: 'The Legacy of Babasaheb Ambedkar' Upendra Baxi and Bhikhu Parekh (eds), 122–49 (New Delhi: Sage).

——(1994): *Inhuman Wrongs and Human Rights: Unconventional Essays* (Delhi: Har Anand).

——(1994): *Mambrino's Helmet?: Human Rights for a Changing World* (Delhi: Har Anand).

——(1993): *Marx, Law and Justice* (Bombay: N.M. Tripathi).

——(1989): 'Taking Suffering Seriously: Social Action Litigation Before the Supreme Court of India', in *Law and Poverty: Critical Essays* 387–415 (Bombay: N.M. Tripathi).

——(1986): *Inconvenient Forum and Convenient Catastrophe: The Bhopal Case* (Bombay: N.M. Tripathi).

——and Thomas Paul (eds)(1985): *Mass Disasters and Multinational Liability: The Bhopal Case* (Bombay: N.M. Tripathi).

——(1982): *The Crisis of Indian Legal System* (Delhi: Vikas)

Beck, Ulrich (1998): *Democracy Without Enemies* (Cambridge: Polity Press).

——(1992): *The Risk Society* (London: Sage).

——(1996): *The Reinvention of Politics* (Cambridge: Polity Press).

Becker, Gary (1981): *A Treatise on the Family* (Cambridge, Mass.: Harvard University Press).

Benthall, Jonathan (1993): *Disasters, Relief and the Media* (I.B. Tauras and Co. Ltd.).

Bourdieu, Pierre (1993): *The Field of Cultural Production* (New York: Columbia University Press).

——(1977): *Outline of a Theory of Practice* (Cambridge: Cambridge University Press).

Boutros-Boutros Ghali (1993): 'The Common Language of Humanity', in *United Nations: World Conference on Human Rights, the Vienna Declaration and Program of Action* (Vienna).

Brenner, Robert (1998): 'The Economy of Global Turbulence: A Special Report on the World Economy, 1950–98', 229, *New Left Review.*

Brown, Wendy (1995): *States of Injury: Power and Freedom in Late Modernity* (Princeton: Princeton University Press).

Buchanan, Allen (1991): *Secession: Morality of Political Divorce* (Boulder: Westview Press).

——(1982) *Marx and Justice: The Radical Critique of Liberalism* (London: Methuen).

Burk, Dan L. and Barbara A. Boczar (1994): 'Biotechnology and Tort Liability: Strategic Industry at Risk', 55, *University of Pittsburgh Law Review*, 191.

Burley, Justin (ed.) (1999): *The Genetic Revolution and Human Rights: The Oxford Amnesty Lectures 1998* (Oxford: Oxford University Press).

Butler, Judith (1990): *Gender-Trouble: Feminism and the Subversion of Identity* (London: Routledge).

Cassels, Jamie (1993): *The Uncertain Promise of Law: Lessons from Bhopal* (Toronto: University of Toronto Press).

Castells, Manuel (1997) *The Power of Identity* (Oxford: Blackwell).

——(1996) *The Rise of Network Society* (Oxford: Blackwell).

Caufeld, Catharine (1996): *Masters of Illusion: The World Bank and Poverty of Nations* (New York: Henry Holt).

Cavell, Stanley (1997): 'Comments on Veena Das's Essay "Language and Body: Transactions in the Construction of Pain"', *Social Suffering*, 93.

Charnovitz, Steve (1997): 'Two Centuries of Participation: NGOs and Human Rights', 18, *Michigan Journal of International Law*, 183.

Chomsky, Noam (1994): *World Orders: Old and New* (New York: Columbia University Press).

——(1996) *Power and Prospects: Reflections on Human Nature* (Boston: Southend Press).

Cohen, Stanley (1995): *Denial and Acknowledgement: The Impact of Information About Human Rights* (Jerusalem: The Hebrew University).

Commission on Human Rights (1997): *The Realization of Economic, Social and Cultural Rights: The Relationship between Enjoyment of Human Rights and Income Distribution* (Final report of the Special Rapporteur Jose Bengoa), UN Doc. E/CN.4/Sub2/1997/9, 30 June 1997.

——Commission on Human Rights, Sub-commission on Prevention of Discrimination and the Protection of Minorities (1990): *Study Concerning the Right to Restitution, Compensation, and Rehabilitation for Victims of Gross Violations of Human Rights and Fundamental Freedoms* (Theo von Boven, Special Rapporteur) UN DOC E/CN.4/SUB.2/1990, 10, 26 July 1990.

——Commission on Human Rights (1990): *Report on the Consequences of Impunity*, UN Doc. E/CN.4/1990/13.

Copjec, Joan (ed.) (1996): *Radical Evil* (London: Verso).

Cover, Robert (1987): 'Foreword: Nomos and Narrative,' 97, *Harvard Law Review*, 62.

Cranston, Maurice (1983): 'Are There Any Human Rights', 112, *Daedalus*, 1–17.

Daniel, E. Valentine (1997): *Chapters in an Anthropology of Violence: Sri Lankans, Sinhalas, and Tamils* (Delhi: Oxford University Press).

Das, Veena (1997): 'Language and Body Transactions in the Construction of Pain', *Social Suffering*, 67.

——(1995): *Critical Events: An Anthropological Perspective on Contemporary India* (Delhi: Oxford University Press).

——(1994): 'Moral Orientations to Suffering', L.C. Chen, N. Ware and A. Klienman (eds), *Health and Social Change* (Cambridge Mass.: Harvard University Press).

Davison, James Dale and Rees-Mogg (1997): *The Sovereign Individual* (Touchstone Books).

Debord, Guy (1970): *The Society of Spectacle* (Detroit, MI: Black & Red).

——(1990): *Comments on the Society of Spectacle* (London: Verso).

Derrida, Jacques (1994): *The Sceptres of Marx: The State of Debt, the Work of Mourning and the New International* (London, Routledge).

——(1992): 'The Mystical Foundation of Authority', *Deconstruction and Possibility of Justice*, 3, Drucilla Cornell, Michel Rosenfeld and David Gray Carlson (eds) (London: Routledge).

Donnelly, Jack (1985): 'In Search of a Unicorn: The Jurisprudence and Politics of the Right to Development', 15, *California Western International Law Journal*, 473.

Duggard, John (1999): 'Reconciliation and Justice: The South African Experience', *The Future of International Human Rights*, 399–422.

Eco, Umberto (1995): *Apocalypse Postponed*, Robert Lumley (ed.) (London: Flamingo).

Esposito, John L. (1995): *The Islamic Threat: Myth or Reality?* new edn, (Oxford: Oxford University Press).

Esteva, Gustava and Madhuri Suri Prakash (1998): *Grassroots Postmodernism* (London: Zed Books).

Falk, Richard (1995): *Explorations at the Edge of Time: The Prospects for World Order* (Princeton: Princeton University Press).

Featherstone, Mike (1995): *Undoing Cultures: Globalization, Postmoderism and Identity* (London: Sage).

Ferry, Luc (1992): *The New Ecological Order* (Chicago: University of Chicago Press).

Fitzpatrick, Peter (1993): *The Mythology of Modern Law* (London: Routledge).

Food First Information and Action Network (FIAN) (1996): *Twelve Misconceptions About the Right to Food* (Heidelberg).

Foster, Kenneth R. and Peter M. Huber (1999): *Judging Science: Scientific Knowledge and the Federal Courts* (Cambridge, Mass.: The MIT Press).

Foucault, Michel (1989): *Foucault Live Interviews 1966–84,* Sylvere Lotringer (ed.) (New York: Semiotext).

Frankena, William K. (1963): *Ethics* (New York: Prentice Hall).

Frug, Mary Jo (1995): 'A Postmodernist Feminist Legal Manifesto', *After Identity: A Reader in Law and Culture*, Dan Danielson and Karen Eagle (eds) 7–23, (London: Routledge).

Galtung, Johan (1994): *Human Rights in Another Key* (Oxford: Blackwell).

Gauthier, David (1986): *Morals by Agreement* (Oxford: Oxford University Press).

George, Susan (1994): *A Fate Worse than Debt* (Hammondsworth: Penguin).

Gewirth, Allan (1996): *The Community of Rights* (Chicago: University of Chicago Press).

——(1977): *Reason and Morality* (Chicago: University of Chicago Press).

Gibson-Graham, K.J. (1996): *The End of Capitalism (as we knew it): A Feminist Critique of Political Economy* (Oxford: Blackwell).

Giddens, Anthony (1990): *The Consequences of Modernity* (Cambridge: Polity Press).

Gillies, David (1996): *Between Principle and Practice: Human Rights in the North-South Relations* (McGill: Queens University Press).

Gilligan, Carol (1982): *In a Different Voice: Psychological Theory and Women's Development* (Cambridge: Harvard University Press).

Giorgetti, Chiara (1999): 'From Rio to Kyoto: A Study of the Involvement of Non-governmental Organizations in Negotiations on Climate Change', 7, *New York University. Environmental Law Journal*, 199–244.

Glasman, Maurice (1996): *Unnecessary Suffering: Managing Market Utopia* (London: Verso).

Glendon, Mary Ann (1991): *Rights Talk: The Impoverishment of Political Discourse* (New York: Free Press).

Gold, Richard E. (1996): *Body Parts: Property and Ownership Over Biological Materials* (Washington: Georgetown University Press).

Goldmann, Daniel Jonah (1996): *Hitler's Willing Executioners: Ordinary Germans and the Holocaust* (Boston: Little Brown).

Gorz, Andrew (1982): *Farewell to the Working Class: An Essay on Postindustrial Socialism,* Michael Sonenscher (trs.) (London: Pluto Press).

Gouldner, Alvin (1976): *The Dialectic of Ideology and Technology: The Origins, Grammar and Future of Ideology* (Basingstoke: Macmillan).

Granier, Jean (1985): 'Perspectivism as Interpretation', *The New Nietzsche*, David B. Allison (ed.), 190, (Cambridge, Mass.: The MIT Press).

Greer, Jed and Kenny Bruno (1996): *Greenwash: The Reality Behind Corporate Environmentalism* (Penang: Third World Network; New York: The Apex Press).

Guha, Ranajit (1988): *Subaltern Studies: Writings on South Asian History and Society* (Delhi: Oxford University Press).

Gutto, Shadrack B. (1993): *Human Rights and Peoples' Rights for the Oppressed: Critical Essays on the Theory and Practice from Sociology of Law Perspectives* (Lund: University of Lund Press).

Habermas, Jurgen (1996): *Between Facts and Norms: Contributions Towards a Discourse Theory of Ethics,* William Rehg (trs.) (Cambridge, Mass.: The MIT Press).

Hannum, Hurst (1996): *Autonomy, Sovereignty and Self-Determination: The Accommodation of Conflicting Rights* (Philadelphia: University of Pennsylvania Press).

——(1993) 'Rethinking Self-Determination', 34, *Virginia Journal International Law*, 1.

Haraway, Donna . (1997): *Modest_witness@ Second Millennium. Femaleman©_Meets_Oncomouse™* (London: Routledge).

——(1991): *Simians, Cyborgs and Women: The Reinvention of Nature* (New York: Routledge).

Harr, Jonathan (1997): *A Civil Action* (New York: Vintage).

Harvard Human Rights Program (1997): *Truth Commissions: A Comparative Assessment.*

Harvey, David (1996): *Justice, Nature and the Geography of Difference* (Oxford: Blackwell).

Hayner, Priscilla (1997): 'Fifteen-Truth Commissions, 1974 to 1994: A Comparative Assessment', 16, *Human Rights Quarterly*, 597.

Heller, Agnes (1990): 'The Contingent Person and Existential Choice', in *Hermeneutics: Critical Theory in Ethics and Politics*, M. Kelly (ed.), 52–69 (Cambridge, Mass.: The MIT Press).

Herskovits, Melville J. (1955): *Cultural Anthropology* (New York: Alfred Knopf).

Hirst, Paul and Grahame Thompson (1996): *Globalization in Question: The International Economy and Possibilities of Governance* (Cambridge: Polity Press).

Huber, Peter W. (1993): *Galileo's Revenge: Junk Science in the Courtroom* (New York: Basic Books).

Jacobson, David (1996): *Rights Without Borders: Immigration and the Decline of Citizenship* (Baltimore: The Johns Hopkins University Press).

Jagger, Allison K. (1983): *Feminist Politics and Human Nature* (New York: Rowman and Littlefield).

Jameson, Fredric (1981): *The Political Unconscious: Narrative as a Socially Symbolic Act* (North Carolina: Duke University Press).

Juma, Calestous (1989): *The Gene Hunters: Biotechnology and the Scramble for Seeds* (Princeton: Princeton University Press).

Kazanov, M. (1995): *After the USSR: Ethnicity, Nationalism and Politics in the Commonwealth of Independent States* (Madison: University of Wisconsin Press).

Kelsey, Jane (1999): *Reclaiming the Future: New Zealand and the Global Economy* (Auckland: Bridget Williams Books).

——(1995) *The New Zealand Experiment: A World Model for Structural Adjustment?*, reprinted as *Economic Fundamentalism* (London: Pluto Press).

Kennedy, Paul (1993): *Preparing for the Twenty-First Century* (New York: Harper and Row).

King, Kelvin M. (1998): 'A Proposal for the Effective International Regulation of Biomedical Research Involving Human Subjects', *Stanford Journal of International Law*, 163.

Kleinman, Arthur and Joan (1997): 'The Appeal of Experience; The Dismay of Images: Cultural Appropriations of Suffering in Our Times', in *Social Suffering*, 1.

Kothari, Miloon (ed.) (1999): *Development and Social Action* (London: Oxfam Publications).

Krimski, Sheldon (1991): *Biotechnics and Society: The Rise of Industrial Genetics* (New York: Praeger).

Kritz, Neil J. (ed.) (1995): *Transitional Justice: How Emerging Democracies Reckon with Former Regimes*, 3 vols. (United States Institute of Peace).

Kundera, Milan (1991) *Immortality* (New York: Harper).

Kymlica, Will (1995): *Multicultural Citizenship: A Liberal Theory of Minority Rights* (Oxford: Oxford University Press).

Laclau, Ernesto (1996): *Emancipation(s)* (London: Verso).

——(ed.)(1994) *The Making of Political Identities* (London: Verso).

——and Chantal Mouffe (1985), *Hegemony and Socialist Strategy Towards a Radical Democratic Politics* (London: Verso).

Ladd, John (ed.) (1973): *Ethical Relativism* (Belmont, California: Wadsworth Publishing Company).

Lash, Scott and John Urry (1994): *Economies of Sign and Space* (London: Sage).

Leuprecht, Peter (1998): 'Innovations in the European System of Human Rights Protection: Is Enlargement Compatible with Reinforcements?, 8, *Transnational Law and Contemporary Problems*, 313.

Levinas, Emmanuel (1994): *Nine Talmudic Readings,* Annette Aronowicaz trs, (Bloomington, Indiana: University Press).

——(1987): *Outside the Subject*, Michael B. Smith (ed.) (Standard University Press).

——(1969), *Totality and Infinity: An Essay on Exteriority,* Alphous Lingis (trs.) (Pittsburg: Duquesne University Press).

Lyotard, Jean Francois (1989): *The Lyotard Reader*, Andrew Benjamin (ed.) (Oxford: Blackwell).

MacIntyre, Alasdair (1988) *Whose Justice? Which Rationality?* (Oxford: Blackwell).

——(1981) *After Virtue*, 2nd edn (Indiana: University of Notre Dame Press).

Mamdani, Mahmood (1996): *The Citizen and Subject: Contemporary Africa and the Legacy of Late Colonialism* (Princeton: Princeton University Press).

Marks, Stephen P. (1998): 'From the "Single Confused Page" to the "Declaration for Six Billion Persons": The Roots of the Universal Declaration of Human Rights in the French Revolution', 20, *Human Rights Quarterly*, 459.

Marquaurdt, Stephen (1995): 'International Law and Indigenous Peoples', 3, *International Journal of Group Rights*, 47.

Mayer, Carl J. (1990): 'Personalizing the Impersonal: Corporations and the Bill of Rights', 41, *Hastings Law Review*, 576.

Mayo, Bernard R.(1958) *Ethics and Moral Life* (Ithaca, New York: Cornell University Press).

Meehan, Johanna (ed.) (1995): *Feminists Read Habermas: Gendering the Subject of Discourse* (London: Routledge).

Mehta, Uday (1998): *Liberalism and Empire* (Chicago: Chicago University Press).

Meyer, Ann Elizabeth (1996): 'Reflections on the Proposed Reservations to CEDAW: Should the Constitution be an Obstacle to Human Rights?', 23, *Hastings Constitutional Law Quarterly*, 727–823.

Minnow, Martha (1998): *Between Vengeance and Forgiveness: Facing History After Genocide and Mass Violence* (Cambridge, Mass.: Harvard University Press).

Mistry, Rohinton (1995): *A Fine Balance* (London: Faber & Faber).

Mouffe, Chantal (1992): *The Return of the Political* (London: Verso).

——(ed.) (1992): 'Citizenship and the Political Community', in *Dimensions of Radical Democracy*, 237 (London: Verso).

Muzaffar, Chandra (1993): *Human Rights and the New World Order* (Penang: Just World Trust).

Myrdal, Gunnar (1963): *Asian Drama: An Enquiry into Poverty of Nations* (Hakmondsworth: Penguin Books).

Nelkin, Dorothy and Andrews, Lori, B. (1998) '*Homo Economicus*: Commercialisation of Body Tissue in the Age of Biotechnology', 28 Hastings Centre Report, San Francisco.

Nietzsche, Fredrich (1954): *The Portable Nietzsche*, Walter Kaufman (ed.) (New York: Viking).

Nino, Carlos Santiago (1996): *The Ethics of Deliberative Democracy* (New Haven: Yale University Press).

——(1996): *Radical Evil on Trial* (New Haven: Yale University Press).

Norris, Christopher (1996): *Reclaiming Truth: Contribution to Critique of Cultural Relativism* (North Carolina: Duke University Press).

Nussbaum, Martha and Cass R. Sunstein (eds) (1998): *Clones: Facts and Fantasies About Human Cloning* (New York: Norton).

Osiel, Marc (1997): *Mass Atrocity, Collective Memory and the Law* (New Brunswick and London: Transaction Publishers).

Parekh, Bhikhu (1997): 'Liberalism and Colonialism: A Critique of Locke and Mill', *The Decolonization of Imagination*, 81–98, Jan Nederveen Pieterse and Bhikhu Parekh (eds) (Delhi: Oxford University Press).

——(1988): 'The Modern Conceptions of Rights and its Marxist Critique', in *The Right to be Human*, Upendra Baxi (ed.) (New Delhi: Lancer Publication and India International Centre).

Peffer, R.J. (1990): *Marxism, Morality and Social Justice* (Princeton: Princeton University Press).

Pollis, Amanda (1996): 'Cultural Relativism Revisited Through a State Prism', 18, *Human Rights Quarterly*, 316.

Ponting, Clive (1991): *The Twentieth Century: A World History* (New York: Henry Holt & Company).

Rawls, John (1993): 'The Law of Peoples', in *On Human Rights: The Oxford Amnesty Lectures 1993*, Stephen Shue and Susan Hurley (eds) 41 (Oxford: Oxford University Press).

——(1993) *Political Liberalism* (New York: Columbia University Press).

Ridgway, James and Jeffrey St. Clair (1998): *A Pocket Guide to Environmental Bad Guys (And a Few Ideas on How to Stop Them)* (New York: Thunder's Mouth Press).

Rifkin, Jeremy (1998): *The Biotech Century* (London: Victor Gollancz).

Robertson, Geoff (1999): *Crimes Against Humanity: The Struggle for Global Justice* (Hammondsworth: Penguin).

Robertson, Ronald (1992): *Globalization: Social Theory and Global Culture* (London: Sage).

Roht-Arriaza, Naomi (ed.) (1995): *Impunity and Human Rights Law and Practice* (Oxford: Oxford University Press).

Rorty, Richard (1993): 'Human Rights, Rationality, and Sentiments', in *On Human Rights: The Oxford-Amnesty Lectures 1993*.

Rowell, Andrew (1996): *Green Backlash: Global Subversion of Environmental Movement* (London: Routledge).

Ruigrok, Winfried and Rob Van Tulder (1995): *The Logic of International Restructuring* (London: Routledge).

Sandel, Michel (1982): *Liberalism and the Limits of Justice* (Cambridge: Cambridge University Press).

Santos, Boaventura de Sousa (1995): *Towards a New Commonsense: Law, Science and Politics in the Paradigmatic Transition* (New York: Routledge).

Sathe, S.P. (2001): *Judicial Activism in India* (Delhi: Oxford University Press).

Sayyid, Bobby (1994): 'Sign O' Times: Kaffirs and Infidels Fighting the Ninth Crusade', in *The Making of Political Identity*, 233.

Schlag, Pierre (1997): 'Rights in the Postmodern Condition', in *Legal Rights: Historical and Philosophical Perspectives*, Austin Sarat and Thomas R. Kearns (eds), 263–304 (Ann Arbor: University of Michigan Press).

Scott, Lash and Ronald Robertson (eds)(1995): *Global Modernities* (London: Sage).

Sedgwick, Sally (1997): 'Can Knat's Ethics Survive the Feminist Critique?', in *Feminist Interpretations of Immanuel Kant*, Robbin Mary Schott (ed.) (Philadelphia: The Pennsylvania State University Press).

Sen, Amartya (1999): 'Human Rights and Economic Achievements', in *The East Asian Challenges to Human Rights*, Joanne R. Bauer and Daniel A. Bell (eds), 88–102 (Cambridge: Cambridge University Press).

Sherry, Suzanna (1986): 'Civic Virtue and the Feminine Voice in Constitutional Adjudication', 72, *Virginia Law Review*, 543.

Shivji, Issa G. (1989): *The Concept of Human Rights in Africa* (Oxford: African Books Collective).

Shklar, Judith N. (1990): *The Faces of Injustice* (New Haven: Yale University Press).

——(1986): *Legalism: Law, Morals and Political Trials* (Cambridge: Harvard University Press).

Sklair, Leslie (1999): 'Social Movements and Global Capitalism' in *The Cultures of Globalization*, Fredrik Jameson and Masao Myashi (eds), 291–331 (North Carolina Duke University Press.)

——(1995): *The Sociology of Global System*, 2nd rev. edn (Baltimore: Johns Hopkins University Press).

Smith, Anna Marie (1994): 'Rastfari as Resistance and the Ambiguities of Essentialism in New Social Movements', *The Making of Political Identity*, 171.

Smith, Steven B. (1989): *Hegel's Critique of Liberalism: Rights in Context* (Chicago: University of Chicago Press).

Spelman, Elizabeth (1988): *Inessential Woman: Problems of Exclusion in Feminist Thought* (Baltimore: The John Hopkins University Press).

Spivak, Gayatri Chakravorty (1995): 'Constitutions and Culture Studies', *Cultural Studies: A Reader in Post (modern) Critical Theory*, Jerry Leonard (ed.) 155 (Buffalo: The State University of New York Press).

Stiglmayer, Alexander(1992): The Rapes in Bosnia–Herzegovina', in *Mass Rape: The War Against Women in Bosnia–Herzegovina*, (Lincoln, Nebraska: The University of Nebraska Press).

Stone, Julius (1965): *Human Law and Human Justice* (Sydney: Maitland).

——(1964) *Legal Systems and Lawyers' Reasonings* (Sydney: Maitland).

Strauss, Leo (1975): *Political Philosophy: Six Essays*, Hilail Gildin (trs.) (Indianapolis and New York: Bobbs–Merrill and Pegasus).

Tambiah, Stanley J. (1964): *World Conqueror and World Renouncer* (Cambridge, Mass: Harvard University Press).

Taylor, Charles (1985): *Philosophical Papers*, Vol. 1 (Cambridge: Cambridge University Press).

——(1999): 'Conditions of Unenforced Consensus on Human Rights', *The East Asian Challenges for Human Rights* Joanne R. Bauer and Daniel A. Bell (eds), 124–46 (Cambridge: Cambridge University Press).

Taylor, Mark (1987): *Altarity* (Lincoln Nebraska: The University of Nebraska Press).

Teńson, Fernando (1985): 'International Human Rights and Cultural Relativism', 25, *Virginia Journal of International Law*, 869.

Thompson, E.P. (1989): *Writing by the Candlelight* (London: The Merlin Press).

Thompson, J.B. (1984): *Studies in the Theory of Ideology* (Berkeley: University of California Press).

Tomasevski, Katarina (1997): *Between Sanctions and Elections: Aid Donors and their Human Rights Performance* (London: Pinter).

——(1994): 'Human Rights and the Wars of Starvation', *War and Hunger: Rethinking International Response to Complex Emergencies* Joanna Macrae and Anthony Zwi (eds) (London: Zed Books, in association with Save the Children Fund, UK).

Traweek, Sharon (1988): *Beamtimes and Lifetimes* (Cambridge, Mass.: Harvard University Press).

Tu Wei-Ming (1996): 'Maoism as a Source of Suffering in China', *Social Suffering*, 149–80.

Unger, Roberto M. (1996): *What Should Legal Analysis Become?* (London: Verso).

United Nations (1998): *Adverse Effects on the Illicit Movement and Dumping of Toxic and Dangerous Products and Wastes on the Enjoyment of Human Rights*, UN Doc. E./CN.4/ 1998/10, 20 January 1998.

——(1997): *Human Rights: A Compilation of International Instruments,* Vol. 11: *Regional Instruments* (New York: United Nations Publications).

——(1997) *Human Rights: A Compilation of Instruments* (New York: United Nations Publications).

United States Congress, Office of Technology Assessment (1993): *Dismantling the Bomb and Managing the Nuclear Materials* (Washington DC).

——(1988): *New Developments in Biotechnology: U.S. Investment in Biotechnology* (Washington DC).

——(1993): *Aging Nuclear Plants: Managing Plant life and Decommissioning* (Washington DC).

Walzer, Michael (1983): *Spheres of Justice: A Defence of Pluralism and Equality* (Oxford: Blackwell).

Weingberg, Alvin M. (1972): 'Science and Trans-science', 10, *Minerva*, 209–22.

Weston, Burns H., Falk, Richard A., Charlesworth, Hilary (eds.) (1997): *International law and the World Order: A Problem Oriented Case Book* (St Paul, Minnesota: West Publishing House).

——(1997): Human Rights, 20, *Encyclopaedia Britannica*, 56 (15th edn.)

Wiesberg, Richard (1992): *Poethics and Other Strategies of Law and Literature* (New York: Columbia University Press).

William, Raymond (1983): *Keywords* (Hammondsworth: Penguin Books).

Woodiwiss, Anthony (1998): *Globalization, Human Rights and Labour Law in the Pacific Asia* (Cambridge: Cambridge University Press).

World Bank (1996): *NGOs and the Bank: Incorporating FY95 Progress Report on Cooperation Between the World Bank and the NGOs* (Washington DC: The World Bank).

——(1994) *Governance: The World Bank's Experience* (Washington DC: The World Bank).

Wright, Susan (1994): *Molecular Politics: Developing American and British Regulatory Policies for Genetic Engineering 1972:1982* (Chicago: University of Chicago Press).

Yongun, Han (1913): *Treatise for Reform of Korean Buddhism* (Seoul, Korea).

Young, Iris Marion (1990): *Justice and the Politics of Difference* (Princeton: Princeton University Press).

Žižek, Slavoj (1999): *The Ticklish Subject: Absent Subject of Political Ontology* (London: Verso).

Author Index

Theme Index